# J.D. Edwards® OneWorld® Xe: Object Management Workbench

Allen Jacot and Kimberly Jacot

**McGraw-Hill**/Osborne

New York   Chicago   San Francisco
Lisbon   London   Madrid   Mexico City   Milan
New Delhi   San Juan   Seoul   Singapore   Sydney   Toronto

**McGraw-Hill/Osborne**
2600 Tenth Street
Berkeley, California 94710
U.S.A.

To arrange bulk purchase discounts for sales promotions, premiums, or fund-raisers, please contact **McGraw-Hill**/Osborne at the above address. For information on translations or book distributors outside the U.S.A., please see the International Contact Information page immediately following the index of this book.

## J.D. Edwards® OneWorld® Xe: Object Management Workbench

1234567890 DOC DOC 01987654321

ISBN 0-07-219254-2

**Publisher**
Brandon A. Nordin

**Vice President & Associate Publisher**
Scott Rogers

**Editorial Director**
Gareth Hancock

**Project Editor**
Jennifer Malnick

**Acquisitions Coordinator**
Jessica Wilson

**Technical Editors**
Gregory Borges
Tod Keiffer

**Copy Editor**
Robert Campbell

**Proofreaders**
Linda and Paul Medoff

**Indexer**
Claire Splan

**Computer Designer**
Jean Butterfield

**Illustrator**
Michael Mueller
Lyssa Wald

**Series Design**
Roberta Steele

**Cover Designer**
Ted Holladay

This book was composed with Corel VENTURA™ Publisher.

For the things we have to learn before we can do them,
we learn by doing them.

—Aristotle


The authors would like to dedicate this book to our family, who have given us undivided support over the years, and to those individuals who have taken the time to train us, assist us, and help us to develop our skillsets. Without your help, this could not have been possible.

# About the Authors

**Allen Jacot** is a OneWorld Certified CNC Specialist with J.D. Edwards, and has supported numerous OneWorld implementations since its original beta release in 1996. Allen has worked within J.D. Edwards, developing and leading the J.D. Edwards OneWorld NT Technical Customer Support team as well as providing global leadership around the CNC practice. Currently, Allen is pursuing a master's degree in Computer Information Systems at the University of Denver.

**Kimberly Jacot** is a OneWorld Certified Developer and XPIe Integration Specialist with Deloitte & Touche. Prior to joining Delottie & Touche, Kimberly was a Senior Developer for J.D. Edwards, and has been working with OneWorld since 1997. She has supported and managed several OneWorld implementations, XPIe, and Interoperability integrations with various third-party applications. Currently, Kimberly is sitting for her CPA and is pursuing a master's degree in Computer Information Systems at the University of Denver.

# About the Technical Reviewers

**Gregory Borges** started working at J.D. Edwards in June, 1998. He initially maintained Object Librarian and Batch Version in the B7332 release of OneWorld, and was one of the primary developers who architected and created the Object Management Workbench. He took over as lead developer after its internal rollout at JDE and has continued to maintain, enhance, and support the software as well as teach OMW classes.

**Tod Keiffer** has worked in the J.D. Edwards OneWorld Unix/NT Platform Support Team, and, more recently, as part of the OneWorld Upgrade and Object Management group. In addition to his support and testing role, Tod has taught CNC courses, written supplemental documentation and White Papers, and led in the development of multimedia Internet Presentations for training clients and business partners on the new enhancements in OneWorld Xe. Tod has contributed several White papers and SageCam multimedia presentations for both OMW and the new Electronic Software Update process.

# Contents

# Foreword

With the advent of J.D. Edwards OneWorld B7.3.3.3 (commonly known as Xe), J.D. Edwards introduced an unparalleled version of OneWorld that represents a major step in the evolution of their collaborative enterprise suite. The J.D. Edwards design philosophy has always focused on maximum flexibility, which is enhanced by equipping customers with a robust set of design tools for enabling it beyond other "out-of-the-box" solutions. This ability to customize the software solution for an individual organization is one of the most powerful options provided by OneWorld and has enjoyed a major enhancement in the Xe release. No longer do multiple developers face the possibility of overriding each others' work; no longer do developers forget what objects are required for their projects; and organizations no longer need to fear that anyone with access to the object librarian can force changes throughout the enterprise.

Of course, with change comes the need to understand the rationale behind the enhancement. There is more to effectively using the product than merely setting it up—there are strategies based on what your organization is trying to accomplish, there are strategies based on the size of your organization, and there are even strategies that can simplify the overall development process. To the end goal of understanding and creating the optimal methodology for your organization, you will find *J.D. Edwards OneWorld Xe: Object Management Workbench* an invaluable tool. It provides an in-depth analysis of the functionality, the tools, and the considerations necessary in making the Object Management Workbench (OMW) not just work for your company, but truly enhance your developer's ability to provide solutions that meet and exceed your company's requirements.

Before agreeing to write the foreword for this book, I had the opportunity of getting to know the authors and understanding the team assembled to bring this invaluable tool to you. The authors are some of the best J.D. Edwards technical talent available. They have over fifteen years of OneWorld experience between them regarding all aspects of OneWorld technology and development. One of the technical editors is even responsible for writing the code for the OMW application itself, providing an authoritative document that is a must for any organization implementing Xe. As the global J.D. Edwards practice leader for Deloitte & Touche, I have had the opportunity to work with many organizations implementing the OneWorld suite of applications, and it is rare that I find as useful or timely a book as this one. I highly recommend *J.D. Edwards OneWorld Xe: Object Management Workbench* and know that you will find it the same quality of work I have.

As the OneWorld product continues to grow, meeting the needs of organizations like yours, the J.D. Edwards Press will continue meeting your need to understand how to implement, configure, and make it work for you.

—Jeffrey Plewa
   Global J.D. Edwards Leader, Deloitte & Touche LLP

# Acknowledgments

There are a number of people we would like to acknowledge with regard to this book. Some of them provided intellectual capital, while others provided support and inspiration professionally as well as personally. Although we don't have enough room to list each contribution separately, we want to at least list their names to express our gratitude for their contributions.

| | | |
|---|---|---|
| Joseph Miller | Steven Hester | Eric Cowherd |
| Michael Saucier | Craig Ledonne | Gareth Hancock |
| Stephen Berthe | Michael Jacot | Deloitte & Touche |
| Jessica Wilson | Jennifer Malnick | Brian Stanz |
| Roberta Steele | | |

J.D. Edwards World Solutions Company

The entire support staff at Osborne/McGraw-Hill

## NOTE

Please reference www.jdedwardspress.com to download the Out-of-the-Box Allowed Actions and Activity Rules appendix, as this document will be a useful reference as you read through the book

# CHAPTER 1

# Object Management Workbench Fundamentals

The Object Management Workbench (OMW) is a change management system consisting of models, methods, techniques, and other tools for OneWorld development. Prior to OMW, all change management was performed using manual procedures and/or third-party tools. The OMW system automates many of those processes, allowing you to more effectively manage change. OMW gives you a way to track required changes in a planned and systematic fashion, giving you better control of OneWorld objects. It provides an integrated and simplified graphical user interface (GUI) for OneWorld development. Much unlike its predecessor, Object Librarian (OL), OMW employs projects, user roles, and object tokens to provide better overall control of your development process.

The main GUI, the configuration system, and the logging system are critical pieces in change management for OneWorld development. OMW includes both the repository of information and the functionality that was available to you using OL. OMW, however, has expanded search capabilities; and the concepts, including the repository of information and OL functionality, have been built into a functional change management system. The GUI is what connects all development into one user interface. It simplifies processes such as object check in and check out, and object transfers. (These concepts are covered in the "Working with Objects" section in Chapter 2.) The configuration system controls all development from one central point, by implementing careful planning of your software development life cycle. It is in the configuration system that the system administrator sets up, for example, check in and check out locations—that is, the path codes or data sources where objects reside. The complexity of this process now resides with the system administrator, and the user interface is simplified. Finally, the logging system tracks all changes to the system automatically, thus being proactive in tracking change not only at the project level, but also at an object level.

In this chapter, you will learn about the basic concepts, or fundamentals, of OMW and what it does for your company. It is important to first understand the fundamentals, before you move into using OMW in a true development environment. In the following chapters, we will tie the fundamentals into real examples of using OMW, as well as provide you with a strategic case study.

# Projects

What constitutes a project and why use projects? In OneWorld, a *project* is made up of a group of OneWorld objects that have been modified or created by a user, usually a developer. Projects allow you to methodically group OneWorld objects so as to complete or resolve a problem or task. There are no special rules to follow for small, medium, or large development efforts, however. In the past, developers had to track changed objects using a multitude of forms; this is now simplified by using the concept of a project in OMW. By tracking your changes in the context of a project, you can more readily track all modifications needed for a specific change, and identify specific modifications made to a particular object during any given time—and it's all automated!

All work on objects within OneWorld must be done within the context of a project. In OMW, there are two types of projects. There are projects that you, as a user, add to track specific groupings of objects; and there are default projects, which are created automatically by the OMW system for each OneWorld user. All projects also have statuses, such as "pending review" and "in programming." These statuses are used to determine the types of actions that can be performed on objects within those projects. The "Working with Projects" section in Chapter 2 discusses these statuses in more detail.

# Default Projects

What is a default project and when is it used? The *default project* is your (as the user) personal project. It is commonly used for research and development, although most development is done within a user-created project, allowing for more efficient tracking of the complete assigned task. The status of the default project cannot be changed; thus, objects cannot be transferred using a default project. It does, however, perform much like a user-created project. When a user runs OMW for the first time, a default project is created and named with the user's sign-on ID.

To reiterate a previous statement, all work on objects within OneWorld must be done within the context of a project. Objects may be developed using the default project, and moved into a user-created project when the object is complete and ready to be transferred. It is not recommended, however, that you develop using the default project, as you do not have full development capabilities. As OneWorld is configured out of the box, development capabilities are limited due to the allowed action restrictions on the default user role. In addition to the allowed action restrictions, default projects cannot be advanced to a different project status, eliminating the possibility of object transfer. If an object is selected or newly created, and is to be added to a project but a project is not selected, the object will be added to your default project. This process will be explained in more detail in Chapter 2.

If development work is done on objects outside of OMW—for example, UDC edits, menu selections, and adding of Batch or Interactive Versions (Non–Object Librarian [Non-OL] objects)—those objects are added to the OneWorld user's default project so that changes are captured and better control is maintained across your system. Because changes of Non-OL objects are done through a project, these changes are first validated through the Object Management Workbench configuration. For example, this means that when you are adding a version through Batch Versions, behind the scenes, OneWorld is validating these actions through the OMW-allowed actions for the default project user role and the activity rules for the project status.

The most common reason for using the default project is for researching issues and/or creating proof of concepts for your work. Issues that are commonly researched, on request of a user group, include information about logic behind a field shown on a form and where default information is set, if not in the data dictionary. A proof of concept is a simple interactive application (APPL) or batch application (UBE) that is created to test the logic within an object. Quite often, the authors will create a proof of concept to test required parameters needed in business function (BSFN) calls. Chapter 2 goes into more detail on creating objects in OneWorld.

# Objects

In OneWorld, an *object* has traditionally been defined as a reusable entity, created by the OneWorld tool set. Objects include Object Librarian (OL) objects, such as (but not limited to) interactive applications (APPL), batch applications (UBE), data structure (DSTR) objects, and—yes—even tables (TBLE). Although the structures around these objects differ, they are objects nonetheless.

In OMW, the definition of objects has been expanded to include other Non–Object Librarian type objects, or data source–based, rather than path code–based, objects. Other than the data in the tables themselves, just about everything created in OneWorld that performs a function is an object. For a detailed discussion on data sources and path codes, please refer to *J.D. Edwards OneWorld: The Complete Reference* by Joseph Miller, Allen Jacot, and John Stern (Osborne/McGraw-Hill, 2000).

OneWorld objects include the following OL and Non-OL objects:

- OL objects:
  - Interactive applications
  - Batch applications
  - Data structures
  - Business functions
  - Business views
  - Named event rules

- Media objects
- Tables
- Non-OL objects:
  - Data dictionary (DD) items
  - Interactive and batch versions
  - User-defined code (UDC) items
  - Workflow items
  - Menus
  - User overrides

With the inclusion of Non-OL objects into OMW, this means that you have better control over the changes that are made to your system. You no longer have to track UDC and DD item changes using dreary forms that are often hard to read and track. This is done automatically by moving these objects into a user-created project once the change is made and the project is ready for transfer. We will go through an example of adding objects and transferring them from the default project into a regular project in Chapter 2.

# Owners

In OneWorld, an *owner* is a user that is assigned a specific role in a project. Owners usually possess an attribute, knowledge, or skill that allows them to accomplish a task. By setting up owners, you have greater control over access and management of the project itself. Having owners also allows you to appropriately staff personnel on other projects according to their current workload. By simply viewing those projects in an active status for each user, you can put together a more well-rounded team project plan. A discussion on roles played and how they tie into the owners concept is covered in the next section.

The Search tab is used to locate OneWorld users to add to a project in an assigned role. Owner search capabilities are covered in "The Object Management Workbench Form," later in this chapter.

# Roles

Knowing what function, or part, you play in a particular task is directly tied to user roles. User *roles* are set up for all the persons that can or do participate in a project. The role essentially defines the user's function within the project organization. Project managers will generally assign a user to a project. When they do so, they will indicate what role that user will be playing. User roles defined in the base system, and a description of how they are used, are shown in the following table. You can also configure or customize the user roles to meet your organization's specific business requirements. This is done by adding or removing values to or from the System (Product Code) H92, UDC UR (OMW User Roles) and UDC (H92/UR).

| Role ID | Role Description | Definition of Role |
| --- | --- | --- |
| 01 | Originator | User that originated the project. When a project is added, the user that signed into OneWorld and created the project will automatically be added as the originator. |
| 02 | Developer | User(s) that create and work with the project. There may be more than one developer assigned to a project. |
| 03 | Manager | User(s) that manage the project. This code is commonly used to store the person or persons ultimately responsible for keeping the project on time and on budget. |
| 04 | Quality Assurance (QA) | User(s) that test the project's functionality. This code is commonly used to store the person or persons that will perform process testing and system testing of the functionality after the developer has completed coding and unit testing. |
| 05 | Product Support | User(s) that relay statuses to outside persons. This code can be used to store individuals responsible for communicating the status of a project to persons outside of the project community. |
| 06 | PVC Administrator | User(s) that are responsible for maintaining version control over the OneWorld Development Tools releases. When projects contain Non-OL objects, the PVC (Product Versions Control) administrator commonly maintains control of the pristine version of the change, as well as updating the objects in the appropriate locations. |
| 07 | Training | User(s) responsible for maintaining training manuals and creating training sessions. This code is used to store individual(s) responsible for updating training materials, as well as incorporating new enhancements into existing materials or new training classes. |

| Role ID | Role Description | Definition of Role |
|---------|-----------------|--------------------|
| 08 | Documentation | User(s) responsible for updating or creating documentation on a change made to the OneWorld system. This code is commonly used to store the documentation supervisor or multiple documentation editors who will be automatically informed (e.g., using the e-mail process built into OMW), once the project has reached a certain status, that a change must be made to documented materials. |
| 09 | Supervisor | User(s) that supervise a portion of the project. This code is commonly used to store the person or persons responsible for tracking the progress of smaller portions of a project. The supervisor can also be set up to play a role similar to a manager. |

Chapter 4 discusses allowed actions and activity rules that enable you to further define these roles.

Quite often, a user is asked to assume and is assigned multiple roles on a project. So, the ultimate question is, can I assign more than one user to a specific role in OMW? The answer is, yes, you can. OMW encompasses many of the everyday tasks that you would perform as a project manager, two of which are assigning tasks and assigning roles. You can easily add more than one developer, or any other project role, to a project. Quite often, in a development environment, no one developer can complete a task in the time frame given, and no one QA can complete a full functionality test prior to the release of the project. Thus, it is common to assign multiple owners to multiple roles on a project. The owners folder will show the user and the role that the user plays. Searching and viewing owners to add to a project or that are assigned to a project is discussed in "Object Management Workbench Form," later in this chapter, and in Chapter 2.

# Allowed Actions

What is an allowed action in OMW? Allowed actions are rules that spell out what actions a specific user may perform on an object in a project. These allowed actions are defined for each project status and for each object type. An *action* is an event or series of events, such as design and transfer—actions that are common within a development environment. Perhaps this is more easily explained in an example: An allowed action for a developer is an authority or privilege that comes with the job description, also called a user role in OMW. The developer role would have allowed actions defined for the actions that the developer would need in order to complete his or her daily job duties. A manager, for instance, may have more authority than the person performing the work (the developer). OMW can be configured to allow the manager to deem the development and testing cycles complete and ready for promotion to your production environment.

These rules (allowed actions) are configured by the system administrator for each object type and for each project status in the OMW configuration application. They are discussed in more detail in Chapter 3.

# Tokens

As discussed in the "Objects" section, earlier in the chapter, all projects can contain OL objects and Non-OL objects. OL objects use *tokens* to minimize the possibility of one user overwriting another user's changes to an object. Only one project can hold a token to an object at any one time. Non-OL objects do not carry a token; rather, the system administrator or product versions control administrator commonly updates the object in the correct environment.

The token management system organizes application development by providing a single check out environment. Tokens are assigned to the project, if it is available, when the object is checked out. If the token is not available, the user may add their check out request to the token queue to receive the token when it is available (inherit the token). Tokens provide a change control solution in a system that doesn't support merging or versions of specifications. Chapter 2 discusses tokens and the actions you can perform around tokens, as they relate to objects, in the "Working with Tokens" section.

Okay, so you really don't understand what a token is. Fair enough, we've been supplying you a lot of information. Think back to when you were a kid, at band camp, and it was one of those rare moments when they let you out of the practice rooms to enjoy the weather. You're sitting around the campfire telling ghost stories. Each person around the fire is contributing to the story, but you're allowed to speak only if you hold the marshmallow (the token). If someone else tries to speak while you're holding the marshmallow, no one else can understand or hear what you're saying, and the story will get confusing. A token has a similar idea. If someone else has the ability to make changes to your object while you're working on it, the code will no longer be the same, the two versions cannot be merged simply, and you are left with a sticky mess in the bottom of the fire pit. Thus, a token is like holding the key, or the permission slip, to be allowed to make changes to the system. If another user tries to check out an object when you hold the token, they will be placed in a queue until you release the token (usually once the object is promoted into production). Token switching, which allows you to switch a token in the middle of the development process, will be discussed in Chapter 2.

# The Object Management Workbench Form

To access the Object Management Workbench (OMW) form, run OMW from the Fast Path (type **OMW**) or choose Object Management Workbench from menu GH902. You may also launch OMW by typing **OL** in the Fast Path (this must be configured by your system administrator). The OL application is no longer available in the Xe release of OneWorld. This may trouble or perplex some of you; however, once you learn to use the new tools available, you'll learn to love them. This section only begins to touch upon the features available in OMW; Chapter 2 will really focus on the differences in more detail. The OMW form is shown in Figure 1-1. It is displayed prior to clicking

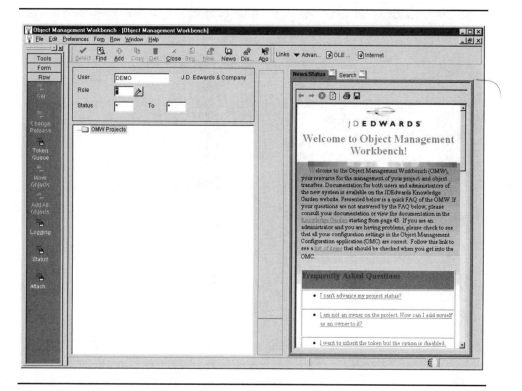

**FIGURE 1-1.**   Object Management Workbench form News/Status window

Find. You will see the News/Status tab in focus, which is easily customized to fit your business needs. The default Web page that is displayed is stored in the OMW media object queue. You may change the Web page that is displayed with the processing options of the OMW application (P98220). There are also options to default information into the filter fields on the OMW form. These filters are discussed in more detail in the next section, "Project View Search." Common information contained within the News section may be internal Web sites with project time-line information, breaking news events, build schedules, or any other data your system administrator or project manager feels is pertinent for your business.

After you click Find, the OMW form will be displayed in Project view, as shown in Figure 1-2. Any development work will be done with this form. For typical development, it allows the user to create a project and add objects and owners to that project. In the past, developers—or even managers, for that matter—were never allowed to transfer objects. Managers gave permissions to transfers objects, but a system administrator or

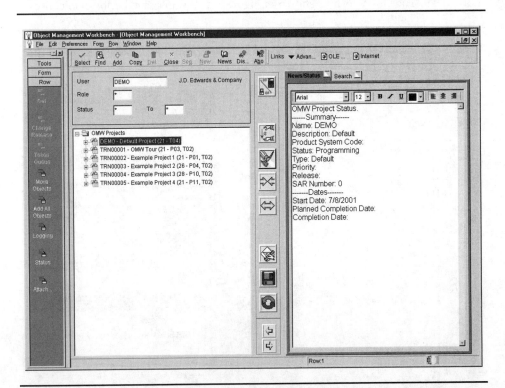

**FIGURE 1-2.** Object management Workbench form in Project view

product promotion administrator was the only individual allowed access to the transfer process. In OMW, users may access the design tools and other object management tasks depending on how the administrator configured each role that they play in the project. OMW also allows the administrator to define where objects are checked out from and checked in to, without you, as the user, having to keep track of this information and enter it manually. OMW also has automatic transfers of objects when the project's status is advanced to a certain status. See Chapter 2 for everyday uses and examples of OMW.

From left to right, the OMW form contains:

- **Tools, Form, and Row function tabs and icons**    These are displayed if the preference to view the exit bar is selected.

- **The Project View window**    This window contains the OMW projects folder. When this folder is opened, it displays a list of available OneWorld projects and their related objects and owners, for the user signed into OneWorld. You can limit your search by entering a user, role, and/or status.

- **The center column of action buttons**    These buttons are displayed for specific allowed actions. When the project and/or objects are at a status for which the user is allowed to perform that action, the button will be displayed. These actions and how they are used are discussed in detail in Chapter 2.

- **The News/Status and Search window**    This window can display a Web site (URL or Web page stored in the OMW media object queue), project status and OneWorld release information, and object search results. When selected, the Search tab displays the category, search type, search fields, and the Results window. This tab, as well as advanced search options, is described in more detail in the Search sections in this chapter.

# Project View Search

The Project view is shown in the left-hand window of the OMW form. It consists of the user, role, and status filtering fields, as well as a project list for the specified user. You can view your projects and the objects, as well as the owners those projects contain, using this window. You can also view the projects for any other OneWorld user. This is useful should you, as a project manager, wish to see newly created projects or the status of a project. You will commonly select a project, an object, or an owner from this window in order to select actions to perform on them.

To search on a project in which you play a role, simply click Find with the User field filled in with your user ID. By filling in just the user and nothing else, you will see the projects you are listed as owner of, or those you play a role in.

Should you wish to narrow your project search, you can choose to filter by user role and/or filter by project status. Filtering by user role will show only those projects in which you play a specific role. To filter, enter in the roles filter field the role you want to use in your search. The visual assist will aid in selecting a valid role. Then when you click Find, only those projects in which you play that role will be displayed. You can also view only those projects that have a certain project status. You do so by filling in the status fields, Status (from) and To. Again, the available visual assist will aid in selecting a valid status. Clicking Find will display only those projects that are at or between the statuses you entered. The default project will also be displayed regardless of whether it meets the search criteria. If you have left the role filter field populated, you will see the projects at or between the statuses entered when you play the role indicated. Figure 1-3 shows an example of how these filters function in the stand-alone version of OneWorld Xe.

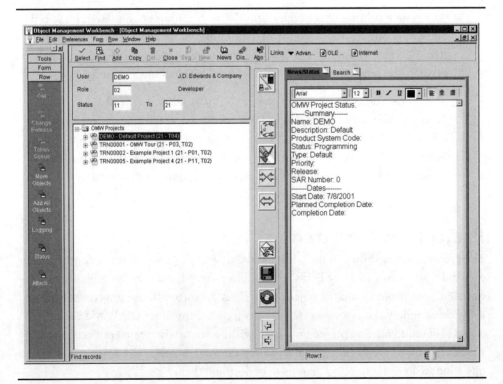

**FIGURE 1-3.**   Project view search

# Project View Advanced Search

There are times when an advanced search is required. For instance, you may be having issues with a particular object, say P4210, and you may want to see all projects included in the P4210 application. This would allow you to better determine which project, or which change, caused the issue you are seeing. There are three advanced search types or forms that can facilitate this search. These can be accessed by clicking Form | Exit, Advanced Search, or Search by Object.

With the user filter field populated, click Advanced Search. The OMW Project Search and Select by Project User form is displayed (see Figure 1-4). This form displays all projects and user roles for which a specific user is entered as an owner.

If the Project view user filter field on the OMW form is blank when Advanced Search is chosen, all projects across the OMW system are displayed when you click Find. This can be very helpful if OMW encounters an error when adding a user to a project at the time it is created, or when changes are made to the project. You can limit your search by using any of the Query By Example (QBE) fields.

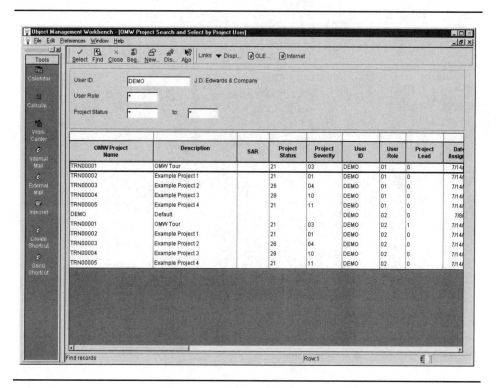

**FIGURE 1-4.**   Project Search and Select by Project User

If you select Form | Exit, Search by Object, the OMW Project Search and Select by Object form is displayed. When you click Find, all objects contained within all projects will be displayed. You may use the QBE fields to limit your search to a specific object name, object type, project, etc. An example of the Search by Object form is displayed in Figure 1-5. In our example, we are searching on all projects that include a business view (BSVW) that is in system code 01 (V01*).

### TIP

*The Project View Advanced Search forms are multiselect forms. After you have located your desired projects or objects, you may select multiple rows and click Select. These records will be returned to the OMW form and displayed in the project list.*

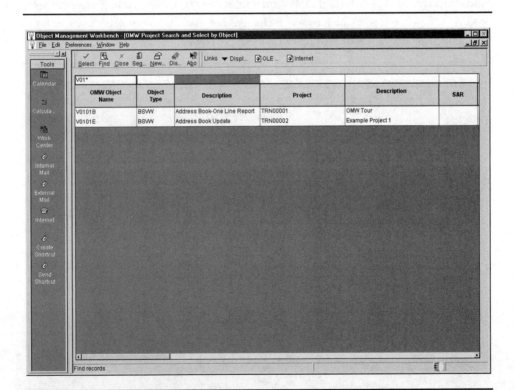

**FIGURE 1-5.** Project Search by Object

# News/Status View

The News view is selected when you open the OMW form. This tab can display an Internet Web page (URL) or an informational HTML page stored in the OMW Media Object Queue that your administrator has set up to provide you with details the administrator feels you need to know. It can also contain important links you may need to access.

When a project is selected in the Project View window, the News/Status tab will show information about the selected project. The right-hand window will display project status and release information consisting of the project name, description of the project, product system code, status of the project (e.g., In programming, Ready to Transfer, QA Test, or Rework), type (e.g., Enhancement or Bug), priority, release, SAR (Software Action Request) number, start date, planned completion date, and completion date. Not all fields will be populated or relevant. (Project statuses are covered in Chapter 4.) The start date, planned completion date, and actual completion date are excellent tools for tracking if your project is moving along as scheduled. They can be changed at any time during the project. You can also add attachments to your project; these will stay with the project for its entire project life cycle (i.e., until it reaches a completed status). These attachments, which are useful for tracking issues, risks, kudos, and so on, are also discussed in Chapter 2. Figure 1-6 displays a project with the status information showing. To return to the News tab at any time, you may choose the Form | Exit to News option or click News.

When an object is selected in the Project View window, the News/Status tab will show information about the selected object. To view an object's status, click Find. The OMW Projects folder is displayed. Drill into OMW Projects by double-clicking it or clicking the plus sign for a list of valid projects. Choose the project that contains the object you wish to view. Objects are contained within the Objects folder in a specified project. Select the object to be viewed. The status summary data will appear in the right-hand window.

*NOTE*

*If another display was selected, the status can be re-displayed by selecting Row | Exit status.*

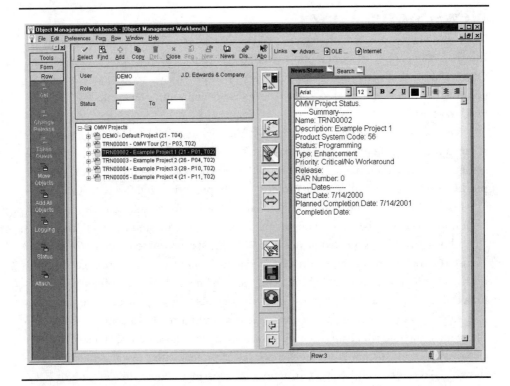

**FIGURE 1-6.** Status view

You will see the object name, description, product code, product system code, creation date, and OneWorld release. Objects may also contain location information, check out information, and token information if they are Object Librarian objects. Objects will appear in the Project view with or without a check mark, and in different color schemes. At a glance, you can see which object you have checked out and which objects hold tokens in a project. You can also see which objects hold a token but are not checked out. This will be discussed in Chapter 2. It is important to understand this scheme so that you aren't inadvertently forced to override changes you have made to your objects. Figure 1-7 displays an object's status information for an Object Librarian object. Figure 1-8 displays an object's status information for a Non–Object Librarian object.

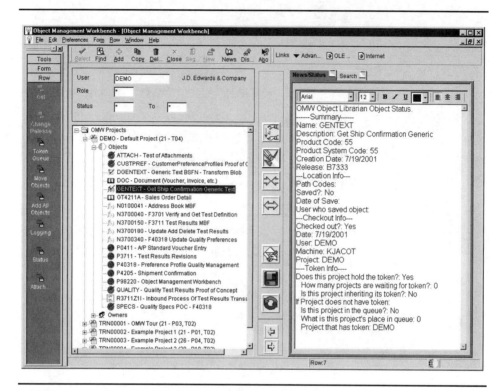

**FIGURE 1-7.** Object Librarian Object Status view

When an owner is selected in the Project view, the News/Status tab will show information about the selected owner. To view owner status information, click Find. The OMW Projects folder is displayed, as well as other projects for a user. Open up the project containing the desired owner. In the Owners folder, highlight the owner in which you wish to display information. The owner's status summary will appear in the right-hand window. It includes data about the date the project was assigned, the time it was assigned, the user group, and whether the owner is a lead. The lead option is future functionality. It can, however, be used to mark which supervisor has ultimate responsibility over a team, but it will not allow any special privileges to this user. The owner summary data is typically useful when you wish to view the user group information. If an owner is not contained within the appropriate user group, rules should be applied such that projects follow correct change management guidelines.

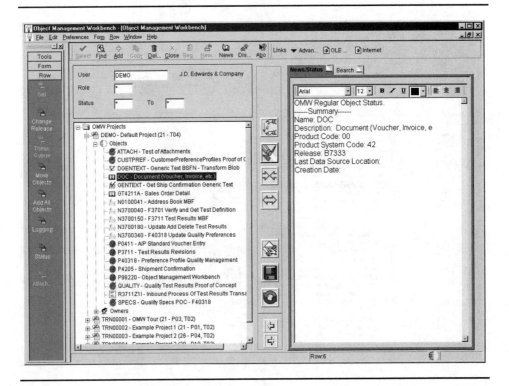

**FIGURE 1-8.** Non–Object Librarian Object Status view

The last piece of data included in the summary is estimated hours. By entering estimated hours for an owner, as well as planned completion dates and other data into the project, a manager can easily review the projects in the system for information such as how long a development effort is taking and whether the task will be completed on time. Again, the attachments to a project, as well as category codes, can be used to further track pertinent project data.

## Search View

Performing an efficient search is the first step in adding objects or owners to a project. Searches are done by clicking the Search tab in the right-hand window. You can then, as a user, fill in the appropriate object search criteria fields.

## Basic Search

A basic search is performed by selecting values first in the Category field. A drop-down list will give you the valid values. Select from Data Dictionary, Menus, Object Librarian, OMW Projects, Owners, User Defined Codes, User Overrides, and Workflow. In the Search Type field, select one of the search types from the drop-down list. This list displays only those search types that apply to the selected object category. You can also enter more search criteria information in the Search field to further specify your search results. What you enter in this field is determined by the Search Type selected. An example of a basic search (not added to a project at this time) is given in the following steps and shown in Figure 1-9.

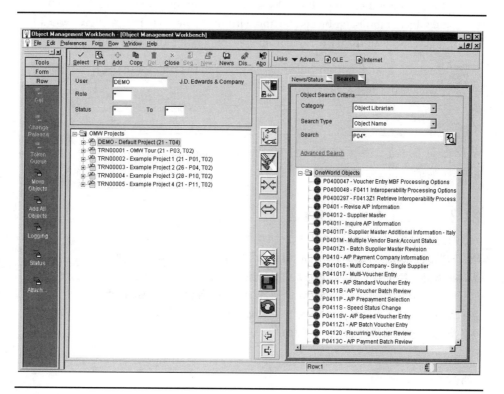

**FIGURE 1-9.**   Search view example

We will discuss adding objects to projects in Chapter 2. You add objects to a project using the arrows in the center column of action buttons:

1. Click the Search tab on the right side of the OMW form. This will display the Object Search Criteria fields and results (once retrieved).

2. Click the Category field. Select an object category from the pull-down menu. (Owners is not an object category; this is covered in the next section.) For this example, choose Object Librarian.

3. Click the Search Type field. Select a search type from the pull-down menu. For this example, choose Object Name.

4. In the Search field, type P04*. By doing this, you have limited your search to all Object Librarian objects starting with the value P04. This will give you all applications in the 04 (or Accounts Payable) system/product code.

5. Click the Search button (magnifying glass) to the right of the Search field to display your results.

**N O T E**

*When using the Search field, depending on the database you are using, it is case sensitive.*

**N O T E**

*You use the pipe (I) to specify a suffix to search for. For example, entering* **R0006PIXJDE\*, with Category = Object Librarian and Search Type = Object Name|Version Name** *searches for all XJDE versions of Object R0006P (see Figure 1-10). The advanced search functionality, however, is easier to use when searching for versions. Examples of this type of search are shown in Figures 1-15 through 1-17, at the end of this chapter.*

## Owner Search

The Search view is also used to locate OneWorld users (such as DEMO) to add to a project in an assigned role. To search on an owner, click Owners in the Category field. Select a valid Search Type in the drop-down list. Valid types are Address Book

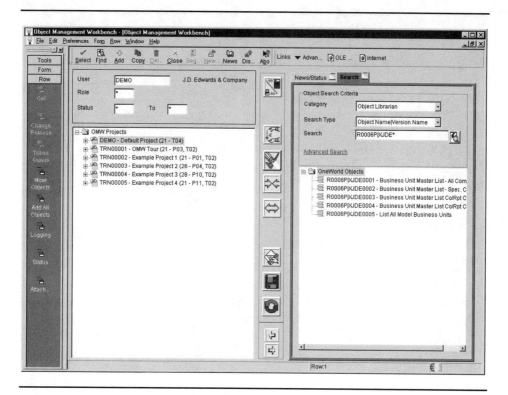

**FIGURE 1-10.**   Search view Delimiter example

Number, Alpha Name, and User ID. You can also enter more search criteria information in the Search field to further specify your search results. Figure 1-11 displays search results where Category = Owners and Search Type = User ID. The Search field further specified this search when we entered *D*. When you click Search, the system shows user IDs that contain the letter *D*.

## Advanced Search

The advanced search function allows you to search for objects and owners using search capabilities over a wider range of values. This may be necessary if the search types provided for basic searching do not allow you to narrow your search far enough. To perform an advanced search, you must fill in the Category and Search Type fields.

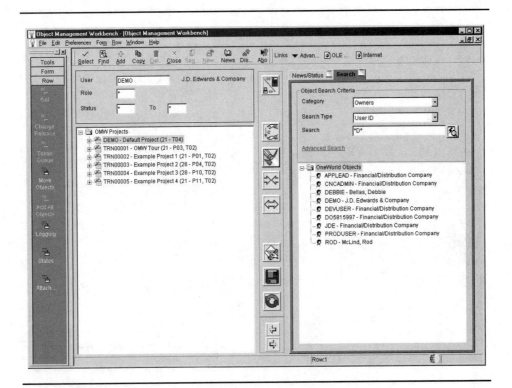

**FIGURE 1-11.** Search view owner example

These fields will be used to indicate the type of search form that will be displayed. Figures 1-12 through 1-14 show an advanced search on a User Defined Code (UDC).

Click the Advanced Search link just below the Search field. The appropriate Search and Select form will display according to the Category and Search Type fields that you entered. You can then use the QBE fields to search for your objects.

Once you have located the desired object, you can select one or multiple grid rows to return to the Search View window on the OMW form.

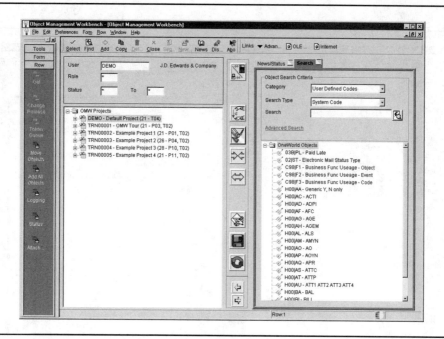

**FIGURE 1-12.**    Advanced search UDC OMW form

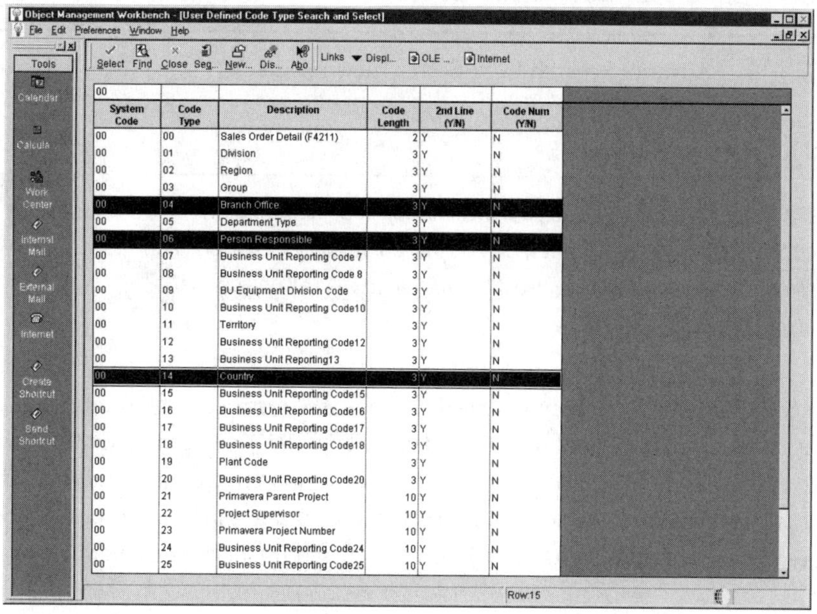

**FIGURE 1-13.**    Advanced search UDC search and select

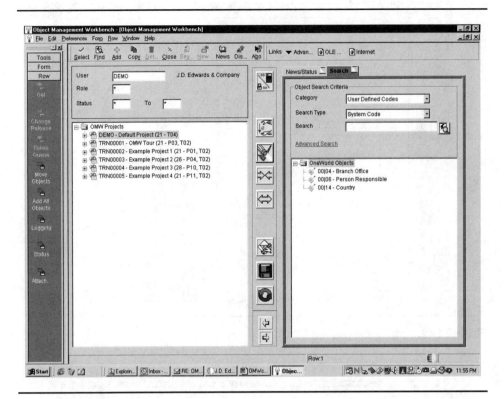

**FIGURE 1-14.** Advanced search UDC Search view results

*N O T E*

*Page at a Time processing is enabled within the Object Search window, meaning that there may be only a few objects that are actually displayed upon completing your search. You must use the scroll bar to view all objects that were returned from your search.*

Once the records have been returned to the OMW form, Row | Exit, Add All Objects can be used to add all the selected records to the project in view. This can be used to add multiple records to a selected project; however, keep in mind that this will add all objects that meet the search criteria entered, and not just the records that are displayed in the window. Add All Objects is discussed further in Chapter 2.

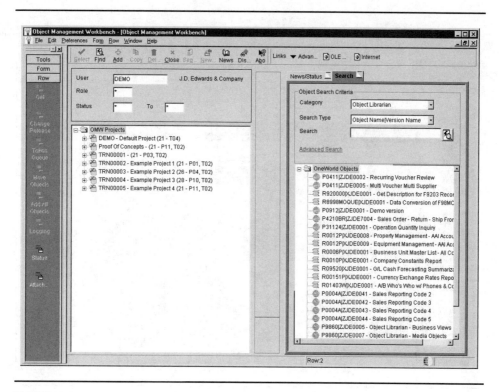

**FIGURE 1-15.**   Advanced search versions OMW form

Figures 1-15 through 1-17 show an advanced search on versions for UBE R0006P. This is especially useful when there may be versions that users created with another naming convention. For example, if you want to see more than just the XJDE versions of a UBE, or select multiple versions into your project for modification, you may use the advanced search forms. The advanced search and select form for versions also shows you the user that created the version, who made the last modification, when it was last changed and executed, the check out status, whether it resides on the server, security information and a description, and the version list mode. This screen will appear differently depending upon the type of object on which the search is performed. In order to move the selected objects into a project, you must select a project in the Project View window.

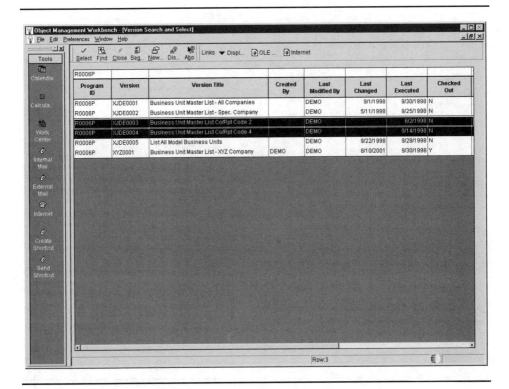

**FIGURE 1-16.** Advanced search versions search and select

# Summary

In this chapter, we have just begun to discover the benefits of the OMW change management system. We have discussed the basic concepts, or fundamentals, necessary for change management to occur in your development environment. We have also covered the Object Management Workbench form, which is key to beginning the development project life cycle, as well as key to pulling everything together in a planned and systematic fashion, all the while providing automation to meet your needs in a more effective manner.

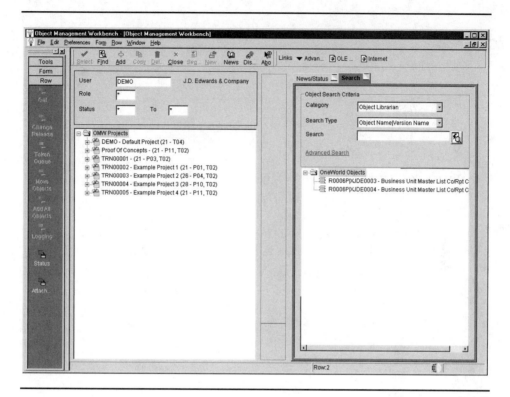

**FIGURE 1-17.**   Advanced search versions search view results

# CHAPTER 2

# Developing with Object Management Workbench

Working with Projects

Working with Objects

Working with Tokens

Working with Owners

Developing objects with the Object Management Workbench (OMW) is much different than with the Object Librarian (OL). With the introduction of projects, user roles, and object tokens, OMW provides a much more complex system that you must learn. When you hear the word "complex," you often think, "difficult." Truth be told, since the introduction of these concepts, it is much simpler to manage your work, to make sure that no one else has made changes to the same object you are working on while you're working on it, and to group all of the objects that are affected by your modification. These are just a few of the benefits that you receive as a developer. OMW also gets rid of a lot of the manual processes you had with OL. Do you recall all of the paper forms you had to fill out, and all of the approvals you had to go through just to transfer an object? With the OMW, the activity rules and transfer procedures are built into the system. You no longer have to worry about which path code to choose when checking an object out and in, or worry that you chose the wrong path code. The system is configured to worry for you.

In this chapter, you will learn how to work with projects, objects, tokens, and owners. All of the tools that you need as a developer are contained within one easy-to-use interface. Throughout this chapter, you will be shown how to use OMW in the development of your objects, and you will be given examples of when to use each of the tools.

# Working with Projects

Projects allow you to methodically group OneWorld objects so as to complete a problem or task. By tracking your changes in the context of a project, you can more readily track all modifications needed for a specific change. This section describes how to use OMW to create a project, modify project properties, view project logs, add all objects, move objects, and advance a project to the next status in the software development life cycle.

## Creating a Project

Creating a project in OneWorld in order to track all modifications for a specific task is fairly simple. When you create a new project, you can create one based on your own project naming conventions, or create one based on a link to your Software Action Request (SAR) system. Because you probably won't have a link into a SAR system, we will touch on it only briefly throughout this chapter by references to such a system. Keep in mind that actions that you can perform on a project not linked to a SAR also hold true for those that are linked to a SAR. To create a project, follow these steps:

1. Click Add. The Object Management Workbench – [Add OneWorld Object to the Project, <Project Name>] form displays.

2. Click the OMW Project button in the Object Management Workbench group box.

3. Click OK. The Object Management Workbench – [Project Revisions] form displays.

4. On the Summary tab, fill in the Project ID, Description, Type, Severity, Product System Code, and Release fields. These fields are described in detail following these steps.

5. On the Dates tab, fill in the Date Started and Planned Completion Date fields. The Date Entered and Completion Dates are disabled, but will populate automatically for you to the date the project was entered and the date the project reaches a completed status, respectively.

6. On the Category Codes tab, fill in the desired category codes. These codes can be set up to meet your project needs. The UDC H92/C1-C0 (10) is used to customize the data that is tracked per project. Examples of category codes that you might want to set up include data tracking the estimated and actual hours for the development of the entire project above and beyond the dates that are used on the Dates tab, third-party involvement, and legacy system references.

7. On the Attachments tab, you can add text comments to your project. These attachments will carry through for the life of the project. You may also access these attachments from the OMW form. To view project attachments, perform the following steps:

    1. From the OMW form, click Find to display your projects.

    2. Click the project you wish to view attachments on.

    3. Click attachments from the Row | Exit. Your attachment data will display in the right-hand window (see Figure 2-1).

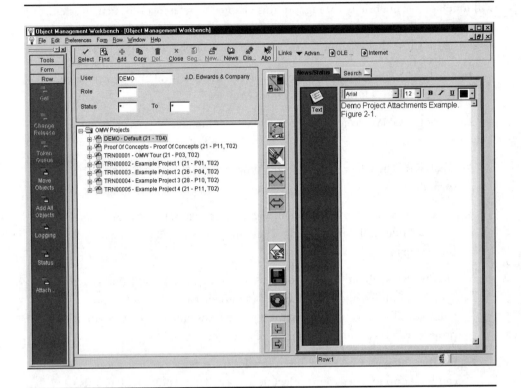

**FIGURE 2-1.** Project attachments

*T I P*

*To save your attachments, you must be in Design view. Although you are able to type in the News/Status window, you cannot save your attachments in this view. To get to Design view after you have already created your project, click the Design button in the center column of action buttons (T square). Click the Attachments tab. Make your changes, and then click OK to save those changes.*

## Project ID

The Project ID is the unique project identifier. It commonly appears in direct relation to the description of your modification. In our example, the Project ID equals

ProofOfConcepts, which is a duplicate of the Description (see Figure 2-2). Long project IDs can, however, become cumbersome to manage; thus, as part of your change management process, you may want to devise a naming convention for projects (e.g., FPI09ALLOC or MPI48INTXX, where FPI = Financials Process Improvements, 09 = Originating System Code, ALLOC = A short description of the type of modification [ALLOC = Allocations]; and where MPI = Manufacturing Process Improvements, 48 = Originating System Code, INTXX = Integration with XX system [third-party software product code]). At J.D. Edwards, a SAR system is used to track projects; that is, project IDs have the same value as a SAR entered into the SAR system. If you have a SAR or Call Tracking system, this is another option for naming conventions within OneWorld projects. Integrating OMW with a SAR system is part of the setup and configuration discussed in Chapter 3.

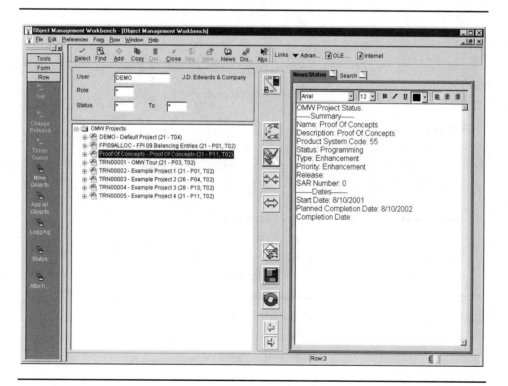

**FIGURE 2-2.**   Create a project

## Description

Description is a more detailed description of your project. FPI09ALLOC could be expanded to have a description of FPI 09 Balancing Entries. The description field is limited to 30 alphanumeric characters.

## Type

Type describes the type of project you are creating. User Defined Code (UDC) H92/PT (Project Type) stores the valid values. Base OneWorld comes with the project types listed in the following table. These are available for you to view; the OMW allows you to select only type 01 or type 02. You will receive an error if you choose another type that is delivered, or if you choose a type that you add to the UDC H92/PT.

| Project Type | Project Description |
| --- | --- |
| 01 | Bug |
| 02 | Enhancement |
| 04 | Default |
| 05 | Tracking/Parent Bug |
| 06 | Tracking/Parent Enhancement |

## Severity

Severity describes the severity of the project you are creating. UDC H92/SV (OMW Project Severity) stores the valid values. Base OneWorld comes with the following severity levels; you can modify these to meet your project needs.

| Severity Level | Severity Description |
| --- | --- |
| 01 | Critical/No Workaround |
| 02 | Critical/Workaround |
| 03 | Not Critical/No Workaround |
| 04 | Not Critical/Workaround |
| 10 | Critical Enhancement |
| 11 | Enhancement |
| 12 | Low-Priority Enhancement |

## Product System Code

Product system code is the system code in which the project is located, as well as where, most likely, the objects are located. For custom development work, system codes 55–59 are used. It is recommended that all custom work is done within this range of systems.

## Release

Object release values directly correlate with the transfer (activity) rules; however, the release value of the project is independent of object release values and of the transfer (activity) rules. When working with OneWorld Xe, the release is B7333.

## Status

The status field will automatically default to the status defined by the administrator. The standard configuration default value of a new project is 11 New Project Pending Review. Again, you can change this during setup and configuration. This means that when your project is created, it will automatically have a status of 11 New Project Pending Review.

## SAR Number

The SAR Number field is grayed out and disabled unless your system is configured to integrate with a SAR system.

# Project Properties

Over the course of your project, you can change project properties. This includes items such as descriptions, dates, and severity. You may want to change these properties if the type of project you are working on has changed. For example, if the project is no longer required for go-live, the severity may change from 01 Critical/No Workaround to 03 Not Critical/No Workaround. To change the properties of a project, you do a find on the OMW form, choose the project you wish to change, and then click the Design button (T square) in the center column of action buttons or click Select on the toolbar.

## Summary Tab

The Summary tab allows you to change the description of your project, the type, the severity, the product system code, and the OneWorld release. Again, note that the release is independent of the object release values and of the transfer (activity) rules.

### Dates Tab

The Dates tab allows you to change the date the project started, as well as the planned completion date.

### Category Codes Tab

The Category Codes tab allows you to change any of the category code values you have previously set up.

### Attachments Tab

The Attachments tab allows you to add to the text attachments data. The Attachments tab is often used to store information such as meetings and attendees, as well as sign off procedures and dates.

# Logging

The logging system allows you to view changes made to a project and/or an object. These changes include information such as whether a project was advanced and when, object check out, check in, and so on. Because the system is structured on two levels, you can view either project messages or object messages. The first level defines the action being logged, the object being acted upon, and the project the object belongs to. The second level contains log information for each action defined in the first logging level. This means that if you advance a project to the next project status, you will see, in the logs, the request for advancement (transfer) and the objects that were transferred. To view project logs, you must select the project for which you wish to view logs. At this point, choose Row | Exit Logging. The Object Management Workbench – [Work With Project Logs] form displays. Click Find to display the log records for the project selected. To show only the last logging action, you can select the Show Only Last Action check box. See Figure 2-3 for an example of actions performed on our project Demo.

To view object logs, you must select the project and the object you wish to view logs on. At this point, choose Row | Exit Logging. The Object Management Workbench – [Work With Object Logs] form displays. Click Find to display the log records for the object selected. To show only the last logging action, you can select the Show Only Last Action check box. See Figure 2-4 for an example of an object log.

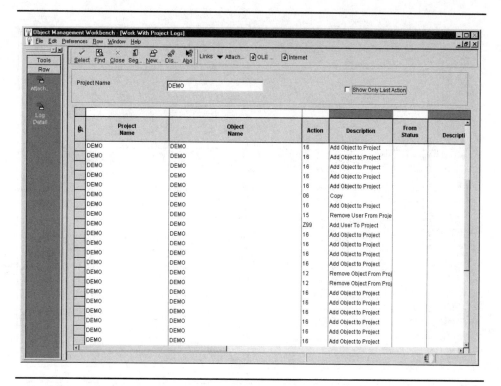

**FIGURE 2-3.** Project logging

---

### N O T E

*It is very important to differentiate between project-level logging and object-level logging. To determine why a user received an error when, for example, advancing the status of a project that involved a transfer, the project level logs should be used to determine which objects received an error, and subsequently look at the object level logs for those objects to determine why they failed to transfer successfully.*

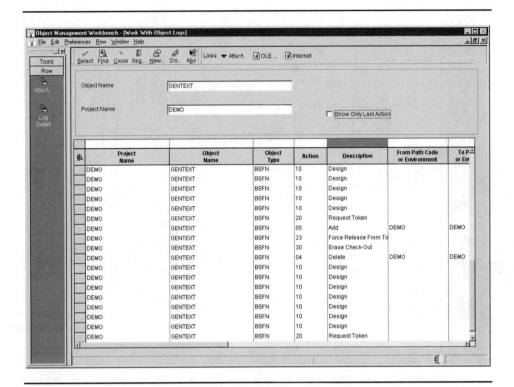

**FIGURE 2-4.**   Object logging

# Add All Objects

With OMW, you get some new functionality that can be useful when deciding which objects need to be modified to meet your business process requirements. The Add All Objects Row | Exit allows you to add a group of objects to a project. An example would be a search on all P13* objects, or all equipment-related interactive applications. You would perform this type of search if you wanted to review each of these applications and modify them, for instance, to add a form control pertinent to your everyday business. You would perform the search, highlight the project you wish to add these objects to, and then choose Row | Exit Add All Objects (see Figure 2-5).

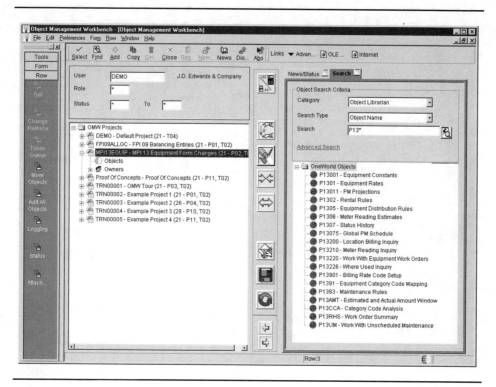

**FIGURE 2-5.** Add All Objects Search results

**N O T E**

*Page At A Time processing is enabled within the object search window, meaning that only a few objects may actually be displayed upon completing your search. You must use the scroll bar to view all objects that were returned from your search.*

This Row | Exit can be used to add multiple records to a selected project, but keep in mind that this will add all objects that meet the search criteria entered, and not just the records that are displayed in the window (see Figure 2-6).

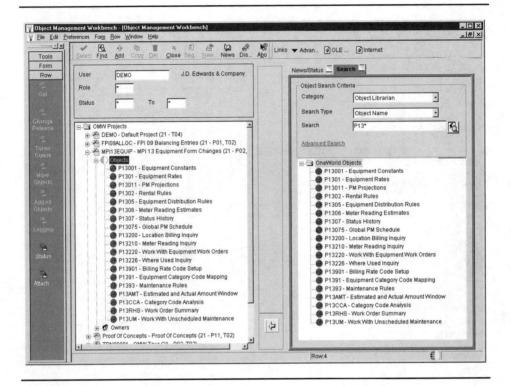

**FIGURE 2-6.** Add All Objects Project view

---

*CAUTION*

*You can choose Row | Exit Add All Objects without having performed a search. If you do this, you could potentially be adding all objects that exist in your system to the project that is chosen.*

# Move Objects

There may be times when you wish to move an object from a project—for instance, if you have not finished developing an object but wish to advance the project, or if you simply added the object to the wrong project. You can move objects from one project to another by dragging and dropping them, or by using the row exit; but make sure that both projects and the object are visible in your Project view. This action can also be used to move users from one project to another, or to move a project under another project. Moving objects involves moving an object or moving multiple objects.

As stated, to move an object, in the OMW form Project view, click the object you want to move. Drag the object over to the target project, and drop the object. The object will be removed from the source project and will be visible only in the target project. If the object you are trying to move is checked out, OMW will validate that the target project is at a status that allows check out. It also checks that the sign-on user is allowed to check the selected object out.

To move multiple objects, click the project containing the objects you want to move. From the Row | Exit menu, choose Move Objects. If you use Row | Exit, Move Objects is within the Advanced option. In the To Project field, enter the project you wish to move the selected object. On the Search & Select form, choose the objects you want to move and click Select (see Figure 2-7). The system will move the objects from the source project and will be visible only in the target project. Depending upon the number of objects you are moving, this process could be quite lengthy.

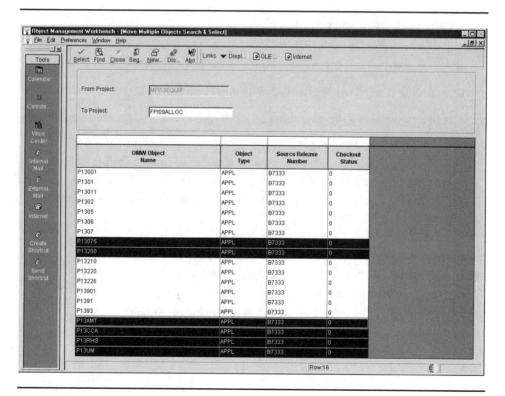

**FIGURE 2-7.**  Move Multiple Objects

There is a distinction between moving an object between projects, and removing an object from a project and adding it to another project. When an object is moved, if it was checked in under the source project, the check-in record will be updated with the project name of the target project. When an object is removed from the source and added to the target, this check-in value will not be updated. OMW will transfer an object only if the check-in record indicates that the object was modified under the current project that is being transferred. Without this system check, OMW could potentially transfer changes that were not associated with the current project. Should this happen, OMW will make an object-level log entry indicating that the object was not modified by the current project.

## Advance a Project

The project status is advanced as you complete work on a project. OMW may be configured with Allowed Actions for each user role to allow users to perform certain actions only when a project is at a specific status. Advancing a project status will advance its associated SAR status, if SAR integration is enabled. A project status change can also kick off object transfers to move objects between specified path codes or data sources. To advance a project, perform the following actions:

1. From the OMW form, click Find to display the project list.

2. Click the project to be advanced.

3. Click the Advance Project icon at the top of the center column of action buttons. This button will be enabled only if you play a valid role on the project in which you are attempting to advance. The Object Management Workbench – [Confirm Project Status Change – <Project ID>] form will be displayed (see Figure 2-8).

### CAUTION

*You are cautioned as to whether you want to advance this project to the next status, as it may kick off an object transfer process you may not want to occur. For example, if an object in your project isn't fully developed and you are advancing the project, it may be transferred to another environment and path code, such as production. You don't want an undeveloped object in production, especially if it updates data in tables in an untested manner. Read this form carefully.*

4. Enter the status that you want to advance the project to. You will be allowed to enter only a status that has been set up in the OMW configuration as a valid

Next status. You may click the visual assist to see what valid next statuses are currently set up for your user signon. The status you will choose is most likely what the software development life cycle says is the Next Valid Status. (This is also shown in Figure 2-8.)

*N O T E*

*You can check the Validate Only box to validate the status change without actually advancing the project. This allows you to verify that the project is valid before attempting any object transfers. If a project status change is going to kick off a transfer, the user may want to validate that the project and its objects are ready to be transferred. Any subproject or projects linked through token inheritance will also be validated at this time.*

5.  Click OK. If you did not click the Validate Only box, you will actually change the project status and kick off any object transfers. If you clicked the Validate Only box, project status validation only will run. The OMW form will reappear.

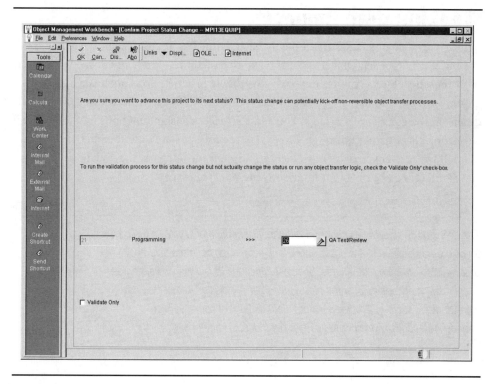

**FIGURE 2-8.**   Advance project

## Deleting a Project

If you add a project in error, you may delete it from the system. When you delete a project, the system removes all objects and owners from the project. If you delete a project that contains objects that are checked out, the system erases the check out on each object before deleting the project. If the project holds any tokens, the system also releases the token for those objects. This action will not delete any objects left in the project.

With the standard OMW configuration, you may delete only projects that are at a status of 11 New Project Pending Review. Quite often, users ask to delete projects that are at a 01 Complete status so that they may more easily search the system for past projects. It is not recommended that you purge these projects; however, as part of your system back-up and change management plan, you will want to discuss the longevity of storing these projects for audit purposes. To delete a project, on the OMW form, highlight the project you wish to delete and then click Delete. Click OK to confirm the delete.

## Working with Objects

In OneWorld, an object has traditionally been defined as a reusable entity created by the OneWorld tool set. Objects are the backbone of all development efforts. Without these reusable objects, you do not have a workable product. You can create a new object, view and modify an existing object, or delete an object from within OMW. You do this in the context of a project. You can also access design functions for a object and check objects out and in through OMW. These processes are described in the sections that follow. Also covered are object icons and their meanings as they relate to OMW, and maintaining objects in multiple software releases.

### N O T E

*The definition of objects has changed with the introduction of OMW. In the past, an object was defined as including only OL objects, such as interactive and batch applications, data structures, business functions, business views, named event rules, media objects, and tables. Now objects include OL objects and Non-OL objects. Non-OL objects include data dictionary items, versions, user-defined codes, workflow items, user overrides, and menus.*

# Creating a New Object

During the development process, you may want to create a new object to enhance your business requirements. The process to create a new object is as follows:

1. Do a find on the OMW form to view all projects for your user ID.

2. Click the project in which you wish to add a new object.

3. Click Add. The Object Management Workbench – [Add OneWorld Object to the Project, <Project Name>] form displays. If the Add button is grayed out, your user role may not have rights to perform this function. See the "Allowed Actions" section in Chapter 3 for more information on configuring your system for this operation for your user ID.

4. Click the desired object type you wish to add, and click OK.

5. If the object is an Object Librarian object, the Object Management Workbench – [Add Object] form displays.

6. Fill in the Object Name, Description, Product Code, Product System Code, and Object Use, and click OK to create the new object. These fields are described in detail following these steps.

7. Once you click OK, the object is created and added to your project. Click the Design Tools tab on the form that displays to perform development or design functions on that object. The design features available to you are explained in more detail in the "Design Functions" section.

## Object Name

The Object Name is a combination of the type and system code, as well as an indication of the type of process you will be running. For example, P0411 is an interactive application (P), in system code 04 (Accounts Payable). R52425 is a batch application (R), system code 52 (Contract Billing). An example for a custom batch application would be R5652425; a batch application (R), system code 56 (custom), system code 52 (originating system). This object would most likely be a modification to the existing R52425 object to meet the business needs without changing the vanilla J.D. Edwards OneWorld product.

## Description

The Description is a basic depiction of the object in which you are creating.

## Product Code and Product System Code

The Product Code and Product System Code are usually the same; they will be within 55–59 for custom objects.

## Object Use

Use the visual assist to determine your object use. It is not recommended that you customize these values; rather, choose from the list according to the function of the object.

# Viewing and Modifying an Existing Object

To view or modify an existing object, you must add that object to a project. You will need to first search for your object and then add it to your project. Most often, if you are viewing an existing object, that object is added to your default project. If later you determine that you need to modify that object by adding additional functionality through additional code or through a plug-n-play, you can drag and drop it into your active project. The process of adding an existing object to a project is described here:

1.  Do a find on the OMW form to view all projects for a user.

2.  Click the project in which you wish to add an object.

3.  In the search window, perform a search on the object in which you wish to view. Search capabilities were discussed in Chapter 1 in the "Object Management Workbench Form" section.

4.  Once you've located that object, highlight the object and click the arrow that points left in your center column of action buttons to add it to your project. You can also double-click the object to add it to your project. When the object has been added to the project, OMW will automatically click Find to refresh the tree information. If the left arrow does not appear in your center column of action buttons, you may not have rights to view and/or change existing objects. See Chapter 3 for more information on configuring your system.

# Removing and Deleting an Existing Object

You may want to remove an object from your project during the software development life cycle. Objects are removed when you've reviewed the information and no longer wish to have it in your project list. Often, the default project contains so many objects that it is cumbersome and difficult to manage; thus, you can remove objects from the project. Removing objects from your project does not delete them from your system; it simply removes them from your view. You may also want to remove an object from your project if a change is no longer required on that object. Deleting objects from OneWorld is discussed later in this section.

## Removing an Existing Object

To remove an object from your project, follow these steps:

1. Select the object that you want to remove in the Project View window.

2. Click the arrow that points to your right in the center column of action buttons.

3. Verify that the object was removed from the project by doing a find on the OMW form.

### N O T E

When an object is removed from a project, the token will be released and the check out erased, if the object is checked out at the time. With the standard J.D. Edwards OneWorld OMW configuration, the only time an object is allowed to be removed from a project is in a project status of 21 In Programming.

### T I P

To remove all objects from a project, the R98222B UBE may be used. The user that runs this report (UBE) must play a role on the project from which objects are being purged.

## Deleting an Existing Object

There are times when an object is no longer needed, or more often, that object was added by mistake. At this point, you will want to delete the object from your system. You can delete an Object Librarian (OL) object from the server, from your local machine only, or from the save location, or you can mark it to be deleted completely from the system when the project is advanced. Non-Object Librarian (Non-OL) objects have two different levels of deletion. You can delete an object from the server (this is the default setting), or you can mark the object to be deleted completely from the system when the project is advanced.

For an OL object, you can delete the local specifications and/or, if the OL object is checked in, the checked-in version of this object. Also, if the OL object was saved to the check-in location, it can be deleted from that location as well. In order to delete the object from its administratively defined check-in location, the Object Management Configuration (OMC) transfer (activity) rules for object deletion must point to the same location as the check-in location. See the "Activity Rules" section in Chapter 3 for more information about this process. OL object deletion from any other location can be done by marking the object to be deleted completely from the system. The object will then be deleted when the project in which it resides is advanced. This means that if the object status indicates that it is to be deleted, then when the project is advanced, instead of the object being transferred, it will be deleted. The OMC transfer (activity) rules must be of type 03 (transfer or delete) or 02 (delete only).

To delete an object:

1. Do a find on the OMW form to view all projects for a user.

2. Click the project in which you wish to delete an object.

3. Click the object you wish to delete. Objects are listed under the Objects portion. The plus signs (+) are used to expand the lists.

4. Click the Del(ete) button in the toolbar. The Object Management Workbench – [Delete of <Object Name>] form displays. It displays differently for OL or Non-OL objects, as shown in Figures 2-9 and 2-10.

5. Click one of the check boxes. Click OK to implement your deletion choice. Objects that are marked to be deleted completely will be **bolded** in your project.

## CAUTION

*You should delete the object from the system, by marking the object to be deleted from all locations, only if you are absolutely sure this needs to take place. There is no undo button. Once the object has been marked for deletion, to remove the delete flag, the object must be removed from the project and then re-added. Once the delete flag is set, the object will be deleted from the other path codes and environments as the project status is advanced. To view the location where objects will be deleted when the Delete Object From Server check box is selected, click View Locations and a form will display these locations. The locations that display are based on the OMC transfer (activity) rules that are defined by your system administrator.*

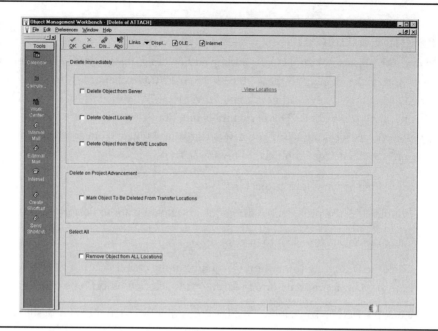

**FIGURE 2-9.** Delete OL object

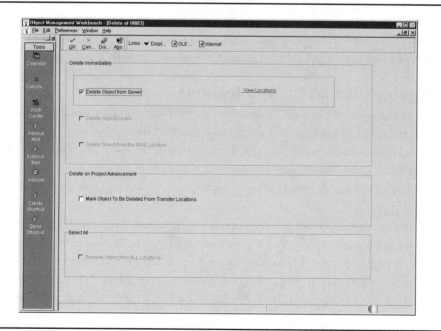

**FIGURE 2-10.** Delete Non-OL object

# Design Functions

Working with objects not only entails adding and deleting objects, but you will most likely want to make changes to these objects. To make these changes, you will use the design tools built for OneWorld development. With OMW, you are just a few clicks away from these design tools. The design tools functions that display are based on the object type you are working with. You can design a new object from scratch or modify existing objects. To design an object, follow these steps:

1. Click Find to view your project list.

2. Double-click the project containing the object you want to design.

3. Click the object you wish to develop.

4. Click the Design Action button (T square) in the center column of action buttons. The appropriate design form for the selected object type displays.

5. Click the Design Tools tab to display the available design tools for designing the object type you selected.

Part of any development effort is understanding and using the design functions available for each object. The following sections illustrate the design functions available for each object type. For more information about using these tools, as well as the other tools mentioned in this chapter, please refer to *J.D. Edwards OneWorld: A Developer's Guide* by Chris Enyeart and Steven Hester (Osborne/McGraw-Hill, 2000).

## Designing Interactive Applications

Once you've clicked the Design Tools tab for an interactive application object, you can start Form Design Aid (FDA), Browse Event Rules, Run the Application, exit to the Versions List, run Vocabulary Overrides, View the Forms for the application, or perform a Visual ER Compare (see Figure 2-11).

FDA allows you to modify your interactive application using the OneWorld FDA tool.

Browse Event Rules gives you the opportunity to review the event rules used within the application without having to enter the FDA. The Browse Event Rules tool is useful if you wish to quickly locate where a form control is used and how the value is assigned. For example, if you wish to see where the search type field is assigned within the address book application (P01012), you would click the Browse Event

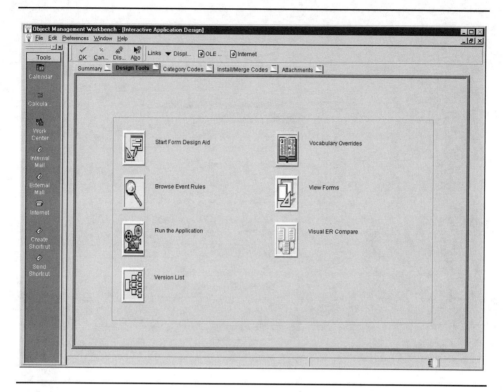

**FIGURE 2-11.** Interactive application design functions

Rules button. At this time, you will see a listing of all the event rules for the P01012. Right-click the name of the application and choose Search. Type **Search Type** and uncheck Match Case. Once you click the Find Next button, the tool will perform a search for everywhere the words "Search Type" are used (see Figure 2-12).

You can run an application from OMW by clicking the Run The Application button. This is useful when first designing an application. If you run an application from the Design Tools tab, it will allow you to quickly test your changes without having to add the object to a menu. It is recommended that you exit out of FDA prior to running the application; however, it is not always necessary. You can also run the application by typing the object ID (e.g., **P0411**) in the fast path, or from a menu. To run the object from a menu, you will need to create a new menu or add the object to an existing menu.

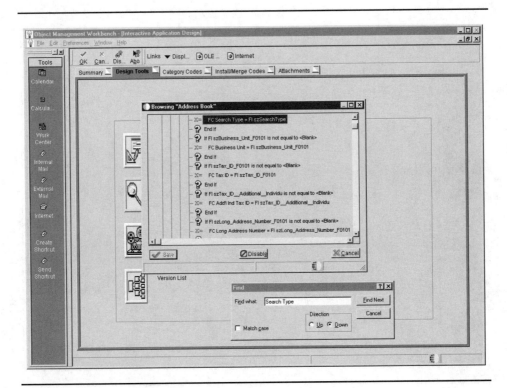

**FIGURE 2-12.**   Interactive application browser event rules

When performing continuous development, meaning you are making multiple changes and testing those changes numerous times during one session, it is recommended that you use the Run button on the Design Tools tab. When an object is run, OneWorld will load the specifications for the object into cache. This cache is used the next time the application is run, until OneWorld is exited. When you are using the Run button on the Design Tools tab, OMW will clear this cache so that fresh specifications are used each time; therefore, the user will see the latest changes that were made to the application the last time it was saved.

From the Design Tools tab, you can exit to the Versions List for your interactive application. When you click this button, you will be brought to the Object Management Workbench – [Work With Interactive Versions] form. Here you can run a specific version of the application you are developing or modifying, add a new version, change the properties of a version, or change the print options. You can also display only those versions that you created, or all versions within the system. If versions are modified or added, they will be added to the current project that the user is working in.

When choosing Vocabulary Overrides, you will be brought to the Object Management Workbench – [Work With Vocabulary Overrides] form. You must have proper authority to make vocabulary override changes to enter this form. Vocabulary Overrides allow you the ability to change—for instance, and most commonly—the glossary for a particular data item on a form that will make it more descriptive of the module you are using. This is useful when you want to change a column description in one or two applications, but not across the entire system. If you change the description of the data dictionary item, the change is seen across the entire system.

*CAUTION*

*Objects cannot be checked out when Vocabulary Overrides are changed, since the changes are made directly to central objects. Checking in the object after modifying Vocabulary Overrides results in overwriting the changes that were just made.*

The View Forms button gives you an opportunity to make changes to a form's properties without entering FDA. By clicking this button, you are brought to the Object Management Workbench – [Work With Forms] screen. Here, you will see a list of all the forms contained within that interactive application. When you select a form, you can change the form information. This includes the description of the form, the type of form, the application, the product code, the help ID, the help filename, and a series of five category codes. We do not recommend making changes at this level, as they could alter the look, feel, and functionality of an application in drastic ways. It is recommended that all changes of this nature be made within FDA. You can add category code information here to track things such as where the application is called from. For example, you could set up Categories 1 through 5 (UDC 98/F1-5) to contain all system codes, and then choose all codes—up to five—where this application is used. These category codes are not readily available to the users, and custom reports would need to be developed in order to view this data; thus, they are not highly used. The Cross Reference facility on OneWorld has a similar concept, and is widely used.

Visual ER Compare is new functionality that was introduced in the Xe release of OneWorld. It allows you to visually compare code from the local machine and a path code, or from one machine to another. You will find yourself using this quite often when wanting to compare the changes another user made to what exists on your local machine. We use this tool quite often when wanting to understand what changes were just made to the system. For example, if functionality that was previously working is no longer working, you may want to compare the new code to the old code to see what has changed that may have affected your business process. Visual ER Compare is also used to see whether electronic software updates (ESUs) were applied to an object. By comparing the new code to the old code, you can see whether an object has been changed.

## Designing Batch Applications

From the Design Tools tab within a batch application (UBE), you can start Report Design Aid (RDA), Browse Event Rules, view Vocabulary Overrides, view the Versions List, or perform a Visual ER Compare (see Figure 2-13).

RDA allows you to modify your batch application using the OneWorld RDA tool.

The Browse Event Rules, Vocabulary Overrides, Versions List, and Visual ER Compare work very similarly to those described in the "Designing Interactive Applications" section, earlier in the chapter.

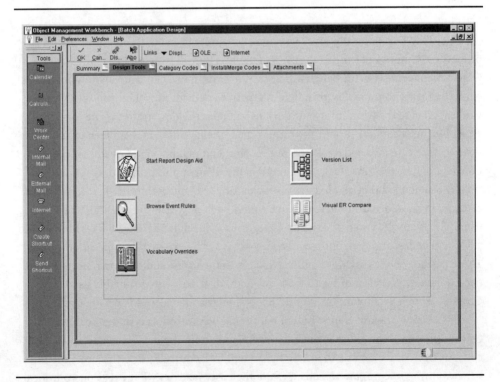

**FIGURE 2-13.**    Batch application design functions

Another form of batch application is a table conversion. To mark a UBE as a table conversion, the table conversion check box should be checked upon creation of the object. The tool that you use to create table conversions is the Table Conversion Design Aid. It performs much differently from RDA and requires a separate learning process. To access design, simply click the Start Table Conversion Design Aid button on the Design Tools tab.

## Designing Tables

From the Design Tools tab within a table (e.g., F40318), you can start Table Design Aid (TDA), start Table Trigger Design Aid, Build Table Triggers, Browse Table Trigger Event Rules, Generate the header file, or perform a Visual ER Compare (see Figure 2-14). Also note that the column prefix is displayed on this screen. When viewing a table in the database, each data dictionary item included in the table will be preceded by this prefix.

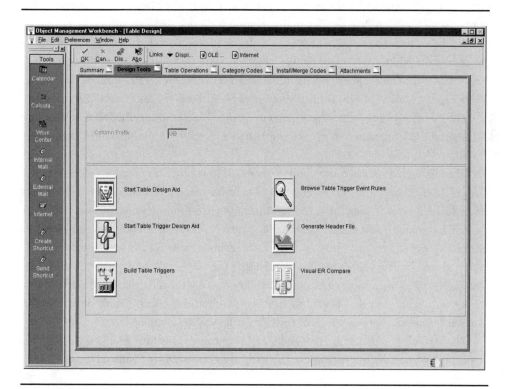

**FIGURE 2-14.**    Table design functions

Starting TDA allows you to design the table, that is, to add data dictionary items to an existing or new table. A common table function is to add a new index to the table. Adding a new index will give you quicker and better search-and-selection capabilities, depending upon your business needs.

The Table Trigger Design Aid allows you to add triggers to a table. A table trigger is code that is added so that when a table is viewed, the columns within the table will appear in a certain manner. Another table trigger would be such that when a record is added to a table, the record is written to a flat file that is picked up by a third-party application.

The Browse Table Trigger event rules button allows you quick access to the event rules that are used within the table trigger itself. That means that you do not have to go into table trigger design in order to see the code.

Clicking the Generate Header File button allows you to generate the file/table. This function is used when the table is new and you would like to view the contents in your database, or if the table was not generated correctly.

Visual ER Compare works as previously described in the "Designing Interactive Applications" section. Please refer to this section for a detailed example.

Before we move into the next design tools function discussion, it is important to first cover the additional functionality available to you on the Table Operations tab for a specific table. These operations include Generate Table, Generate Indexes, Remove Table From Database, Copy Table, Default Oracle Parameters, and Oracle Parameters.

The Generate Table option will generate your table in the specified data source. It is important to understand, however, that when you generate a table, all the data that resides in that table will be purged.

The Generate Indexes option will generate all indexes that you have defined for your table. This option will not cause the data to be purged. Generating indexes should be performed prior to using that index within other design functions.

Click Remove Table From Database to remove the table from the data source entered on the screen that appears after clicking this option. Tables are sometimes removed from a data source prior to performing the Copy Table function.

The Copy Table option gives you the ability to copy the data that resides in your table within a data source into another table. You should use Copy Table only when you are certain the specifications of the from and to tables match.

The Default Oracle Parameters and Oracle Parameters options give you the opportunity to define information such as storage allocations for your table and table indexes.

## Designing Business Functions

From the Design Tools tab, you can start Business Function (BSFN) Design Aid or Build the Business Function. You can also open BusBuild, to build any function, from OMW (see Figure 2-15). Also note that the Source Language, Parent DLL, and Business Function Location (C/S) are displayed on this screen. The Source Language is either C or NER, and is set up when the BSFN is created. The Parent DLL is the specification location of the BSFN. The Function Location is either Client Only, Client/Server, or Server Only. Client Only indicates that the BSFN is meant to run only on a local machine and will not be included in a server package build. Server Only indicates that the BSFN should be run only on the server. Client/Server indicates that the BSFN can be run local or on the server.

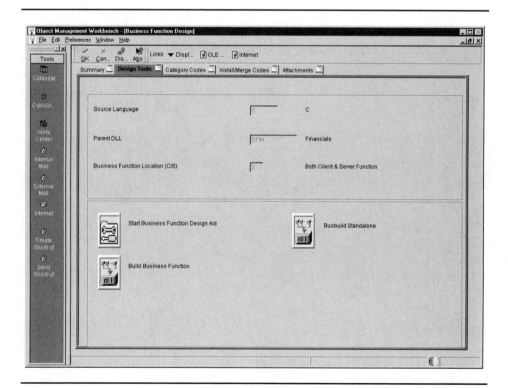

**FIGURE 2-15.**  Business Function Design Aid functions

Business Function Design Aid is used for C functions, as well as for Named Event Rules (NER). Within this tool, you will add Data Structures to use within your BSFN.

The Build Business Function button gives you quick access to the build function. If you would like to generate your code and check for errors or warnings, you will click this button.

The BusBuild function allows you to launch the BusBuild executable. BusBuild is a tool that allows you to build a particular function, rebuild libraries, or build all functions.

## Designing Data Structures

The user can Start Data Structure (DSTR) Design, Create a Type Definition, or enter the Named Mapping function. If your DSTR is a Generic Text or Media Object DSTR, you will be given the same options as you would for a DSTR, except the object type is Media Object Data Structure (GT), rather than DSTR (see Figure 2-16). If your DSTR

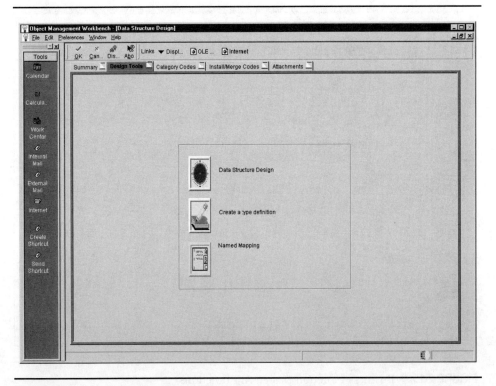

**FIGURE 2-16.** Data structure and media object design functions

is a Processing Option DSTR, you will be given the options to Start Processing Option Design Aid and Create a Type Definition (see Figure 2-17).

The Start Data Structure Design button gives you access to making changes to a data structure object type. A DSTR is a list of parameters, or data dictionary objects, that are used to pass data between applications, tables, or forms. DSTRs are either system generated or user generated. A system-generated DSTR is one that is used within FDA or RDA. It is used to pass data between other forms and sections. User-generated DSTRs are those that you create to pass data into a BSFN or NER, as well as for Processing Options and Media Objects.

To create a type definition, you will click the Create A Type Definition button. The type definition is loaded into cache and can be pasted into the desired document. A type definition, or typedef, is a list of your DSTR parameters, with their corresponding types and lengths. For example, the typedef for GT4211A is shown in Figure 2-18.

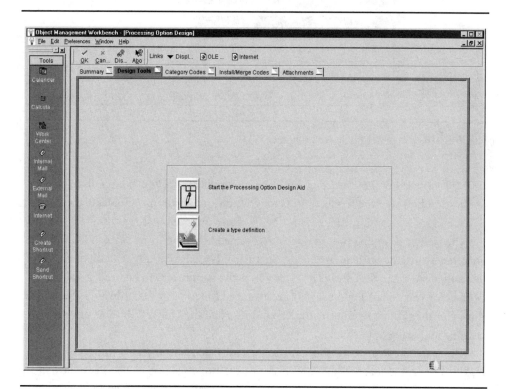

**FIGURE 2-17.** Processing Option Design functions

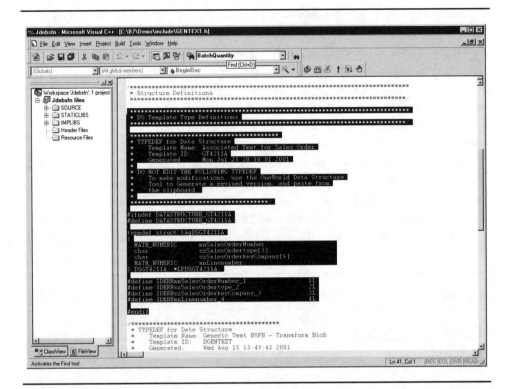

**FIGURE 2-18.** typedef for Media Object DSTR

GT4211A is used within the Ship Confirmation application (P4205) to tell the application how to store media objects for a Ship Confirmation. A media object DSTR commonly contains the keys to the file that your data is stored in.

The Named Mapping button opens the Named Mapping form. Named Mappings are often associated with Smart Fields. Smart Fields are essentially data dictionary items that call a BSFN that uses a DSTR where the parameters to be used are already defined for you. Smart Field usage is an advanced function in J.D. Edwards OneWorld; thus, you should have a definite understanding of all the OneWorld tools prior to creating and using Smart Fields.

The Start The Processing Option Design Aid (PDA) button gives you access to making changes to a processing option data structure object type. The PDA allows you to create the form that you see when running processing options on an interactive or batch application. Here, you add data dictionary items that are used and passed into your application. You have the option of choosing data dictionary items that contain, for instance, visual assists and default values. You can also add a processing option glossary item to your processing option form control so that you have more descriptive help on what the processing option is used for.

To create a type definition, you will click the Create A Type Definition button. The type definition is loaded into cache and can be pasted into the desired document. This produces the same type of listing as for a DSTR or GT object type. Processing Option typedefs are also used, for example, in BSFNs to set default values for a particular option for a type of application. A common example of this is how, within the Voucher Entry Master Business Function (B0400047), the processing option values are fetched. If a Voucher Processing Version is not entered by the user, the BSFN defaults a value of ZJDE0001. See Figure 2-19 for an example of this code. If the fetch of the ZJDE0001 Processing Option Values is successful, the values are assigned to a DSTR that is used to pass the information back into the calling form or function.

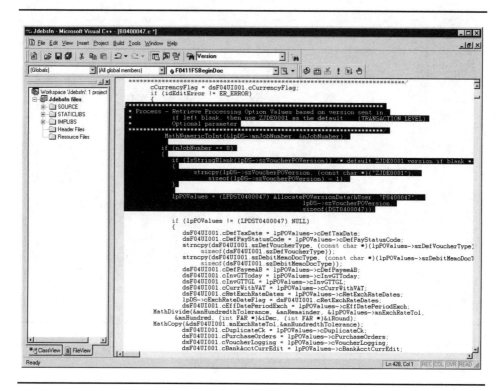

**FIGURE 2-19.**   Processing option default version code

## Designing Business Views

From the Design Tools tab within a business view (BSVW), you user can Start the
Business View Design Aid or Create a Type Definition for the view (see Figure 2-20).

BSVW Design Aid allows you to add or change a new or existing BSVW. A BSVW is
a selection of data items from one or more tables. Here, you would select the data items
from the table that you need to use within your interactive or batch application. Because
you select only those data items that are required in an application, there is less
movement of data over the network. Creating a typedef for a BSVW produces the
same results as it does for a DSTR.

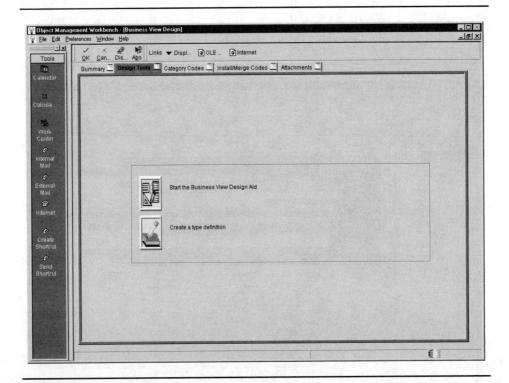

**FIGURE 2-20.**　Business View Design functions

## Designing a Workflow Process

From OMW, you can create or modify a workflow process. Searching on an existing workflow process involves choosing the Workflow Category, and Process Name|Process Version Search Type on the Search Tab. See Figure 2-21 for an example of these search criteria as they relate to the Batch Approval Process for Accounts Payable. You have other Search Type criteria available to you as well. To view all Search Type criteria, use the down-pointing arrow that is part of the form control. Clicking the Design Action button will display the Design Tools form. This allows you to Change the Workflow Status and gives you the option to go to Workflow Revisions. See Figure 2-22 for an example of this form.

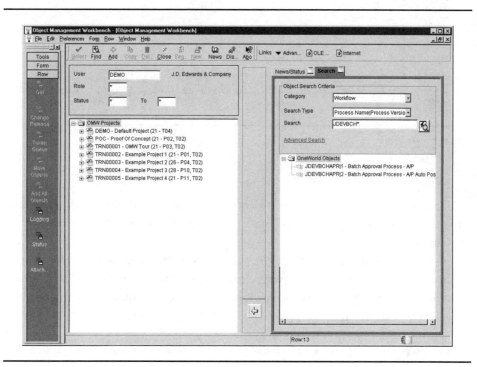

**FIGURE 2-21.** Workflow process search

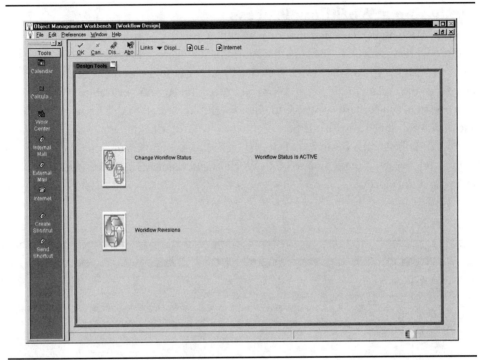

**FIGURE 2-22.** Workflow process design functions

The Change Workflow Status button activates or deactivates the workflow process that you have chosen. The status of your workflow process is shown to the right of this button.

The Workflow Revisions button gives you access to the Workflow Revisions application. In other words, this is where you can view the Process Master Data and Relationship Data. Designing Workflow Processes is another process in itself and is discussed in more detail in *J.D. Edwards OneWorld: A Developer's Guide.*

## Managing Menu Revisions

From OMW, you can create or modify a menu. Searching on existing menus involves choosing the Menus Category and Menu ID Search Type on the Search tab. See Figure

2-23 for an example of this search criteria as it relates to 1099 Annual Processing. You have other Search Type criteria available to you as well. To view all Search Type criteria, use the down-pointing arrow that is part of the form control. Clicking the Design Action button will display the Object Management Workbench – [Menu Header Revisions] form. This allows you to make changes to the menu header. See Figure 2-24 for an example of this form. You can also exit to the Work With Menu Selection form or the Title Overrides. Menu Selection allows you to make changes to the content of the menu, and Title Overrides allow you to make changes to how the items appear on the menu.

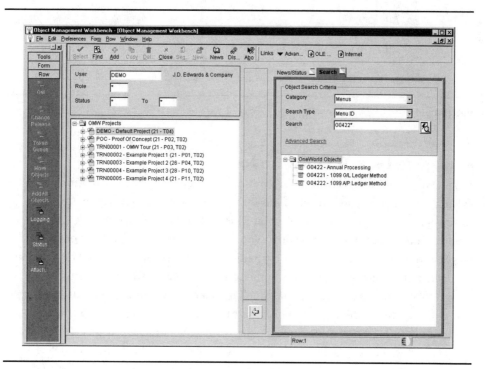

**FIGURE 2-23.**    Menu search

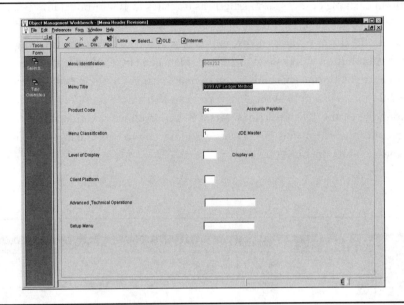

**FIGURE 2-24.** Menu design functions

## Managing User-Defined Codes

From OMW, you can create or modify a user-defined code (UDC). Searching on an existing UDC was discussed in the "Advanced Search" section of Chapter 1. Clicking the Design Action button will display the Object Management Workbench – [User Defined Code Types] form. This allows you to make changes to the description and length of the UDC. You can also state whether you wish to see the second description line, and define whether the UDC is numeric and right-justified, or alphanumeric and left-justified. There are other ways in which to make these changes, but this is a simple place to recall where these types of changes can be made. See Figure 2-25 for an example of this form as it relates to the Sales Management Price Category Type. You can also exit to the User Defined Code form where you can add, modify, or delete values contained in this UDC. By having a UDC listed in your project, you let the system administrator know that you have made a change to a UDC that needs to be added to the PRISTINE environment. You can also have the UDC automatically transferred when the project's status is advanced.

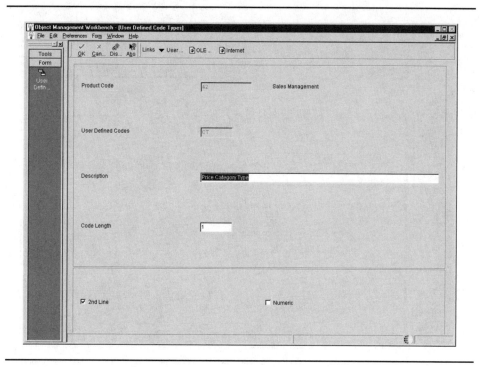

**FIGURE 2-25.**   User-defined code design functions

## Managing Data Dictionary Changes

From OMW, you can create or modify a data dictionary (DD) item. Searching on an existing DD item requires changing the Category to Data Dictionary and the Search Type to a value contained in the drop-down list on the Search tab. Searching for a data dictionary item in OMW is similar to the same search you would perform using the DD application (P92001). Clicking the Design Action button will display the Data Item Specifications for the DD item you choose. This form gives you access to making changes to the description, glossary, default value, and so on. We recommend that all DD changes be performed by a system or DD administrator. This is to ensure that no changes are made that will interrupt the flow of business, as DD changes could and do affect all users of the OneWorld system, regardless of the environment into which they logged. Figure 2-26 shows the DD specifications for data item QTYINV.

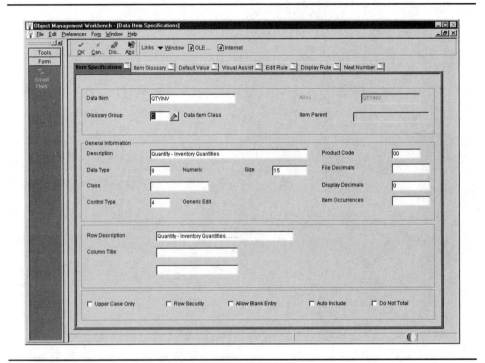

**FIGURE 2-26.** Data dictionary design functions

# Object Properties

Object Properties can be updated in OMW just as they could be in Object Librarian. The object's properties, previously located in OL on the Object Codes Row | Exit and the "Work with" forms, are now located on one form. To view and maintain object properties:

1. With the OMW form displayed, click Find to display your projects.

2. Double-click the project.

3. Click the plus sign (+) next to objects to expand the tree node, and then click the object you wish to update.

4. Click the Design Action button (T square) in the center column of action buttons. The design form for the object type selected is displayed.

You can modify the requested fields on the Summary tab, Category Codes tab, Install/Merge Codes tab, or Add/View Attachments. If you modify object fields, changes will be saved only if you click OK and return to the OMW form.

# Checking Out Objects

When you are working with objects, it is a given that you will want to check out the current specifications for an object. This process is especially common if more than one developer is working on an object. One developer will commonly save the object into the save location, and another will check out the changes and continue the work. Or you may want to check out the latest changes to perform a quality review of work done up to the current date.

## Get Feature

The Get feature allows you to get an object's specifications without actually checking the object out. This is advantageous when you just want the latest specifications, but you don't want to change the object. For example, a tester will perform a Get on an application to get the latest specifications for testing rather than waiting for the transfer process to occur, and a package to be built and deployed. Further object testing is usually required, and this feature allows quality analysts to get changes made to the software or to assist the developer in making sure changes are accurate. To perform a Get, do this:

1. Click Find on the OMW form.

2. Double-click the project in which your object resides.

3. Click the plus sign (+) next to objects to expand the tree node, and then click (highlight) the object you wish to perform a Get on.

4. Click the Get button (hand) in the center column of action buttons. The object's specifications will pass to your local machine according to predetermined object transfer (activity) rules for the project's current status, set up by the administrator in OMW configuration. This is the same location where objects are checked out, for the project's current status, if check out has been authorized within Allowed Actions.

You may always go into design for the selected object to view specifications; however, since you do not have the object checked out, you cannot check the object back in and have your changes take effect.

## Advanced Get Feature

Choosing Advanced Get allows you to specify the location from which you want to retrieve the specifications for the object. Users may want to do this when they would like to view objects in locations other than the check-out location, or to restore objects in the check-in location from versions that are in other path codes. To perform an advanced Get, follow these steps:

1. For OL Objects, click Row | Advanced – Get. The path code search and select form displays. Performing an advanced Get on Non-OL objects is not recommended and has been disabled since the initial release of Xe; however, should you perform this action, the data source search and select screen will appear and allow you to choose the data source location where your specifications are stored.

2. Double-click the desired path code or data source that you want to retrieve specifications from onto your local machine.

3. You may now go into design and make changes to the selected object. However, since you do not have the object checked out, you cannot check the object back in and have your changes take effect.

## Check Out

The check-out function allows you to check out an OL Object (and batch versions). If an object is already checked out by another user, you will be given the opportunity to be added to the token queue for this object or inherit the token (see later sections on inheriting tokens). If e-mail addresses have been configured within J.D. Edwards OneWorld Address Book (P01012) Who's Who (P0111) Electronic Addresses (P01111) information, once the token is available, you will be notified with an e-mail message. See Chapter 3 for object notification setup.

*TIP*

*If you modify an object without having the token and checking the object out, you will not be allowed to check in that object. Once you check in an object, you still have the token.*

If someone else holds the token, you can still perform a Get on the object and continue developing while you wait for the token. When the token is available, you can save your specifications, check out the object, and get the token. Then you can restore the object to get your changes. In most cases, this type of action occurs because you do not want to wait for the token. The other developer has completed work and the object is in the process of being transferred, but the object transfer process is not yet complete.

*CAUTION*

*Be sure not to overwrite changes another developer has made. See the "Working with Tokens" section, later in the chapter, for a discussion of tokens. Once you check out an object, if you do a restore, you need to be aware of any changes made after you performed a Get on the object, and the changes must be reimplemented in the specifications that were restored from the save location. Visual ER Compare can be very helpful during this process.*

To check out an object, follow these steps:

1. From the OMW form, click Find.

2. Double-click the project in which your object resides.

3. Click the plus sign (+) next to an object to expand the tree node, and then click (highlight) the object you wish to check out.

4. Click Check Out in the center column of action buttons to check out the object to your local machine. If the object is not available, a query displays asking whether you would like to be added to the object's token queue or inherit the token.

5. Click Yes to add your user ID to the token queue and automatically receive it when it becomes available; otherwise, click No (we will discuss inheriting tokens later). If the token is available, the object will be checked out.

6. Ensure that the object's icon is colored and now has a check mark on it, indicating that the object has the token and has been checked out.

## Erase Check Out

Should you no longer wish to perform development on an object, or if you are just viewing the code and another developer wishes to make changes to that object, you can erase the check out. To do this, you must select the checked-out object by highlighting it in the Project View window. Then click the Erase Checkout button in the center column of action buttons.

The OMW indicates an object is no longer checked out by removing the checkmark superimposed over the object's icon when it was checked out.

# Checking In Objects

Once you have completed development of an object, or if your system administrator has required check in due to system backups and mandatory packages, you will want to check in your objects. Objects can be checked in only after they have been checked out. For OL objects, use the check-in function to check the specifications for an object into the check-in location. The check-in location is determined by your system administrator within the OMC transfer (activity) rules. See Chapter 3 for configuring your check-in location. To check in an OL object, follow these steps:

1. From the OMW form, click Find.

2. Double-click the project in which your object resides.

3. Click the plus sign (+) next to objects to expand the tree node, and then click (highlight) the object you wish to check out.

4. Click Check In in the center column of action buttons to check the object into the check-in location. This button will be enabled only if the object has been checked out to the current machine.

# Save and Restore

Often, you will want to save the changes you have made to an OL object, but you are not ready to move them to the check-in location, or you may have a machine that has specifications on it that you want to save and later restore to get them into the check-in location. In this case, you may use the Save button to save the specifications off to a predefined save location, and the Restore button to restore those specifications at a later time.

## Save Function

To save your specifications to the predefined save location, perform the following steps:

1. From the OMW form, click Find.

2. Double-click the project that the object is currently in, and then click the object you would like to save.

3. Click Save, second to the bottom in the center column of action buttons, to save the object specifications that are on the local machine.

## Restore Function

If you did a client install or want to put the specifications on another machine, you can use the Restore button to retrieve the specifications from the save location. To restore an object, perform the following steps:

1. From the OMW form, click Find.

2. Double-click the project that the object is currently in, and then click the object for which you would like to restore specifications to the local machine.

3. Click the Restore button at the bottom of the center column of action buttons to restore the specifications from the save location to the local machine.

**N O T E**

*To check in specifications that are on the local machine before a check out has been performed, you should perform a save to move the local specs into the save location, perform a check out to receive the token and a check-out record, and restore the specifications to the local machine with those specifications that were placed in the save location. Since this potentially replaces specifications that were updated in the check-in location since the user last retrieved them, the user should validate that there are no other changes to the object, other than their modification, before checking in. Visual ER Compare can be very helpful when performing this validation.*

# Object Icons

The color of an OL Object icon can tell you a great deal about its check-out, check-in, and token statuses. Non-OL objects will always have a colored object icon. The icon colors and the related meanings are described in the following table. All information that is displayed according to the different icons can also be seen in the object status display window.

| Icon | Icon Description |
|------|------------------|
| Gray Object Icon with Checkmark | Someone else has the token for this object, and it is currently unavailable for check out. |
| Colored Object Icon (not gray) | The object's project has the token for this object. That is, the project that this object currently resides in has the token. |
| Colored Object Icon with Checkmark (not gray) | The object's project has the token for this object, and the object is checked out. |
| Gray Object Icon | This object has not been checked out, and no other project has the object's token. |

**N O T E**

*Objects marked to be deleted are marked in* **bold** *and will hold the token.*

# Maintaining Objects in Multiple Software Releases

Same-named objects in different software releases can be modified in the OMW in the same project. For example, if you are maintaining two systems and an object needs a change, you can modify that object in both systems using the same project. After adding the first object to the project (it will be added at the current release level of your system), when you add the same object to the project the second time, the user will be prompted to specify at which release level they would like to add the object to the project (these release levels are based on the OMC transfer [activity] rules that exist for different release levels for the current object type). If an object has been added to the project for the current release level and you would like to change it to a different release level, use Change Release Row | Exit.

*CAUTION*

*Changing and maintaining objects in multiple releases can cause problems due to OneWorld object inter-dependencies. Changing an object in one version and then updating the object in another version to match might cause dependent objects to malfunction. For example, if you change the Accounts Payable Master Business Function (MBF), you must be aware of other processes, such as Purchase Order Entry, that are affected by your change. Proper testing procedures should be in place.*

Once the objects exist in the project, you can maintain them independently, or you can update one to match the other. When working with objects from separate releases, the OMW handles check out, check in, and transfer file paths for you according to the OMC discussed in Chapter 3. Simply perform the necessary modifications and use the OMW functions as you would normally. For example, check-in objects and advancing projects do not change; only the configuration behind the scenes has changed, and there are no differences in how you see these objects, other than that the code itself may be different because of the release level.

*NOTE*

*If you attempt to add an object to a project in which it currently resides, you will be prompted for the release level of the object you are trying to add. If you are not maintaining objects at multiple release levels, the object already exists in your project. You should scroll through your object list in the project to find the object.*

# Working with Tokens

OL objects use tokens to minimize the possibility of one user overwriting another user's changes to an object. The token management system organizes application development by providing a single check-out environment. The concept of a token was first introduced to you in Chapter 1. This section explains more fully the actions that you perform within token management.

## The Token Management System

The Token Management System controls modifications to OL objects by requiring a project to hold a token for the object before checking out the object, and requiring the project to have the token in order to check-in the object. Once a project has a token, the token will stay with the project until it is manually released or the project is advanced to a status, indicated in the Transfer (Activity) Rules, that will release the token. When the token is released, it will be assigned to the next user in the token queue. We recommend that tokens be released automatically by OMW only when objects have been transferred into the production path code. To reiterate, tokens are assigned to the project when the object is checked out, if the token is available. If the token is not available, you may enter the token queue to receive the token when it becomes available, or you may inherit the token when the project that contains that object reaches a certain status. The object may be checked out only if the token is assigned to the project, and the object may be checked in only after it has been checked out. This process enforces that the next user modifying the object receives the previous user's changes.

There are three things you can do while your project holds the token:

1. Allow another user to inherit the token.

2. Switch the token with another project.

3. Release the token.

*N O T E*

*There is only one token per object, per release.*

## Token Inheritance

Allowing another user to inherit the token forces both projects to be advanced together as if they were one project. When the status of one project is advanced, all other projects inheriting tokens will be advanced also. In order for tokens to be inherited across projects, all projects must be at the same status. Inheritance with a default project is not allowed. Objects in all inheriting projects must be ready to be advanced, and the user advancing the projects must play a role in all inheriting projects that are authorized to advance the project. This allows multiple fixes to be applied to one object. Quite often, the inheritance functionality is used when your project is taking a considerably long time to complete. In order that you do not hold up other development to that object, you may want to allow another user to inherit the token; that user can check out the object once your changes are complete without waiting for the project to advance through the project life cycle.

## Token Switching

Switching an OL object's token to another project allows an emergency fix to be applied immediately. This action releases the token and pushes the project currently having the token back onto the queue as the first project waiting for the token. The selected project is then given the token. Switching the token is a polite word for "stealing" the token. If this is done, communication should be made with the user that the token was taken from because that user may have had the object checked out. Taking the token will erase their check out. If they did have the object checked out, they may need to save their specifications, re-check-out the object, restore their original specs, and then reimplement the emergency fix to their restored specs. This action should be restricted to a specific role to ensure security of the objects. Within a large development organization, it is recommended that the "switch token" action be allowed only for the manager or supervisor roles to prevent developers from "stealing" tokens from each other. To switch the token, perform the following actions:

1. From the OMW form, click Find.

2. Double-click the project that the object is currently in, and then click the object that holds the token.

3. Click the Switch Token (four hands) button in the center column of action buttons. The project token queue search and select form displays.

4. Click Find, and select the project to which you wish to assign the token.

5. Click Select to switch the object's token from the current token holder to the project selected.

## Releasing the Token

While a project holds an OL object's token, no other projects may check that object out. Therefore, if you have checked out an OL object, and your project is assigned the token, and if you no longer desire to develop the OL object further, you may release the token and assign it to the next person in the queue. When the object's token is released, OMW will erase the check out, if the object was checked out. By releasing the token, you are indicating to other users that the object is available for them to check out and make any necessary changes they may have. In order to prevent issues with project advancement and object transfer, tokens should be released by OMW only when the object is promoted into the production path code. Releasing the token gives up the token and allows the next project in the queue to get the token. Releasing the token often occurs manually when the severity of your project has changed, and thus you must allow for the completion of other projects first. You may also want to release the token if the design specifications are not yet complete for your enhancement to the object to allow for bug fixes in the interim, or if you have inadvertently received the token and want to release it for others to use.

### CAUTION

*Potential project advancement issues can arise because OMW updates the check-in record with the project name that it was checked in under. OMW will transfer an object only if the check-in record indicates that the object was modified under the current project that is being transferred. Otherwise, OMW could potentially transfer changes that were not associated with the current project. By releasing the token before the object has been transferred to the next path code, other users can check in the object and update this field with their project and prevent this project from successfully advancing. If this happens, OMW will create an object-level log indicating that the object was not modified by the current project.*

To manually release the token, perform the following steps:

1. From the OMW form, click Find.

2. Double-click the project in which your object resides.

3. Click the plus signs (+) next to objects to expand the tree node, and then click (highlight) the object you wish to release the token for.

4. Click the Release Token button in the center column of action buttons to release the object's token.

Tokens are automatically released by OMW on a project status advancement (this is the recommended method); however, keep in mind that the OMW may have been configured to release tokens for different objects at different Project Status changes. Therefore, all object types may not give up their tokens during the same change in Project Status.

### NOTE

*There is one restriction on forced token release. You cannot release a token from a newly created object.*

# Working with Owners

This section describes how to use OMW to perform the following owner-related functions: adding owners to projects and viewing and maintaining owner properties.

## Adding Owners to Projects

In order to perform actions on a project, or the objects within the project, a user must be assigned as an owner of the project. When these users are assigned, each user is given a specific role to play. This role dictates the kind of actions you can perform on the project or the objects in it. If e-mail addresses have been configured within your J.D. Edwards OneWorld Address Book (P01012) Who's Who (P0111) Electronic Addresses (P01111) information, the added user will be notified with an e-mail message indicating which project they have been added to. To add users to projects, perform the following steps:

1. In the OMW form, click Find to open the project list.

2. Double-click the desired project to open it, and then click the Owners icon.

3. Click the Search tab.

4. In the Category field, click Owners.

5. In the Search Type field, you can click Alpha Name, Address Book Number, or User ID.

6. If you have a particular user in mind, enter his or her Alpha Name, Address Book Number, or User ID in the Search field. This entry must match the search type specified in the Search Type field.

7. Click the Search button to the right of the Search field to display your search results.

8. Click the user to be added to the project. Ensure the Owners icon or the desired project is still highlighted in the project list.

9. Click the left-pointing arrow in the center column of action buttons. The Add User To Project form displays.

10. You must indicate what role the user you are adding to the project is going to play. Enter that role in the Role field.

11. If the user is to be a lead, select the Lead check box. The lead option is future functionality. It can, however, be used to mark which supervisor has ultimate responsibility over a team, but it will not allow any special privileges to this user.

12. Click OK to add the user to the project and return to the OMW form.

# Viewing and Maintaining Owner Properties

The properties of a user, such as user role, estimated hours, and lead indicator, can be modified for the project users. For example, the Estimated Hours to Complete a Project/SAR may be maintained for each user on the project. Updating the Estimated Project Hours for Completion automatically updates the SAR with the total of all estimated hours for all users assigned to the project, if you have an integrated SAR system. To view and maintain user properties, follow these steps:

1. In the OMW form, click Find to open the project list.

2. Double-click the desired project to open it.

3. Double-click the Owners icon to open the owners list.

4. Click the Owner whose properties are to be changed.

5. Click Select. The project User Details form displays.

6. You can do three things:

   a. Change the user role by filling in the User Role field.

   b. Set up the user as a project lead by checking the Lead check box.

   c. Change or enter the estimated number of hours this user will work on the project. Fill in the Estimated Hours field.

7. Click OK when you've finished to save your changes and return to the OMW form.

When updating a User Role and SAR integration is turned on, be sure not to violate SAR integrity rules. For example, the Assigned To field is required for SARs at a status greater than 20. If this is the case, and the role (Owner A) being modified is the role that is mapped to the Assigned To field in the SAR, changing this role will result in the Assigned To field being blank. To prevent this violation, another owner (Owner B) assigned to this role should be assigned to the project before the original owner's (Owner A) role is changed. When the Owner (Owner A) is updated, the other owner (Owner B) for this role will be swapped with the updated owner (Owner A) on the SAR.

# Summary

In this chapter, we have discussed how to develop using the Object Management Workbench. This chapter gives you a start at understanding all of the functions available to you as a developer and how they are used. We have discussed working with projects, objects, tokens, and owners. Working in the context of a project allows you to readily track all modifications needed for a specific change. Working with objects involves the tools that are used to modify your objects, as well as how to check out those objects, check them in, and advance them into production, among a great deal of other functions. Working with tokens involves understanding the Token Management System and how tokens work in OneWorld. And, finally, working with owners involves how owners are used in the software development life cycle. Being a developer using OMW is only one piece of the puzzle. It is not always a bad idea to also understand how the system is configured and how it affects your role on the project team. The following chapters discuss configuring your system and will enable you to bring everything you've learned thus far into a system that works for you.

# CHAPTER 3

# OMW Setup and Configuration

What Is Object Management Configuration?

User Roles

Allowed Actions

Activity Rules

Constants

Tables That the Object Management
  Workbench (OMW) Uses

Creating a Save Location

OMW Logging Capabilities

Object Action Notification

OMW Reporting Capabilities

Okay, you now have this brand new functionality to help you track your changes to the OneWorld system. Your company's executives are all excited about this built-in change management functionality and cannot wait to implement it. What does that mean for you as the OneWorld system administrator, developer, power user, or project manager? Well, if you have had experience with OneWorld prior to the OneWorld Xe release, then you are used to installing the system and letting the developers just dive right into the system and start coding. This sometimes caused issues of user-defined codes existing in one environment but not others, code being overlaid, or no one knowing for sure to what environment a fix was applied. With Object Management Workbench (OMW), those days are gone!

This is actually a good thing. Now you will need to plan how you want your modifications to enter your OneWorld environments, decide who will have the authority to move these modifications into higher environments, and evaluate how close the out-of-the-box OMW configuration comes to meeting your company's needs. This means that you will receive input from your developers, power users, testers, and project managers on what their needs are, which may sound like a bit of work. Well, it is—but by the conclusion of this chapter you'll understand why it's worth it!

We would normally schedule an OMW and software development life cycle (SDLC) design session with our clients to get the implementation off to a good start. At a minimum, this session takes at least one to two full days. In this session, the client's development manager, the system administrator, the business analyst manager, and the project director all get together to determine how OMW must be configured to meet their needs. You will get a pretty good feel of what goes on during one of these design sessions as you read through this chapter. In a design session and in this chapter, you learn about

- What object management configuration is
- User roles
- Allowed actions
- Activity rules
- The activity rules director

- Constants

- Creating a save location

- Token inheritance

- Reporting capabilities of OMW

# What Is Object Management Configuration?

As you start to work with the Object Management Workbench, you will hear the term *OMC*. This term, which means *object management configuration*, is used to describe the process of setting up the Object Management Workbench to meet your company's needs. This new functionality—like the rest of OneWorld—was designed to be highly configurable so that, as your business's needs change, the software can change with them.

In previous chapters, we have discussed some of the basics of OMW. These basics include what a project is, what a token is, and what you need to do in order to advance a project. We are now going to get into what a OneWorld system administrator needs to do to ensure that projects can be promoted smoothly and that OneWorld developers have access to the tools that they need within OMW.

When developers access the Object Management Workbench, all they care about is if they can code, check in, promote, and protect their changes. All of this has to be set up behind the scenes. However, your OneWorld system administrator first needs to understand the needs of the development and testing organizations within your company. Once this person has this understanding, then and only then can he or she get to work and configure the system.

To start setting up your OMW configuration, you will need to go to the Object Management Workbench menu (GH9081), shown in Figure 3-1. This menu contains the tools that your system administrator will need to configure and monitor the system. To start, you will need to double-click the Object Management Configuration application (P98230). This will take you into the Object Management Configuration window shown in Figure 3-1. Table 3-1 explains the function of the options in this window.

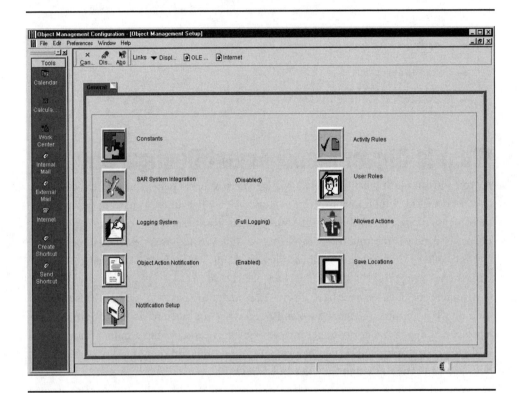

**FIGURE 3-1.**   Object Management Configuration window

| Option | Description |
| --- | --- |
| Constants | This setting allows you to define the constants of the system. This includes what status new projects are placed in, what the default user role will be for the creator of the new project, and what the user's default project status will be. |

**TABLE 3-1.**   Object Management Workbench Configuration Application Options

| Option | Description |
| --- | --- |
| SAR System Integration | This functionality is used by J.D. Edwards development, to hook into their existing SAR (Software Action Request) system when they use OMW to develop future releases of OneWorld. Do not attempt to use this functionality, as it was designed only for internal use. |
| Logging System | This option enables you to set up the detail level of logging on OMW activities that you desire, as well as how OMW will behave if the logging system fails. |
| Object Action Notification | This option enables you to turn the notification system on or off. |
| Notification Setup | This option allows users to subscribe to be notified by e-mail when actions that they define are taken on an object in the system. |
| Activity Rules | This option enables you to set up rules to determine what happens when a user executes actions or activities on OneWorld objects. |
| User Roles | This option enables you to define the users' functions or job roles within the project, and will directly affect what actions they are allowed to perform. |
| Allowed Actions | This option gives you the ability to define what actions users who are assigned a user role are allowed to perform. |
| Save Location | This selection lets you define a location where your OneWorld developer users can save work that is not ready to be checked in. |

**TABLE 3-1.**    Object Management Workbench Configuration Application Options
(*continued*)

We will go over all of the settings of the Object Management Configuration window in this chapter. However, as you will soon see, a lot of these configuration options depend on other configuration options. This is shown in the diagram in Figure 3-2, which describes the approach that should be taken when configuring your Object Management Workbench. You need to follow a logical approach to build your configuration because, as the diagram shows, each step depends on the one before it. If you do not follow this approach, your setup will not be complete. To start, you first need to review your user roles.

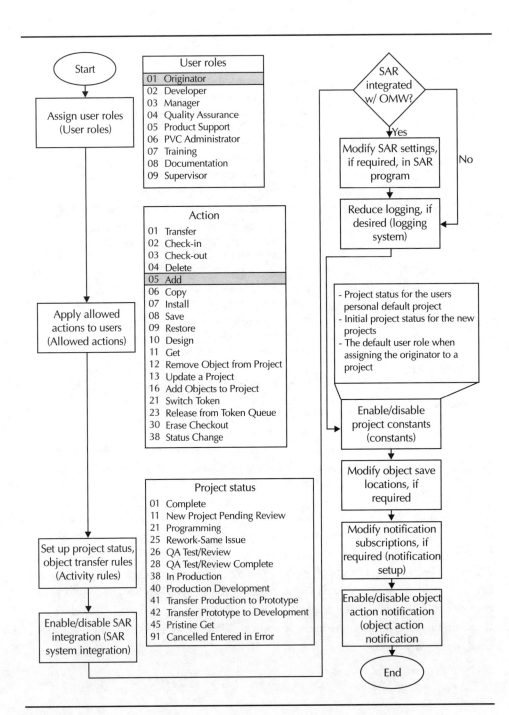

**FIGURE 3-2.**  Object Management Workbench configuration process flow model

# User Roles

Before we get too far into the details of setting up user roles, let's take a minute and define exactly what a user role is and how you would determine whether you require any custom user roles. A user role can be defined as what a particular person does on a project. To break it down to its most basic level, a user role is a job description, such as "developer."

If you were to have a design session to help you set up your object management configuration, one of the first questions asked would be, what type of jobs do you have people performing for your OneWorld implementation? If you are modifying the OneWorld code, you will have developers, and, hopefully, you will have quality assurance personnel. These both are user roles you will need to ensure exist in your object management configuration.

J.D. Edwards ships the major user roles that are typically involved in an implementation. These user roles are important, because they will determine what action each individual user in OneWorld can perform on an object or project. As Figure 3-2 shows, user roles are the foundation of your Object Management Workbench configuration. These user roles tell the system what job functions will be performed and must be in place before you can grant these user roles rights to perform certain actions. This preserves and protects projects and objects from being changed by someone without authority. We will cover how to grant allowed actions in the "Allowed Actions" section later in this chapter.

## Shipped User Roles

J.D. Edwards realizes that their customers are not going to be accustomed to a change management system right off the bat, so they have shipped some default configuration settings. These include user roles that cover the major roles typically used during an implementation. These settings may suit your needs or not, as J.D. Edwards ships them with values intended to meet the usual setup needs for most clients. However, do not worry; this is OneWorld, so you can configure the system to use your own user roles if you desire. The shipped user roles are shown in Figure 3-3 and described in Table 3-2.

As you can see, this list is fairly basic, and may or may not describe all of the user roles or jobs that you have involved with your project. One of the most common roles that we have seen changed is the 03 Manager user role. The main reason is there may be more than one type of manager, and it's not clear what type of manager this is. Is it a development manager or a quality assurance manager? If you refer to Figure 3-2, you

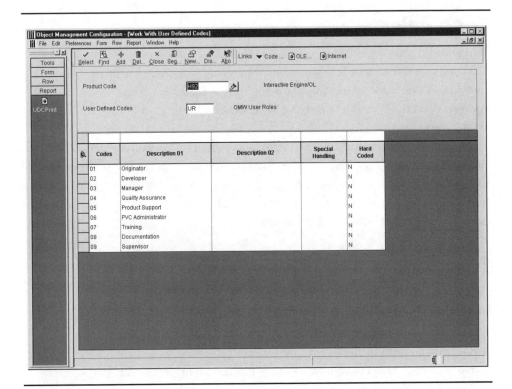

**FIGURE 3-3.**   User roles window

| User Role | Description |
| --- | --- |
| 01 | Originator |
| 02 | Developer |
| 03 | Manager |
| 04 | Quality assurance |
| 05 | Product support |
| 06 | PVC administrator |
| 07 | Training |
| 08 | Documentation |
| 09 | Supervisor |

**TABLE 3-2.**   Shipped User Roles

will see that these user roles are used to determine what an individual's allowed actions are for projects. This means that you need to be sure you have the user roles you really need defined. Do you want the developmental manager to have the same allowed actions as the quality assurance manager? If they are the same person, no problem; however, if they are separately managed groups, you do not want them to accidentally interfere with each other's work. This is why we stated earlier that during an Object Management Workbench design session, you need to have all of the appropriate managers—i.e., decision makers—in one room for this meeting.

## Adding or Removing a User Role

Review the shipped user roles very carefully. Ask yourself, is there a user role in your project that does not appear here, but should? Will someone be performing a job where they cannot share a shipped user role, such as a testing and development manager? If this is the case, then you will need to add a custom user role to meet this need. We recommend that you add only necessary user roles to keep the Object Management Workbench configuration simple, and thus more easily managed.

If you have experience with OneWorld, you are probably looking at Figure 3-3 and saying to yourself that it looks like a user-defined code setup. You would be absolutely correct. User roles are nothing more than user-defined codes. This means that the role, such as 02, is stored in the F0004 and F0005 user-defined code tables.

---

### *N O T E*

*The Object Management User Roles have a ten-character limit.*

---

These user-defined code tables are stored in the control tables data source for each environment. This means that they are environment specific. If you are going to change an OMW user-defined code setting, you will want to ensure that this change is propagated through your other environments. Otherwise, your users may become confused, as the user role descriptions may not match between environments and users may receive "user defined code does not exist" errors when attempting to use OMW functionality in other environments.

## Adding a User Role

To add a user role, you simply click the Add button in the Work With User Defined Codes window, as shown in Figure 3-3. This will take you to the User Defined Codes

window. In this window, you simply click the blank grid line and enter your desired
role into the codes column, a description in the appropriate column, and **N** in the
hard-coded column. You will want to set the hard-coded column to N, because Y tells
the software that you have hard-coded an application to call this UDC value. Since this
is not the case, set this value to N. In our example, we have added a role of 10 Quality
Assurance Manager. Once you have finished defining your role, click OK. This will
take you back to the Work With User Defined Codes window. Click Find in this
window, and you should now see your new role listed.

You may be wondering whether you need to add this user role from the Object
Management Configuration application, since it is only a user-defined code. The
answer is no. You could add this value through the standard User Defined Code
application (P0004A). However, if you added your role through this application instead,
you would need to specify H92 for the product code and UR for the User Defined Codes
field, since these values will not default for you as they do in the Object Management
Configuration application. Once you have placed the values in these fields and have
clicked Find, you can add another user role in exactly the same manner as you would
from the Object Management Workbench application.

When you add or change a user-defined code outside of an OMW project, you
will see the UDC added to your default project (default projects were discussed in
Chapter 2). This means that, if you go into the User Defined Code application and
modify your user roles, you will see this change in the Object Management Workbench.
You can also add this change into an existing or new object management project and
have it promoted to another environment. We will discuss exactly how this happens
in the "Activity Rules" section, later in this chapter.

## How User Roles Relate to OMW Projects

It's important to understand how user roles relate to projects. This is because different user roles enable you to accomplish different types of work. Out of the box, OMW is delivered so that any user can assign himself or herself to a project as any user role. As you can imagine, this could cause problems with your development work. To illustrate this problem, we are going to cover an example of adding an OMW object into a project. Although some of this information was covered in Chapter 2, we will quickly review it here. To do this, first open the OMW application and add a new OMW project (how to add projects is covered in Chapter 2). To do this, press Add. This will take you into the Add OneWorld Object To The Project window (Figure 3-4). In this window, you are presented with several options. You can add new Object Librarian objects, which are interactive applications, batch applications, interactive versions, batch versions,

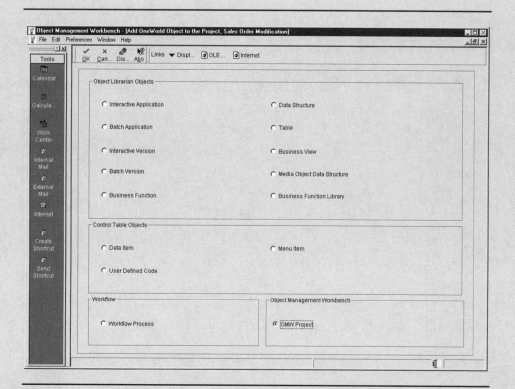

**FIGURE 3-4.** Add OneWorld objects to a project

business functions, data structures, tables, business views, a media object data structure, or a business function library.

You can also add control table objects. These are data dictionary data items, user-defined codes, or menu items. Workflow processes can also be added from this window. Finally, you can add an OMW Project, which is what needs to be done in order to explain how user roles hook into OMW projects. Once you have selected this radio button, click OK. This will take you into the Project Revisions window shown in Figure 3-5. In this window, you give the Object Management Workbench application information about your project. This window has several tabs with fields on them that must be filled out to add an OMW project. These fields are explained in Tables 3-3 and 3-4.

**Category Code Tab**    This tab allows you to attach custom category codes to your project. These category codes can provide greater detail in reporting on OneWorld project statuses.

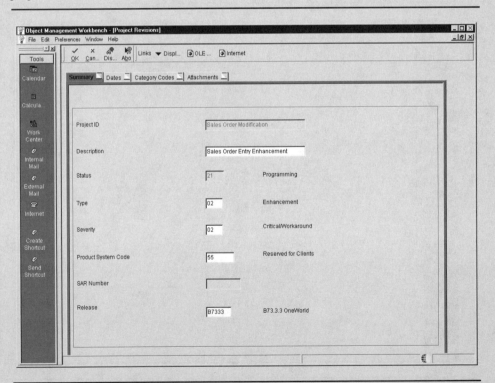

**FIGURE 3-5.**    Project Revisions window

| Field | Value |
| --- | --- |
| Project ID | Place the name of your project here. |
| Description | Enter a description of your project in this field. |
| Status | This field will default with a project status. This project status is defined in the Constants area of the Object Management Configuration window. The Constants section of the Object Management Configuration application will be discussed later in this chapter. |
| Type | This is the type of project being defined. The shipped project types that a user may create are<br>01 – Bug<br>02 – Enhancement<br>However, you will see the following values that you cannot select without receiving an error. These project statuses are used only internally by J.D. Edwards.<br>04 – Default<br>05 – Tracking/Parent Bug<br>06 – Tracking/Parent Enhancement |
| Severity | This field shows the severity of the project. The shipped severity levels are<br>01 – Critical/No Workaround<br>02 – Critical/Workaround<br>03 – Not Critical/No Workaround<br>04 – Not Critical/Workaround<br>10 – Critical Enhancement<br>11 – Enhancement<br>12 – Low-Priority Enhancement |
| Product System Code | This is the system code that the project affects. If you are adding a custom project, you should choose from system codes 55–59. These system codes are reserved for clients. |
| SAR Number | This is a Software Action Request number, which will default only if the SAR system is set to enabled in the Object Management Configuration window. This setting can be used only internally at J.D. Edwards |
| Release | This is the release of OneWorld software you are running on. |

**TABLE 3-3.**   Project Summary Tab

**Attachments**    This tab allows you to add notes about your project and also attach design documents or other documents to your project.

| Field | Value |
|---|---|
| Date Started | This is the date that the project will be started. |
| Planned Completion Date | This is the date that the project is expected to be completed. |
| Date Entered | This field is disabled and is the date that the project was added into the Object Management Workbench software. |
| Completion Date | This field is disabled and will be populated by OMW when the project's status is advanced to 01; it is the actual date that the project was completed. |

**TABLE 3-4.** Project Dates Tab

Once you have filled in the desired fields, click OK to return to the Object Management Workbench window. When you click Find, you will now see your project listed. Expand your project and you will see a folder for objects and one for owners. Since you added the project, you will automatically be listed as an owner of the project. This is shown in Figure 3-6.

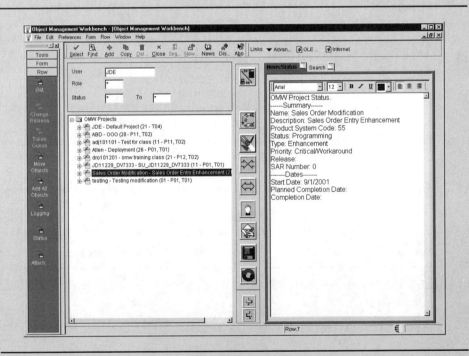

**FIGURE 3-6.** New object management workbench project

You will notice that your OneWorld user ID will be defaulted as a certain user role. This user role is defined through the Object Management Configuration Constants option, shown in Table 3-5. Now comes the part that will make your security administrator's hair stand on end.

If you highlight and select your user under the Owners directory, you will be taken into the Project Users Detail window. From this window, you can change your OneWorld user role on the project, which, as you will see in the next section, gives your user more authority or rights. Use the values shown in Table 3-5.

The scary part is that the user role is just a user-defined code and that, out of the box, your users in OMW can choose any one of these user roles. This means that they will have additional rights on projects if they choose a different role. We will cover exactly what rights they might obtain when we go through the allowed actions in the next section of this chapter.

As a system administrator, you are likely thinking there has to be a way to lock your end users out of selecting at will the role they have on a project. Well, take heart—there is! Remember that the user roles are just user-defined codes. You can restrict users from seeing a value in this table through row security.

| Value | Field |
|---|---|
| Project ID | This field will be grayed out and default with the project name. |
| User ID | This field will be grayed out and list the selected OneWorld user ID. |
| User Role | This option allows you to specify the role a user plays on a project. The default roles are<br>01 – Originator<br>02 – Developer<br>03 – Manager<br>04 – Quality Assurance<br>05 – Project Support<br>06 – PVC Administrator<br>07 – Training<br>08 – Documentation<br>09 – Supervisor |
| Project Lead | This is future functionality. |
| Estimated Hours | This is the estimated hours that the user will work on this project. |
| Date Assigned | This is disabled and is the date that the project was assigned to this user. |
| Assigned to Time | This field is disabled and is the time that the project was assigned to the user role. |

**TABLE 3-5.** Project User Detail Window

## DEFINITION

***Row security*** *is a type of OneWorld security that allows you to restrict OneWorld users from accessing certain data in tables of your choice. For example, you can allow your end users to see employees' names, but not their social security numbers.*

You can set up row security by going to the Security Maintenance menu (GH9052). Double-click the Security Workbench on this menu. This will take you into the Work With User/Group Security application, shown in Figure 3-7. This application allows you to set up a variety of different OneWorld security options. For more information on OneWorld security options, refer to *J. D. Edwards OneWorld: The Complete Reference*.

To add row security restricting your users to only seeing and using certain user roles, go to the form/row button. This will take you into the Row Security Revisions

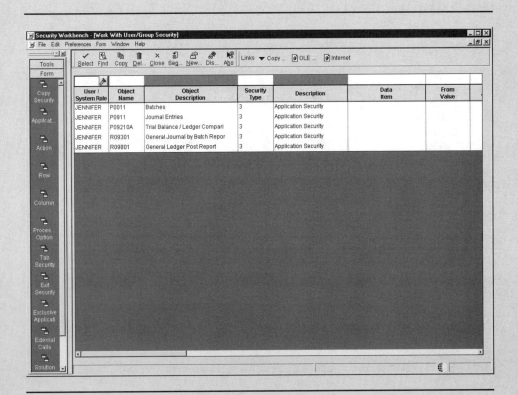

**FIGURE 3-7.**   Work With User/Group Security window

dialog box. It is from this dialog box that you add your row security entry to restrict your users from selecting a role you do not want them to have.

To do this, place the name of the user or group that you want to apply row security to. Once you have placed the name of the user or group in the dialog box, you need to place the name of the table that you are securing in the grid under the table column. You then need to place the data item in the column labeled Data Item. This data item value will be the data dictionary data item that is used for the column of the table that you want to restrict your users from seeing certain data in. In this case, you will want to use the data item of Description001, which has an alias of DL01, because this is the name of the data item that is used for the description of the user roles in the F0005 table.

You may be wondering why you are placing security on the description column of the F0005 User Defined Codes table and not on the data dictionary item that is used for the column that contains the values for the user role. This is great observation. The reason that you are not placing row security on the column that contains the numeric values for the user roles in the Object Management Workbench—for example, 01 for Originator—is because you will lock your users out of other user-defined code values if you do this. To avoid this, you can set up row security for the exact descriptions that you are trying to restrict your users from.

Once you have filled in the data item, you will need to place the restriction on the From Value and the Thru Value. In these fields, you will want to place the exact description of what you want to restrict your users from. So, if you want to lock your users out of the user role of Manager, you place this value in the From and Thru Value fields. You then need to set the Add, Delete, and View fields to N. The Alias field will default based on the value you placed in the Data Item field. Click OK; the grid line will disappear. Click Find, and you should now see your row security record, an example of which is shown in Figure 3-8. Close this application.

## CAUTION

*Use the Cancel or Close button to exit the Security Workbench application. If you just close the window by clicking the X in the upper-right corner, some of your changes may not be saved. This is a rule that you should follow throughout OneWorld. This is because, in some applications, there are event rules, which perform work, on the Close and Cancel buttons. So, if you do not close out correctly, these event rules will never run and you may get undesired results.*

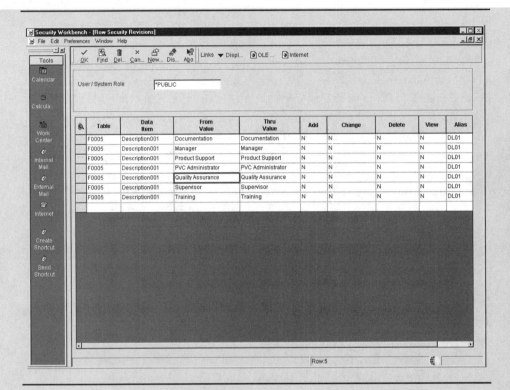

**FIGURE 3-8.** Row security for OMW user roles

## NOTE

*You may get an error saying "Data item not set up for row security." This is because the data item needs to be configured for row security. If you receive this error, you need to go to the GH951 Data Dictionary Design menu. Double-click the Work With Data Dictionary Items application (P92001). This will take you into the Work With Data Dictionary Items dialog. Place the alias of your data item in the Alias field of the query by example line (QBE). Click Find and select the data item. You will see a Row Security check box on the Item Specifications tab. Select this check box and click OK. Now attempt to set up your row security again.*

Once you have finished setting up your row security, log out of OneWorld and then log back in again. The OneWorld security settings are cached, so you will not see your changes until you log out and back into the system. Once you log back into the system, go to menu GH902, Cross Application Development Tools. Double-click the Object Management Workbench application (P98220). Once you are in the Object Management Workbench application, click Find. You will see your default project, named after your OneWorld user ID. Expand this project to see the Objects and Owners directories—these are shown in Figure 3-7. Expand the Owners directory. You will see your OneWorld user ID. Select this user ID to go to the Project User Details dialog box. Click the visual assist button for the User Role field. You now should not be able to see the user role of 03 Manager. This type of row security should be set up as soon as the software is installed and the configuration of the Object Management Workbench starts. This will ensure that a user does not assign their user ID to a project with a user role with more authority than that user should have.

## CAUTION

*If you restrict user roles by implementing row security over the Description field on the F0005 table for user roles, you will also lock these users out of any other UDC values with the same description. To ensure that you are not locking other UDC values down, perform a select statement over the F0005 table for these descriptions. If you find duplicate descriptions, you can either change the OMW user role descriptions to be unique, or set up row security on the F98221 Project Users table to restrict users from adding these values into this table. The downside to this approach is that your users will be able to select any user role; although when they attempt to add the user to the project, they will receive an error.*

# Allowed Actions

Now that you have finished defining all of your job titles or user roles, you can move on to the next step in setting up your object management configuration. The next step is to set up your allowed actions. You have defined what job roles will be involved with your OneWorld development; however, you have not defined what each of these roles is allowed to do. When you set up your allowed actions, you tell the OneWorld system what actions each user role is allowed to perform on each object type for the different project statuses.

We recommend that you take setting up your allowed actions seriously. This is because your allowed actions are similar to your OneWorld security setup in that, if they are not planned and implemented correctly, you will have user roles with allowed actions they should not perform or are not qualified to perform. This can lead to objects being accidentally deleted or becoming corrupted, a condition that can be very difficult to rectify. Normally, you will conduct a planning session with your OMW users to carefully plan out what user roles are allowed to perform what actions. These allowed actions need to be planned out with the assistance of the OneWorld system administrator and the developmental manager. These allowed actions should also be documented and tested during the initial implementation of the OneWorld Xe software to ensure that they have been set up correctly.

## Allowed Actions

To set up allowed actions, go to the GH9081 Object Management menu and select the Object Management Configuration application (P98230). This will take you to the Object Management Setup window. Click Allowed Actions, and you will be taken into the User Allowed Actions window, shown in Figure 3-9. From this window, you tell the Object Management Workbench application what each user role is allowed to do for each different project status. Before we go too much further, we are going to take a moment to explain the different fields on this window and their importance. The numbers in Figure 3-9 match up to the descriptions of each of these fields listed in the following pages.

1. **User Role field**   This field contains the alphanumeric value used to define your user role.

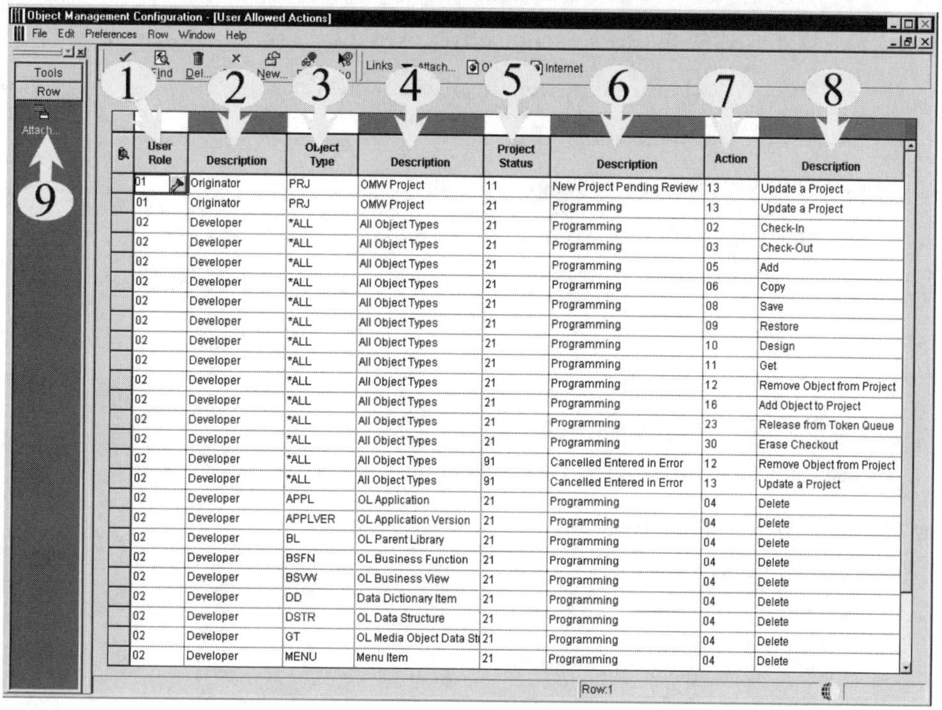
Object Management Configuration - [User Allowed Actions]
File Edit Preferences Row Window Help
Tools
Row
Attach...
Find Del... New...
Links Attach...
Internet
1 2 3 4 5 6 7 8 9
User Role | Description | Object Type | Description | Project Status | Description | Action | Description
01 | Originator | PRJ | OMW Project | 11 | New Project Pending Review | 13 | Update a Project
01 | Originator | PRJ | OMW Project | 21 | Programming | 13 | Update a Project
02 | Developer | *ALL | All Object Types | 21 | Programming | 02 | Check-In
02 | Developer | *ALL | All Object Types | 21 | Programming | 03 | Check-Out
02 | Developer | *ALL | All Object Types | 21 | Programming | 05 | Add
02 | Developer | *ALL | All Object Types | 21 | Programming | 06 | Copy
02 | Developer | *ALL | All Object Types | 21 | Programming | 08 | Save
02 | Developer | *ALL | All Object Types | 21 | Programming | 09 | Restore
02 | Developer | *ALL | All Object Types | 21 | Programming | 10 | Design
02 | Developer | *ALL | All Object Types | 21 | Programming | 11 | Get
02 | Developer | *ALL | All Object Types | 21 | Programming | 12 | Remove Object from Project
02 | Developer | *ALL | All Object Types | 21 | Programming | 16 | Add Object to Project
02 | Developer | *ALL | All Object Types | 21 | Programming | 23 | Release from Token Queue
02 | Developer | *ALL | All Object Types | 21 | Programming | 30 | Erase Checkout
02 | Developer | *ALL | All Object Types | 91 | Cancelled Entered in Error | 12 | Remove Object from Project
02 | Developer | *ALL | All Object Types | 91 | Cancelled Entered in Error | 13 | Update a Project
02 | Developer | APPL | OL Application | 21 | Programming | 04 | Delete
02 | Developer | APPLVER | OL Application Version | 21 | Programming | 04 | Delete
02 | Developer | BL | OL Parent Library | 21 | Programming | 04 | Delete
02 | Developer | BSFN | OL Business Function | 21 | Programming | 04 | Delete
02 | Developer | BSVW | OL Business View | 21 | Programming | 04 | Delete
02 | Developer | DD | Data Dictionary Item | 21 | Programming | 04 | Delete
02 | Developer | DSTR | OL Data Structure | 21 | Programming | 04 | Delete
02 | Developer | GT | OL Media Object Data St | 21 | Programming | 04 | Delete
02 | Developer | MENU | Menu Item | 21 | Programming | 04 | Delete
Row:1

**FIGURE 3-9.** User Allowed Actions window

2. **Description field** This field will be automatically populated; it contains a description of your user role.

3. **Object Type field** The Object Type field contains the type of object that you are setting up an allowed action for. You can use a wildcard value of *ALL to set up your allowed actions for all of the different object types, or you can select just one of the shipped object types. The shipped object types that are valid values for this field are

   - **ACT_DOC (Future Functionality)** ActivEra Documentation
   - **ACT_REL (Future Functionality)** ActivEra Task Relationship

- **ACT_RULE (Future Functionality)** ActivEra Qualifier Rule
- **ACT_TASK (Future Functionality)** ActivEra Task
- **ACT_VAR (Future Functionality)** ActivEra Variant
- **APPL** OL Application
- **APPLVER** OL Application Version
- **BL** OL Parent Library
- **BSFN** OL Business Function
- **BSVW** OL Business View
- **DD** Data Dictionary Item
- **DSTR** OL Data Structure
- **GT** OL Media Object Data Structure
- **MENU** Menu Item
- **PRJ** OMW Project
- **TBLE** OL Table
- **UBE** OL Batch Application
- **UBEVER** OL Batch Version
- **UDC** User Defined Code Type
- **UO** User Override
- **WF** Workflow Process

4. **Description field** This field will be automatically populated; it will contain the description of the object type that you have selected.

5. **Project Status field** This is the object management project status code. There are plenty of shipped project statuses to choose from, or you can even add your own custom project statuses, as these values are just user-defined codes. If you have worked with J.D. Edwards software for a while, you will probably be familiar with a few of these project statuses, as a lot of them are based on the J.D. Edwards Software Action Request (SAR) statuses. The shipped project statuses are listed next.

- *ALL—This is a wild card option that applies the defined allowed action to all project statuses
- 01 – Complete
- 02 – Returned for Clarification
- 06 – Returned–Already Reported
- 08 – Returned–Could not Duplicate
- 09 – Closed–No Further Action
- 10 – Refer to Parent SAR
- 11 – New Project Pending Review
- 12 – Reviewed by Customer Support
- 13 – Reserved by Software Devel.
- 17 – Reserved by Software Devel.
- 15 – Reserved by Software Devel.
- 16 – Reserved by Software Devel.
- 17 – Plan or Research
- 18 – Design
- 19 – Design Review
- 20 – Awaiting Staff
- 21 – Programming
- 22 – Programmer Test
- 23 – Manager Review
- 24 – Transfer to Production
- 25 – Rework–Same Issue
- 26 – QA Test/Review
- 27 – Rework–New Issue
- 28 – QA Test/Review Complete
- 29 – Demo Data
- 2A – Approved by CRB
- 2C – Waiting Programmer Check In
- 2M – Waiting Manager Approval
- 2Q – Waiting QA Manager Approval
- 2W – Waiting CRB Approval
- 30 – Ready for Transfer to Cum
- 31 – Returned–Not Planned
- 35 – Manager Review ESU
- 36 – ESU transfer to PRD
- 37 – Ready for ESU Build
- 38 – In Production
- 39 – To be reviewed with Users group
- 3P – Pristine Updates–OMW
- 40 – Production Development
- 41 – Xfer Production to Prototype
- 42 – Xfer Prototype to Development
- 45 – Pristine Get
- 90 – Completed–Not Tested
- 91 – Cancelled Entered in Error
- 99 – Completed
- MM – Beta Testing–MASTERS
- MP – Alpha Testing–MASTERS

6. **Description field**   This field will be automatically populated; it is the description of the project status that you select.

7. **Action field**   This field shows the action that you are allowing for your user role in a certain project status. The actions that you can grant privileges to are

   - **01 – Transfer**   This allowed action allows users to transfer objects between environments or path codes. However, it is important to note that this allowed action does not need to be defined, as this action is not used within allowed actions; to prevent a user from transferring object, you would simply not allow them to exchange the project's status for a status that would transfer objects.

   - **02 – Check In**   This action allows users to check in the object type that you have defined when it is in a project at the status defined in this window.

   - **03 – Check Out**   This action allows user roles to check objects out when they belong to a project in a certain status.

   - **04 – Delete**   This action allows users to delete objects.

   - **05 – Add**   This action allows users to add new objects in the Object Management Workbench.

   - **06 – Copy**   The copy action enables users to copy existing OneWorld objects within OMW.

   - **07 – Install**   This action is currently not available in OneWorld Xe, as it is future functionality.

   - **08 – Save**   This action allows users to save their objects to a save location.

   - **09 – Restore**   This action allows users to restore their objects from a save location.

   - **10 – Design**   This allowed action allows users to access the design tool for the specified object type. This is what allows your user roles into table design aid, forms design aid, and report design aid.

   - **11 – Get**   This allowed action is new functionality within OneWorld. It allows the user to move the specifications for the object out of the central objects and onto their client machine without checking the object out. This allows developers to review other pieces of code without having to check the object out and tie up the token. This action controls both Get and Advanced Get.

- **12 – Remove Object From Project**   This enables the user role to drop objects out of an Object Management Workbench project.

- **13 – Update A Project**   This gives the user role the ability to add notes to a project, add attachments to a project, change the project description, change the project system code, change the release for the project, change the start date, change the completion date, and select category code values for the project.

- **16 – Add Object To Project**   This allowed action allows users to add objects into an existing object management project.

- **21 – Switch Token**   This action allows the user to take the token away from one project and give it to another project. This type of action is usually reserved for developmental managers or system administrators.

- **23 – Release From Token Queue**   This allowed action allows the user role to release its entry in the token queue. So, if developers queue up for the token and change their mind, they can give up their spot in line for the token.

- **30 – Erase Checkout**   This option allows the user role to erase its check-out record. This can be used when a developer checked something out and did not want to check it back in. The developer can just erase the check out.

- **38 – Status Change**   This allowed action gives the user role the ability to change the status of an Object Management Workbench project.

8. **Description field**   This field will be automatically populated; it is the description of the action that you have chosen to give your user role. This value will default.

9. **Row/Attachments button**   This row exit allows you to place text notes or media object attachments, such as a Word document, on your allowed action records. So, if you are making a temporary change and want to leave another administrator a note, this is a very handy place to do this.

Now that you are familiar with the contents of this window, let's talk about some of the predefined user roles set up with certain allowed actions already defined, which are shipped by J.D. Edwards with the software. These may or may not meet your company's needs. The standard or shipped allowed actions are detailed in the Out-of-the-Box Allowed Actions and Activity Rules appendix, listed on the Web site (www.jdedwardspress.com).

As you look at the above list, you will realize that you do not see certain user roles. These include 05 Product Support, 07 Training, 08 Documentation, and 10 Quality.

This means that these user roles will not be allowed to perform any actions within the Object Management Workbench with the out-of-the-box settings. You can change this if you like to allow these roles certain rights, which you would want to do if you had a project member who has a specific role of training or documentation, and thus needs to be allowed to perform only certain actions.

**NOTE**

*The 06 – PVC Administrator user role is assigned \*ALL (Object Types), \*ALL (Project Statuses), and \*ALL (Actions); this rule will provide the 06 – PVC Administrator user role with complete access within OMW without any restrictions.*

## Adding an Allowed Action

You have probably noticed that there is no Add button in this window, as shown in Figure 3-10. So how do you add a new allowed action? To do this, you need to get to the bottom of the allowed actions shown in the grid. There is a blank line where you can type in your new allowed action. As you look at the table of shipped allowed actions, you are likely thinking, "I have to scroll through all of those!"

Of course, you do not have to scroll through all of these lines, and you can save yourself a lot of time by utilizing the query by example line (QBE). First, decide what type of user role you are going to add an allowed action for. You can place this user role in the query by example line and click Find. You will then see only the allowed actions that are set up for that user role. This list is a lot less to sort through than all of the allowed actions already set up in the table. You can further restrict your search by placing the project status on which you want to set up an allowed action in the Query By Example field. You will then see only the allowed actions for that user role and the specific project status.

In our example, we are going to add an allowed action for the 07 Training User role. First, place the user role 07 in the query by example line and click Find. In this case, you will get no records returned, since we are using an out-of-the-box setup. We can then type our new allowed action in the blank line in the grid to set it up. The purpose for each of these fields was discussed earlier in this section.

In the User Role field, place the user role you want to set up an allowed action on. In our case, this would be 07 for training. Tab through the Description field, and it will default to the appropriate description based on the user role you selected. In the Object Type field, place the object type that you want to set up an allowed action for. You can use a visual assist to view all of the different object types and select the one you desire,

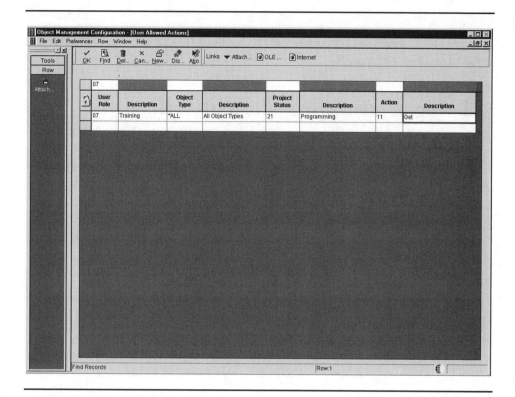

**FIGURE 3-10.**   Adding allowed actions

or you can use *ALL as a wildcard. If you use *ALL, then this allowed action will apply
to all of the different object types. The Description field will default to the description
appropriate to the allowed action that is chosen. The next field is the Project Status
field. This field tells the software on which project status the user role is allowed to
perform the action we are defining. In this example, we are going to use project status
21 Programming. You can also use the *ALL wildcard value in this field to define the
allowed action for all of the different project types. The Action field is the field that
tells the software what action the user role is allowed to perform for the project status
that you have defined. You can use a visual assist to select a different type of action, or
you can use the *ALL wildcard value to allow all actions on the user role and project
status that you have defined. In our example, we are going to define an action of 11,
which is a Get. The Description field will default. Click OK to save your allowed
action definition. You can repeat this procedure as necessary for adding additional
allowed actions.

*T I P*

*Be sure to click OK once you have finished defining your allowed actions, or your changes will not be saved.*

# Deleting or Removing Allowed Actions

Once you add or define an allowed action, it exists forever, right? Of course not—you can remove allowed actions as necessary. In order to remove an allowed action, go to menu GH9081 and double-click the Object Configuration Management application (P98230). This will open the Object Management Configuration window. In this window, select the Allowed Actions button, which will take you to the User Allowed Actions window.

From this window, you are able to remove an allowed action definition. What you need to do is first find the allowed action that you want to delete. You can just click Find, but this will show you all of the allowed actions that have been defined. J.D. Edwards ships 126 predefined allowed actions for the different user roles. Since you probably do not want to sort through all of these allowed actions, you may want to limit your search a little.

You can limit this search by using the query by example (QBE) line. This is the yellow line above the grid. What you will probably want to do is search either on the user role or by project status. In our example, we will go through removing the allowed action that we defined in the preceding section, "Adding an Allowed Action."

To find this allowed action, enter 07, which is the training user role, in the query by example line above the User Role field. Then click Find to see the allowed action records. Once you have found your allowed action record, you can just highlight the record and click Delete. You will then be prompted with the Delete confirmation box. Click OK to confirm deleting the record.

Now you're done, right? The record for your allowed action is gone. Well, not exactly. You have not saved the fact that you deleted the allowed action. In order to do this, you need to click OK in the User Allowed Actions window. This will commit the deletion of the allowed actions record. If you do not click OK, but instead click Find or Cancel, then you will not have saved your changes. Trust us when we say it's easy to forget to do this!

# Copying Allowed Actions

You may have noticed that there is no Copy button in the User Allowed Actions window. Does this mean that you need to manually type in all of your allowed actions setup line by line, over and over again? Well, you could do this if you have lots of free time and not much of a life. However, most of us have better things to do with our time. So we recommend copying existing records whenever possible to save time.

To do this, you first need to find some existing allowed actions that are similar to the new allowed actions you want to set up. For example, if you want to copy all of the allowed actions for your 02 Developer user role, you would first use the query by example line to isolate your records, by entering **02** in the User Role field and clicking Find. You will then see all of the allowed actions that are set up for the developer user role for all projects, as shown in Figure 3-11.

This may be just a few too many allowed action records to sort through, because there are 33 predefined allowed action definitions. You may also want to limit your search by looking for only allowed actions that apply to the developer user role and a specific project status. In our example, we will limit the search to project status 21.

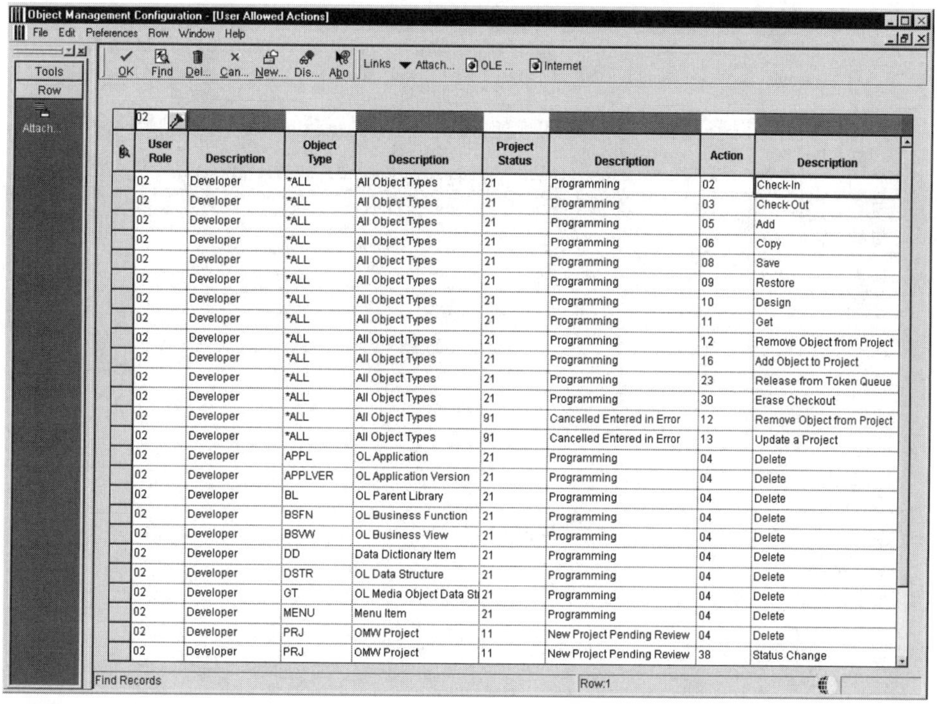

**FIGURE 3-11.**  Copying allowed actions

This limits the records that we see to a limited number and type of actions. You can then highlight the allowed action definition that you want to copy. You can also select multiple allowed action records at the same time. Once you have the allowed action definitions that you want to copy highlighted, press CTRL-C. Then place your cursor in the blank line in the grid for the User Allowed Actions screen and press CTRL-V. This will place a copy of your highlighted records in the grid lines.

Do not click OK at this point; if you do you will get duplicate key errors because, given that you just copied all of these records, they are exactly the same as others that already exist in the table. What you need to do is go through each line and change either the user role or the project status for that user role to set up the desired allowed action. You will notice that the descriptions for some of the values, such as project status and action, are not defaulting correctly. Do not panic, as these will default correctly once you tab or arrow through the field. This is shown in Figure 3-12.

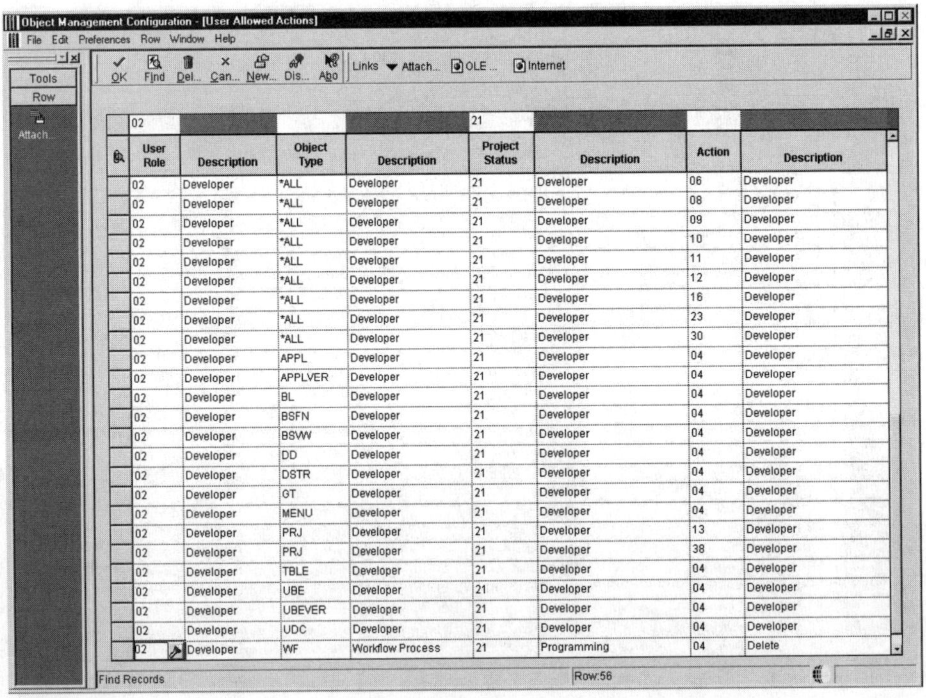


| User Role | Description | Object Type | Description | Project Status | Description | Action | Description |
|---|---|---|---|---|---|---|---|
| 02 | | | | 21 | | | |
| 02 | Developer | *ALL | Developer | 21 | Developer | 06 | Developer |
| 02 | Developer | *ALL | Developer | 21 | Developer | 08 | Developer |
| 02 | Developer | *ALL | Developer | 21 | Developer | 09 | Developer |
| 02 | Developer | *ALL | Developer | 21 | Developer | 10 | Developer |
| 02 | Developer | *ALL | Developer | 21 | Developer | 11 | Developer |
| 02 | Developer | *ALL | Developer | 21 | Developer | 12 | Developer |
| 02 | Developer | *ALL | Developer | 21 | Developer | 16 | Developer |
| 02 | Developer | *ALL | Developer | 21 | Developer | 23 | Developer |
| 02 | Developer | *ALL | Developer | 21 | Developer | 30 | Developer |
| 02 | Developer | APPL | Developer | 21 | Developer | 04 | Developer |
| 02 | Developer | APPLVER | Developer | 21 | Developer | 04 | Developer |
| 02 | Developer | BL | Developer | 21 | Developer | 04 | Developer |
| 02 | Developer | BSFN | Developer | 21 | Developer | 04 | Developer |
| 02 | Developer | BSVW | Developer | 21 | Developer | 04 | Developer |
| 02 | Developer | DD | Developer | 21 | Developer | 04 | Developer |
| 02 | Developer | DSTR | Developer | 21 | Developer | 04 | Developer |
| 02 | Developer | GT | Developer | 21 | Developer | 04 | Developer |
| 02 | Developer | MENU | Developer | 21 | Developer | 04 | Developer |
| 02 | Developer | PRJ | Developer | 21 | Developer | 13 | Developer |
| 02 | Developer | PRJ | Developer | 21 | Developer | 38 | Developer |
| 02 | Developer | TBLE | Developer | 21 | Developer | 04 | Developer |
| 02 | Developer | UBE | Developer | 21 | Developer | 04 | Developer |
| 02 | Developer | UBEVER | Developer | 21 | Developer | 04 | Developer |
| 02 | Developer | UDC | Developer | 21 | Developer | 04 | Developer |
| 02 | Developer | WF | Workflow Process | 21 | Programming | 04 | Delete |

**FIGURE 3-12.** Copied allowed actions grid descriptions

*TIP*

*You may also export the desired allowed actions to an Excel spreadsheet, update the appropriate fields, and then import that data back into the grid.*

In our example, we have copied all of the 02 Developer records for project status 21 Programming. We are now going to change the user role to a 01 for Originator and a project status from 21 Programming to 11 New Project Pending Review. The easiest way to do this is start with the user role column, and just type **01** in the field and arrow down. As you do this, you will see the description change to the correct description for 01 Originator.

In this example, we do not need to change any of the object types, since we copied only the object types that we were interested in. However, you will want to arrow through all of the definitions so that all of your object descriptions show up correctly; then you can tell for sure that you have set up your allowed action records correctly. Once you have arrowed through the Object field, you will then want to tab over to the Project Status field. You need to change all of the project statuses from 21 to your desired project status. In this case, it is 11 New Project Pending Review. Once you have done this, you can then arrow through all of the action settings, so that the description shows up correctly.

# Activity Rules

By now, you may be asking yourself, are we done yet? Well, not quite yet. The beautiful thing about the Object Management Workbench is that, although it takes some time to set up, it actually puts change management controls onto your OneWorld system. In the past, you really just turned the system on; and if you did not manually implement some change management procedures, you hoped for the best. With the Object Management Workbench, you are now able to build most of your change management controls directly into the OneWorld software.

We have already talked about user roles, which can be described as a job description, and we have also talked about allowed actions. These are the first steps that you must go through to set up your Object Management Configuration. Once you have defined your user roles and your allowed actions, you then need to move on to setting up your activity rules. The allowed actions, which we discussed in the preceding section of this chapter, tell the system what each user role is allowed to do at each different project status.

OneWorld will first look to the user role and associated allowed actions to verify whether an action can be performed on a certain object type at a certain project status. Once this "verification" has been performed, OMW will then look to the activity rules for direction as to what central object tables to write changes to when you perform a check in or other Object Management Workbench activity. Object movement is controlled by activity rules defined by project statuses.

Well, that is basically what the object management activity rules are for. These activity rules tell the software where to write changes when a check out or a check in is performed; these rules also tell the software how to transfer objects between path codes. This is why the activity rules are one of the last steps in setting up your object management configuration.

To set up object management activity rules, go to the Object Management menu (GH9081). Double-click the Object Management Configuration application (P98230). This will take you into the Object Management Setup window. In this window, select the Activity Rules button. This will take you into the Work With Object Activity Rules window. From this window, you can tell OneWorld what your software development life cycle is and how objects are promoted from one path code into the next until they finally reach the production path code.

## Shipped Activity Rules

The OneWorld software comes with a series of predefined activity rules already set up. These may or may not meet your business needs, so you do have the ability to modify or customize these rules. In the section "Adding Activity Rules," we will cover how to customize these rules. However, before we get into this, we will cover what the shipped activity rules are and the advantages and disadvantages of this setup.

The shipped J.D. Edwards activity rules include some of the values from the J.D. Edwards software action request (SAR) system. If you have been working with J.D. Edwards World or OneWorld software for a while, you are familiar with entering a SAR and then checking the status of the SAR. The SAR will go through several different statuses as it is worked on. If you are not familiar with the SAR statuses, do not worry; we will go through all of the project statuses as they apply to OMW.

Well, time marches on, and so does progress—J.D. Edwards application development now uses the Object Management Workbench to develop new OneWorld functionality and applications. To do this, they need to have certain activity rules in place. They also realize that their clients will need certain rules in place to implement changes in OneWorld. With this in mind, they developed a base set of activity rules to deliver with the OneWorld Xe software.

To see the shipped activity rules, log into OneWorld and go to the Object Management menu (GH9081). Double-click the Object Management Configuration application (P98230). This will take you into the Object Management Configuration window. Click the Activity Rules button to bring up the Work With Object Management Activity Rules window, shown in Figure 3-13. Once you are in this window, click Find and you will see the OneWorld shipped activity rules. When you see these rules for the first time, they may not make a lot of sense.

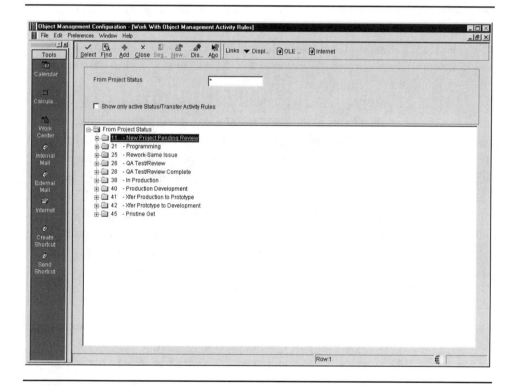

**FIGURE 3-13.**   Shipped OMW activity rules

The folders with the plus sign (+) next to them represent the *project status activity rules*. Before you click the plus and add to any confusion you may have, an explanation of these project status activity rules is in order. As you know, when you have a project in OMW, this project resides in OMW at a certain project status. For example, you may have a project that is at status 21 Programming. If you are assigned to this project status with a Change Status allowed action, you can advance this project to a new status. Your project status activity rules define what list of choices you can advance your project to; they represent your project or software development life cycle. When you click the plus sign (+) by the project status 21 Programming, you will see a list of project statuses that you can advance the project to from 21 Programming; these are transfer activity rules that define what may occur when a project is advanced through its life cycle. Let's make an analogy to clarify this. Imagine project status 21 as a room, and each of the doors exiting that room is a project status that you can advance to from 21. Once out of project status 21, you are in a completely new and different room with different doors, which you can then advance your project through. If you left room 21 and went into room 25, you would then need to look at the 25 Rework-Same Issue main directory, click the plus next to it, and learn what "rooms" you could go to from there.

Each time you pass through a door into the next room, you are changing project statuses. OneWorld then looks to the *object transfer activity rules* to determine whether objects will be transferred from one location to another. Project status activity rules define which statuses or "rooms" you can advance a project to, and object transfer activity rules define object movement when moving to different rooms. You can examine object transfer activity rules by clicking the plus sign (+) on the folders, and then highlighting and selecting one of the possible statuses, or "rooms," that you may advance to. Once you select this room, you will see a list of rules describing what happens to each object type listed when you advance to this room or project status. Details of object transfer activity rules are described in the next sections.

You may now be asking, what about the project status that is the same room number as the one I am in? How can I advance from project status 21 to a project status 21? Well, object transfer activity rules need to be defined for when you advance a project and for when you are doing development work while in a certain project status. When you are in a certain project status, such as status 21, and you are checking objects in or out and doing other development actions, OneWorld will look at the object transfer activity rules under the project folder 21 under the project status 21. This determines where to read and write records during checkout, checkin, or other development activity.

## Shipped Activity Rules for Project Status 11 New Project Pending Review

A OneWorld project, with shipped object management configuration settings, starts in project status 11 New Project Pending Review. This project status is used at J.D. Edwards to see whether the modification will be done. If you expand the folder representing the New Project Pending Review project status, you will see other project statuses. These project statuses are the "doors" to other rooms. When you move a project to another status, you may be changing the project status only for reporting or workflow reasons, or you may actually perform an object transfer between path codes. That is right; with the Object Management Workbench, all object transfers are handled under the covers by the activity rules.

In this project status, the only activity rules that are shipped are ones that allow you to advance your project to another status. No object transfers will be performed when you promote your project to the next status. This means that you have an entry for project status 11 New Project Pending Review and several entries under this folder for other project statuses. The shipped statuses that you can advance your project to are 21 New Project Programming, 40 New Project Production Development, 45 Pristine Get, and 91 New Project Cancelled Entered in Error, as shown here:

| Project Status | Promotion Path Options |
|---|---|
| 11 – New Project Pending Review | 21 – Programming |
| | 40 – Production Development |
| | 45 – Pristine Get |
| | 91 – Cancelled Entered in Error |

# High-Risk Activity Rules

Normally, your OMW project will move from status 11 New Project Pending Review, to 21 Programming, to 26 QA/Test Review, to 28 QA/Test Review Complete, to 38 In Production, and—finally—01 Complete. These project statuses allow you to develop the objects; move them into the PY7333 path code to perform testing; sign off on the testing; and, finally, move the objects into the production path code and environment. Although these are not the only project statuses you will use, they are the major ones. In project status 21, you are allowed to perform development on your OneWorld objects, assuming that your user roles and allowed actions are set up correctly. See the earlier "User Roles" and "Allowed Actions" sections of this chapter for more information. However, J.D. Edwards gives you a couple of other shipped project statuses with activity rules set up for them, which you need to understand. These are 40 Production Development and 45 Pristine Get.

## Project Status 40 Production Development and Emergency Fixes

In our opinion, the project status 40 Production Development should almost never be used. This is because this project status affects your production objects directly; and as *anyone* who programs knows, new code works on the very first try. Well, since code working on the first try really is a rare thing, this project status should be limited to a specific administrator group and should not be allowed to be used by all users. The status activity rule for 40 Production Development was shipped in OneWorld Xe as *PUBLIC. In future releases of the software, this activity rule will be sent out with an ADMIN group value. During an installation and upgrade, sometimes code will be applied directly against the production path code. The project status of 40 Production Development and the project statuses of 40 to 41, 40 to 42, and 41 to 42 status activity rules are intended to allow an object to be promoted backward. These statuses will most likely never be used by customers; however, they are provided just in case modifications are made to an upper path code.

If customers were to use these statuses, they would commit several "sins" that can have severe consequences. One sin is that you have broken your software development life cycle (SDLC). Some people will tell you "So what, we had an urgent issue in our production environment and we needed a fix, which we now have. Life is good, right?" Well, maybe and maybe not. The problem is that you have now made a change to an object in your highest environment. What is going to happen when you promote that object up again from a lower environment, such as PY7333?

What will happen is that you will lose your emergency fix; this may happen weeks or months down the line—so, everything was working and suddenly you don't know why you are having a problem. The other, greater risk here is that you overlay only part of your fix. Now try to figure that out when the production system goes south and the fix was applied weeks earlier by someone else.

The way this should be handled is that you should fix this issue in the development environment and then promote the fix through the higher environments. The reasons for this are simple. You will know for certain that the fix is in your lower environments, and thus it will not be overlaid at a later date by accident. You will also have an opportunity to perform a test on this fix in an environment other than your production environment. This concept is shown in Figure 3-14.

Figure 3-14 shows how an emergency fix should be applied to your production environment. We will walk through each step of this diagram and explain why following this procedure is a best practice that will help ensure the stability of your OneWorld System.

Okay, you have found an issue in your production environment that involves one of your custom objects. This issue needs to be fixed immediately. The first step is to save any current development work that is not ready to be promoted to your save location. This step may or may not be necessary, depending on whether you have performed additional development work on your object.

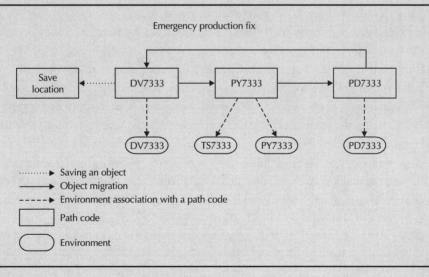

**FIGURE 3-14.**    Emergency fix process flow

Once you have saved your object, you need to create a project, and either manually move your changes out of the object in the DV7333 path code, or restore the problem object or objects from your production path code back to your development path code—assuming you have checked code that is not ready to be promoted into your PY7333 path code. You can now perform the fix on the object in your development environment.

Once your developer has implemented the fix, he or she can then promote this object into the PY7333 path code. Now you need to be aware of something here. If you have code on the object or objects that has yet to be promoted to the production path code, you will need to promote this code again. This is why you need to decide whether you are going to restore the object or manually move your code out of the object.

There may be some concern over impacting your company's testing schedule, since all of the quality assurance testing normally occurs in the PY7333 path code and environment. An emergency promotion may impact your testing schedule, but the impact should be fairly minor. This is because the token should not be released until the object is transferred into the production environment, so any changes you are testing should have been saved by the developer and you can simply promote the objects again.

Also, you will want to perform at least a surface test of your fix in the PY7333 environment. This is because the PY7333 environment is the closest to match your production environment and path code. If the modification does not work correctly, you will want to know now rather than in production.

Once you have performed at least a surface test on your object or objects, you can then promote the object into the production path code and environment. What we have really done here is to ensure that your fix now exists in all of your path codes. Now, you might say, "Wait a minute—didn't we save an object off to the save location, which is not the same as this fix?" This may or may not have happened, depending on your development activities. If this did occur, you now have to combine this fix with your new custom code, but you are doing this in your development environment and it has now become a part of the project itself. If you follow this procedure, you do not have to manually apply the fix to the PY7333 path code, which may require some custom Object Management Workbench configuration setup. Also, you do not have to keep track of where the fix is and where it is not. You have one development contact who is well aware of the difference in the code, since they applied the fix. They now do not have to go through all of the path codes trying to find the delta or difference in the code. If you have worked with the Object Management Workbench application for a while, you may say, "Wait a minute—the shipped activity rules are set up to perform development in production and then I can demote my code change backward through the environments and path codes." Well, we feel this is the wrong approach. You are basically hoping and praying that your code change, in the production environment, does not adversely affect any of your data. That is simply a risk you do not have to take, if you follow the procedure just given. This procedure can be completed very quickly, as long as the correct people are in place.

To this day, it amazes the authors how many clients are willing to risk their production environments. This environment is what runs your business; without it, you are severely limited or you may not even be able to ship any product. We all know that code works perfectly the first time, right? Well, since it does not, you really should not be risking your production data. In a worst-case scenario, you might even cause data corruption. If data corruption happens, we are sure you would much rather it happened in one of your lower environments.

## Project Status 45 Pristine Get

The other status, 45 Pristine Get, is a status that you may or may not use a lot. What this project status allows you to do is perform a Get from the pristine environment. You can do this without having to go through a bunch of different project statuses, if you have only a small number of objects that you would like to get from Pristine. However, if you have a large number of objects you would like to restore from the Pristine path code, it will be easier to add them all to a project and advance it to a status of 45.

### DEFINITION

**Get** takes the object specifications from a path code's central objects and moves them to a client workstation. Unlike a check out, this action does not require you to hold the token or place a record in the Object Librarian detail table F9861.

You should note that in the Object Management Workbench application, on the Cross Application Development Tools menu GH902, there is a row exit named "Get." If you have already read the first two chapters of this book, you know there is also a Get button in the middle of the Object Management Workbench application window, which will appear when the projects are in the correct status.

What is the difference? The difference is that if you use the Get button (which looks like a hand) in the center of the Object Management Workbench application window, you will get the object out of a path code that is determined by the project status. If you use the Row | Get button, you get to select the path code that you want to get the object from. This allows you to leave your project in the status it is in—for example, 21—and still restore the object from the pristine path code.

We recommend that you give the Advanced Get ability to your senior developers, development managers, and development leads. This gives your development group the ability to quickly restore an object, if necessary, without having to go through several different project statuses. You can limit access to this row exit through OneWorld exit security. In case you are concerned that you will now lose visibility of what objects have been restored from the pristine path code, don't worry. You see, the Object Management Workbench has logging that will tell you when a Get is performed, from what path code, by what user, and from what machine. So you really will not lose visibility to the objects that have been restored from your pristine environment.

We mentioned earlier that the Row | Get button allows the developer to choose what path code he or she wishes to restore the object from. This is a very important point. When you have been developing for a while, you probably will not want to restore an object from the pristine path code. The reason is that you now have series of modifications that have made it all the way to production.

Do you want to recode all of those modifications just because you need to restore a single object? We didn't think so. That's why we believe that this Row | Get functionality is so important. Your development staff can now restore an object from your prototyping or development path code, or even from your production path code, depending upon their needs. This also gives them the ability to see what the code looks like in the production environment, if they are troubleshooting an issue. They can simply save from their custom code and then perform a Get from the production environment.

If you have only a small number of objects that you would like to restore from Pristine, you can select them one at a time and perform an Advanced Get, using the Row | Get button, from Pristine for each of them. If you have a large number of objects you want to restore from Pristine, you will find it easier to add them to a project and advance the project status to 45. Then you can simply select the project and click Get. This will perform the Get action on each object in the project and save you from having to do them individually. By selecting the project, you are performing a project-level Get, which performs a Get on all of its objects; the Advanced Get, by contrast, may not be performed at the project level and must be done for each object individually.

## Shipped Activity Rules for Project Status 21 Programming

The next set of shipped status activity rules that we will talk about are for project status 21 Programming. If you follow the "normal" project status path for shipped activity rules, this is the second project status that your project will move into. This is the project status that allows you to perform your development activities on your objects. You can also advance your project from this status to a couple of different project statuses. These are shown as follows:

| Project Status | Promotion Path Options |
|---|---|
| 21 – Programming | 11 – Pending Review |
| | 26 – QA Test/Review |
| | 91 – Cancelled Entered In Error |

Okay, so we made it to the project status where the real work gets done, but what is set up so that this work actually happens? If you look at the shipped activity rules for project status 21, in the Object Management Configuration application, you will notice that there is an entry of 21 under the directory for 21 Programming. When you want to advance your project, you will not see the 21 status, since you are already in the 21 status. The reason this status code is there is to tell the system how to perform actions, which you set or which are shipped in the allowed actions section of the Object Management Configuration application. In the shipped allowed actions, a developer user role is allowed to check objects out, check them in, perform Gets, and perform other design work.

When only the allowed actions are set up, the system does not know anything except that the user role is allowed to perform an action, such as a check in. The activity rules are what tells the Object Management Workbench application where you are checking your objects into. You will see this if you highlight the 21 – Programming status under the 21 Programming directory and click Select. This will take you into the Object Transfer Activity Rules application. This window is shown in Figure 3-15.

You will notice that the grid of this screen has several different columns shown. These include the Active, User, Object Type, Description, From Location, To Location, From Release, To Release, and Allowed Action fields, as well as several different description fields. The Active column tells you whether the activity rule is active or not. The User column tells you for what user or group the activity rule applies. J.D. Edwards ships activity rules only for the *PUBLIC group. We recommend that you set up activity rules only for *PUBLIC, to keep the complexity of your activity rules under

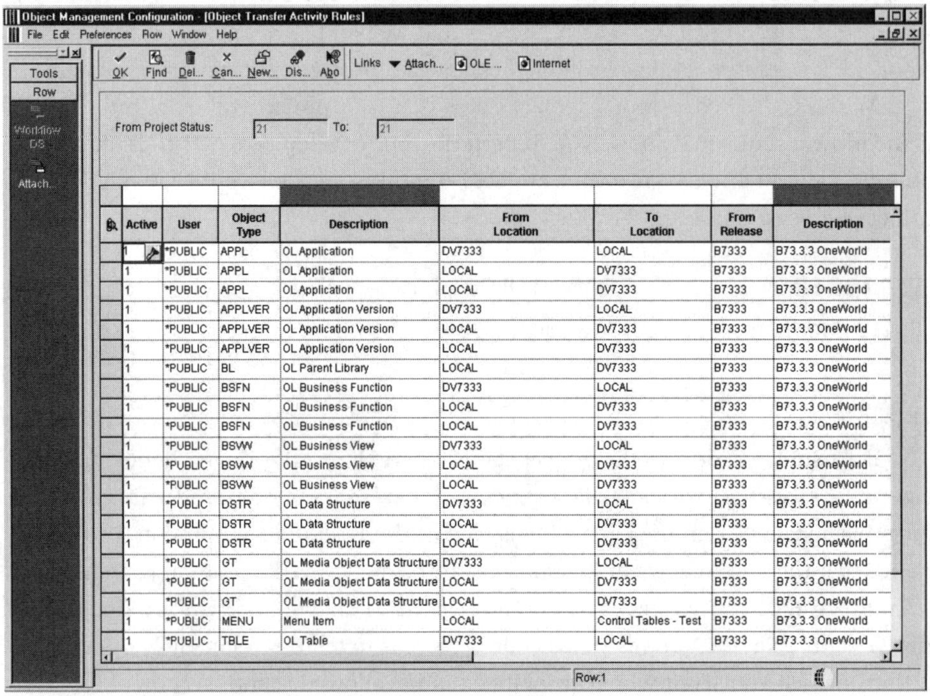

**FIGURE 3-15.** Object transfer activity rules for project status 21

control until you become more comfortable with the activity rules. If you like, however, as you gain familiarity with the software, you can create status changes that are limited to specific users; they can be assigned to a group or a specific User ID. We will discuss this approach in greater detail in the "Adding New Activity Rules" section, later in the chapter. The Object Type column shows you what type of object the activity rule is set up for. You can see the different types of OneWorld objects by clicking the visual assist button when you tab into this field. The next column is a description for the object type. You then see the From Location column. This column is what tells OneWorld where it is getting the information from. So if you are looking at an activity rule for a check out, you will see the DV7333 path code here. The To Location is where the software will copy the information to. In the context of a check out, this will show LOCAL, which is a special value telling OneWorld to copy the information to your developer's workstation. The From Release column shows the release of OneWorld the object is coming from. The Object Management Workbench does allow you to develop in multiple releases, but generally you will leave this as B7333. The software will obey this rule only if the object is at this release level. The To Release column indicates the release you are developing in. The To Release and From Release columns should always match. The Allowed Action column is what tells the software what action the activity rule is set up for, such as a check out. The available actions when the From and To project statuses are the same are 04 Check In, 05 Check Out, and 02 Delete Only.

- When creating check-out rules, the source location will be the central object's path code, and the target location will be LOCAL.

- When creating a check-in rule, the source location will be LOCAL, and the target location will be the path code you want to check the object into.

- The 02 Delete Only rules are used with the Delete From Server option on the Object Delete form. When this option is selected, OMW will look for 02 Delete rules at the current project status and delete the object from the defined target location.

Keep in mind that users may create only one check-out transfer activity rule per object type at each project status (since an object can be checked out from only one location). However, multiple check-in and delete rules can be created if the customer would like to check the object into multiple path codes or delete the object from multiple locations.

Now that you have an understanding of the columns for the grid in this application, let's get back to talking about what you will see here out of the box. The activity rules table, on the Web site, shows you all of the activity rules for the different object types in project status 21. You may customize the activity rules setup if you desire.

You can also advance your project out of the 21 Programming status to a different shipped project status. One option is to set the project status back to 11 New Project Pending Review. This will not perform any action, but will just change the status back to 11, thus restricting actions to the project to the shipped allowed actions.

Another option is to set your status to 91 – Cancelled Entered in Error. This allows your developers to cancel a development project without deleting it from the system. The reason that you may want to use this shipped project status is that you can track and report to management all of the development efforts that have been canceled, so no one will ask later what happened to that modification. Out-of-the-box transfer activity rules are set up to automatically release objects' tokens during this status change, in case any tokens were received and not released before the status was changed to 91. If a token were to be held by a project at 91, a user may end up waiting for it indefinitely. Transfer activity rules can be created to release tokens for objects on a status change while doing nothing else; if the objects do not hold tokens, it will do no harm. To create transfer activity rules to release tokens, create them for each Object Librarian object type, and leave the From and To locations blank while entering 1 in the Release Token field. It is recommended that these release token transfer activity rules exist for any status change that could result in tokens being held for objects where they are not being used—for example, changing a project status from 21 Programming to 91 Cancelled Entered in Error, and 11 New Project Pending Review to 91 Cancelled Entered in Error.

The final project status that you can advance your project to from project status 21, is 26 QA Test/Review. This project status is what actually transfers your OneWorld objects from the DV7333 to the PY7333 path code. The shipped activity rules for this project status tell the software what to copy and where to copy it from and to. When you look at this table, you will notice that the columns are a little different from the activity rules for project status 21. The difference is that the table for status 26 will include a release column, a allowed action, and a mandatory flag. The reason is that the software recognizes that, since this project status is not the same as the status your project is currently in, you are performing a transfer. Now, if you do not have any activity rules set up under the next project status, no objects will be transferred. In this case, however, shipped out-of-the-box transfer activity rules are set up for changing a project status from 21 Programming to 26 QA Test/Review.

The transfer activity rules in the appendix (www.jdedwardspress.com) show the major activity rules columns that will apply to transferring objects from one path code to another. The columns that are not shown are the From Release, To Release, and Description columns for these values. The first column is the active column. The software will obey only activity rules with a value of 1 or active. The user column is the user or group that the activity rules apply to. Again, not to sound like a broken record, we recommend you use only the *PUBLIC group to keep things a little simpler until you have a deeper understanding of the Object Management Workbench. The next column is the object type. This column tells the software what type of object the rule applies to, such as applications, business functions, and UBEs. The Description field gives you a full description of the object type you are setting activity rules up on.

The next two fields are very important. These are the From Location and To Location columns. These fields tell the software from what data source or path code to move your objects, and where to write them. With the shipped transfer activity rules of project status 21 to 26, DV7333 to PY7333 will appear in these columns for most of your object types. The exception will be your menus, user-defined code, data dictionary items, workflow objects, and user overrides, which use data source values rather than path code.

### CAUTION

*When the visual assist is used for the Location field for a UBEVER, you will be prompted whether you want to find a path code or a data source; this feature is unique to UBEVER objects. When a path code is provided, the Version's F983051 record and specifications will be transferred between the From and To locations. When a data source is used, only the F983051 record will be transferred. To ensure that your report versions have the appropriate specifications transferred with them, select the appropriate path code.*

The next column is the Release Token column. In this column will be 1 or 0. This column is important because it determines whether you release the token on your objects, thus allowing another developer to work on that object. The shipped standard is not to release the token until the object is transferred into production. This is why you will see the Release Token Rule field set to 0 for the transfer activity rules from a project status of 21 to 26 with the out-of-the-box configuration. You also will notice that you did not have this option when you looked at the activity rules for a project status of 21 to 26. This is because the software knows that, when the project statuses are the same, you are defining development activity rules, such as where an object is checked in. When the project statuses do not match, the software assumes you are going to transfer an object, or you will leave the activity rules blank and the project status can be used for reporting and approval purposes.

### NOTE

*When transferring an application, OMW will attempt to transfer all \*PUBLIC User Override records that exist for the application. Therefore, a User Override transfer activity rule is required whenever an APPL transfer activity rule is created.*

The next field is the Allowed Action field. Note that this allowed action list is a little different from the allowed actions that you set up for your user roles. Those allowed actions determined what your user role was allowed to do for each project status. The allowed actions for the activity rules tell the software where to write changes once a delete, transfer, check out/get, or check in occurs. You now have the options of

- 01 – Transfer Only
- 02 – Delete Only
- 03 – Transfer or Delete
- 04 – Check In
- 05 – Check Out/Get

The values that you will normally use here are 01 and 03. This is because when you actually have activity rules for a project that is moving from one status to another, e.g., 21 to 26, you are normally transferring objects. The value 01 will just transfer an object. The value 03 is a little different. You see, with OMW, when you delete an object, you can delete the object from your save location, you can delete the specifications on your workstation, you can delete the object from the path code you are working in, or you can mark the object to be deleted at transfer time. If you choose to mark the object to be deleted at transfer time, the object will be flagged for deletion for your upper path codes. As you promote a project that contains this object, you will be deleting the object from each path code as you go. This, of course, is true only if you have your activity rules set up for an allowed action of 03 Transfer or Delete. If the rule was of type 01 – Transfer, nothing would be done with the object flagged for deletion, and objects would be transferred only into this location. The shipped value for your object management configuration activity rules is 03 Transfer or Delete. This activity rule will cause objects that are marked to be deleted to be removed from target path code, as well as transferring the objects.

### NOTE

*Multiple transfer activity rules can be defined for a single status change if you would like to transfer an object to multiple locations. However, you should not attempt to perform multiple transfers such as path code A to path code B, and path code B to path code C, on the same status change. Since the activity rules may be fetched from the database in any order, it is possible that the B to C transfer could occur before the A to B transfer, and this would result in an old object existing in path code C.*

The final column that we will discuss is the Mandatory Flag field. This field will accept a value of zero or one. A value of zero is off, and a value of one is on. This field is used in conjunction with the Active/Inactive field when a rule has been set to inactive. This flag indicates that when a rule has been deactivated and the rule is mandatory, if a project has an object in it that the rule would apply to, the project will not be allowed to advance. It allows the administrator to prevent a project from advancing if it contains a specific object type that he or she has temporarily locked down. The way OMW works, regardless of what the mandatory setting is when a project is advanced to its next status that involves a transfer, all objects must successfully transfer in order for the project to reach the next status. So, for example, if you have 40 applications that you are trying to transfer and one fails, the entire project will not advance to the next project status. Without the mandatory setting, there would be no way to prevent specific objects from transferring while limiting others. With the rule deactivated (without having a mandatory field), OMW would just think that it is not supposed to do anything with the object. The mandatory flag provides a method of indicating that although the rule is inactive, it must have been performed in order for the project to successfully advance. We recommend that you leave this column set to the shipped status of 1.

### *T I P*

*In the GA version of OneWorld Xe, the activity rule to transfer user overrides was shipped incorrectly. It was shipped to transfer user overrides from the Control Tables – Test to the Control Tables – CRP data source. This is incorrect, as the user overrides table, F98950, resides in the central objects data source. You will need to change this activity rule so that the From location is Central Objects – DV7333 and the To location is Central Objects – PY7333.*

## Shipped Activity Rules for Project Status 26 QA Test/Review

Now that we have discussed what happens when you move your Object Management Workbench project to status 26 QA Test/Review, let's talk about what happens from this project status. The following table shows the shipped project statuses that you are allowed to move your project into from project status 26 QA Test/Review:

| Project Status | Promotion Path Options |
|---|---|
| 26 – QA Test/Review | 25 – Rework-Same Issue |
| | 28 – QA Test/Review Complete |

This project status allows your quality assurance personnel to perform integration tests on your modifications. This means that when you go into the Activity Rules application and expand project status 26, you will not see status 26 under this project status directory. They did, however, provide the ability to bring object specifications down to the local machine from the PY7333 path code by providing the allowed actions for the 04 Quality Assurance role to perform a Get. Since all objects that were modified for the fix or enhancement are in the project, and were transferred to the prototype environment, when the project status was changed from 21 Programming to 26 QA Test/Review, performing a Get will bring the specifications down to the local machine and the testing can be performed without having to build a package. For this to function correctly, you will need to add a project status of 26 under your 26 QA Test/Review directory. You then need to set up activity rules telling OneWorld where to get the objects from and where to write them to. This can be a quick way to test projects as they move through the system. However, if you have any objects that need to be tested on a server, you will need to perform a package build.

If the test fails, then the testing team can return the project as a defect, i.e., set the project status to 25 Rework-Same Issue, or they can mark the project as passing their quality assurance tests. Now you will need to decide what types of integration test your company will perform on their system.

Let's start out by talking about moving a project status from 26 QA Test/Review to 25 Rework-Same Issue. If you look at the shipped activity rules for this project status, you will notice that they are blank. What this means is that the project status is only for reporting purposes. This may seem confusing, since we have already moved these objects from the DV7333 path code to the PY7333 path code. This is set up in this manner because you have not released the token on this object. No new development should have taken place on this object when it is set to project status 25 Rework-Same Issue. Your development team can simply monitor their projects through the Object Management Workbench; when they see a project in status 25, they will know that your quality assurance group has found a defect that needs to be corrected and the project can then be moved back to 21, where development work can be redone.

*TIP*

*There are several shipped reports that a development manager may find useful in tracking what statuses the projects his or her team are working on are set to. These can be found on the Object Management menu (GH9083).*

The next project status that you can move your project to, from project status 26 QA Test/Review, is 28 QA Test/Review Complete. This status is also set up solely for reporting purposes, with the shipped activity rules. This means that if you select the activity rule in the Work With Object Management Activity Rules application, there will not be any activity rules set up for this project status under the 26 QA Test/Review folder.

The reason that J.D. Edwards has ship this activity rule set up in this manner is so that you can use this project status, 28 QA Test/Review Complete, as a holding area where a manager can review the OneWorld modifications prior to the modifications being advanced into the production environment. This allows the manager to be the individual performing that status change that promotes objects into production. Later, we will discuss how this status can be used to provide a method for backing up objects in the production path code before they are updated with the objects from the prototype path code.

## Shipped Activity Rules for 25 Rework-Same Issue

The next set of shipped status activity rules that we will discuss are the activity rules for project status 25 Rework-Same Issue. This project status is set up so that your quality assurance group can report defects to your development team. The following table shows the project statuses that you can promote a project to from this project status.

| Project Status | Promotion Path Options |
|---|---|
| 25 – Rework-Same Issue | 21 – Programming |
| | 25 – Rework-Same Issue |
| | 26 – QA Test/Review |

The way that this project status is typically used is as follows: When a defect is found by the quality assurance team or tester, the project status will be set to 25 Rework-Same Issue. The developer responsible for the project will review the notes and move the project from status 25 Rework-Same Issue to 21 Programming. Again, there are no object transfer activity rules for moving a project from status 25 Rework-Same Issue to 21 Programming. This is because you do not need to transfer your objects, since you still have not released the token. The only thing that this project status change really does is allow the developer to place the project in a status where he or she can perform development on the objects contained in this project again. The developer would then move that project back up through the project statuses that we have discussed, from project status 21 Programming.

The developer can also determine that the reported defect really was not a defect. He or she can then tell the quality assurance personnel that the object is functioning as designed. He or she can do this by adding notes to the project and then setting the status to 26 QA Test/Review. Again, this will not transfer any objects, since they already exist in the PY7333 path code and there are no shipped activity rules for this project status change.

The final set of activity rules for project status 25 Rework-Same Issue is 25 Rework-Same Issue. As we have already discussed, when you have a from project status and to project status that is the same in the Activity Rules application, you are setting up activity rules for development activities and not transfers. In this case, however, there are no transfer activity rules set up for this project status. This means you cannot perform any development activities while the project is in status 25 Rework-Same Issue.

### *N O T E*

*We have seen some clients remove the link to project status 21 Programming and place the same activity rules from 21 Programming under 25 Rework-Same/Issue. This gives the client visibility to how many projects being worked on have been returned from the quality assurance team with defects. If you choose to do this, you will also have to duplicate the allowed actions for status 25 to mimic what has been set up for status 21.*

## Shipped Activity Rules for 28 QA Test/Review Complete

Now let's say that your quality assurance team did not find a defect in the code. Then they would move the project from status 26 QA Test/Review to status 28 QA Test/Review Complete. This project status is normally used as a reporting code so that a manager can review the code one last time and then schedule it to be promoted into the production path code. The following table shows the project statuses that you can move the project into from this status.

| Project Status | Promotion Path Options |
| --- | --- |
| 28 – QA Test/Review Complete | 26 – QA Test/Review |
| | 38 – In Production |

In this project status, you really have only two choices. You can send the project back to your quality assurance department, asking them to retest something, or you can promote the code into your production environment and path code.

Let's start by talking about moving the project back to status 26 QA Test/Review from project status 28 QA Test/Review Complete. This former project status has no object transfer activity rules behind it. That means it is set up for reporting purposes only. Since we have not released the token, no new development on these objects can go forward. So, by moving your project status from 28 to 26, you are not transferring any objects; all this really does is tell your quality assurance or testing team to run additional tests.

The next status is the big one. This project status is 38 In Production. This is the project status that actually transfers your code into your production path code. If you take a look at the shipped activity rules (see the appendix at www.jdedwardspress.com), you will notice a few things. One is that they are almost identical to the activity rules for moving a project from status 21 Programming to one of 26 QA Test/Review. The only real difference is that you now have PY7333 in your From location and PD7333 in your To location and you are finally releasing the token. It is at this point that another development project on the objects contained in your project can begin. The transfer activity rules for the project status 26 QA Test/Review to 38 In Production show the activity rules for moving a project from status of 26 to 28.

## Shipped Activity Rules for 38 In Production

The next set of shipped status activity rules we are going to talk about are for project status 38 In Production. At this project status, your project's objects have been transferred into your production path code and the token or tokens have been released. However, you are not done with this project yet.

| Project Status | Promotion Path Options |
|---|---|
| 38 – In Production | 01 – Complete |
| | 28 – QA Test/Review Complete |

J.D. Edwards has set up the shipped activity rules so that you can do two things with a project that is in status 38 In Production. You can mark the project as complete, which means that your modification was successful and you are seeing no issues with it in production, or you can say you have found a defect and set the project status to 28 QA Test/Review Complete.

Project status 01 Complete is another status that does not have any activity rules associated with it. However, this status is hard-coded within OMW and is the only status that OMW currently recognizes as a closed status. The closed status is important, as the OMW software will not allow you to delete any objects in an open project. This status can also be used for reporting purposes to show the projects that have been completed. Now, if you set your project status from 38 In Production to 28 QA Test/Review Complete, well, that is a little different.

This project status code also does not have any activity rules, so it is mainly for reporting purposes, but it can have some consequences. You see, you have already released the token; so if you set the project status back to 28 QA Test/Review Complete, another project with one of your objects may already be in the PY7333 path code, which would invalidate your test. That is why you need to carefully review your development project statuses before setting a project that has made it all the way through production to status 28 QA Test/Review Complete.

### TIP

*Most of the time, it will be easier to start another development project, specifically to fix the defect, and move it through the project statuses instead of demoting the project from the production path code back to the development path code. This also gives you visibility to any defects that were not found until the project was in your live production path code and environment.*

## Activity Rules for the Final Project Statuses

This discussion of shipped activity rules would not be complete without talking about these final project statuses, 40 Production Development, 41 Xfer Production to Prototype, 42 Xfer Prototype to Development, 45 Pristine Get, and their shipped activity rule setup. We have waited to talk about these project statuses until last because they are normally the exceptions to the rule. These are project statuses that should rarely, if ever, be used.

## Shipped Activity Rules for 40 Production Development

| Project Status | Promotion Path Options |
| --- | --- |
| 40 – Production Development | 01 – Complete |
| | 11 – Pending Review |

**Project Status**

**Promotion Path Options**

40 – Production Development

41 – Xfer Production to Prototype

42 – Xfer Prototype to Development

91 – Cancelled Entered in Error

Let's start with one that we feel is not wise for you to use. (This is why these status activity rules should be changed from *PUBLIC to a specific administrator user ID or administrative group so that they are not available to all users.) This is project status 40 Production Development. This project can be reached by moving a project from status 11 New Project Pending Review to 40 Production Development. This project status allows you to perform development activities directly into your production path code. The activity rules are the same as for project status 21 Programming, except that the code will now be checked out and into the production path code.

This project status was designed for emergency fixes. However, we disagree with this logic for several reasons. When you are making changes directly to your production path code, you are taking a huge risk. What you are counting on is that the code will work perfectly the first time, and we all know that programs work perfectly the first time! Your code change could have an issue and even cause possible data corruption, depending on the code change. Why risk this?

We recommend that you follow the normal development life cycle, which means you would start in the DV7333 path code and move the fix through to the PD7333 path code. Now, you can do this fairly quickly using update packages to test your code. Also, the PY7333 environment normally has a subset of your production business data for testing. If you do have a corruption problem, wouldn't you rather you had it in the PY7333 environment's business data?

That said, let's quickly go through the project status that you can move a project to from status 40 Production Development. You can move the project to 01 Complete, which will only release the token. This is because if you are going to perform development in your production path code, you will need to release the token for affected objects when the modification is complete.

You can also set the project to status 11 New Project Pending Review. This does nothing but put the project back at the beginning of your software development life cycle. This could be used if you decide not to modify the object in the production environment and you are going to move the fix through the entire software development life cycle.

The next two project statuses that you can move your project to are a little different. These are 41 Xfer Production to Prototype and 42 Xfer Prototype to Development. Both of these project statuses will transfer the objects contained in the project from your production path code into either the development or the prototyping path code (PY7333). The name of the 42 project status, Xfer Prototype to Development, is kind of confusing. You see, out of the box the activity rules are set up to perform a transfer from your production path code to the development path code, even though the description says transfer from prototyping to development. Since the release of OMW, these status changes have caused a lot of confusion and concern; and as a result, in future releases, JDE will be sending out the status activity rules assigned to the group ADMIN (regardless of whether the customer has an admin group created), and the ability to move a project status from 40 to 42 has been eliminated. The activity rules for both of these project statuses are shipped set up to release the token on transfer and have the mandatory flag set to 1.

Again, these project statuses need to be used very carefully, since objects that are contained in the project may be in development, i.e., in the DV7333 path code, or in testing, in the PY7333 path code. If you use these project statuses, these objects will then be overlaid with the objects that exist in your production path code. This means that you will lose any modifications that exist in the DV7333 path code that do not exist in the PD7333 path code. This could also mean that you can accidentally overlay part of one of your modifications if you do not pay careful attention while using these project statuses.

**Shipped Activity Rules for 41 Transfer Production to Prototype**   Now let's briefly discuss the shipped activity rules for project status 41 Xfer Production to Prototype. The following table shows the promotion path options available to you from this project status.

| Project Status | Promotion Path Options |
|---|---|
| 41 – Xfer Production to Prototype | 01 – Complete |
| | 40 – Production Development |
| | 42 – Xfer Prototype to Development |

This first promotion path option is 01 Complete. This will mark the project as being successfully completed and release the token on all of the objects included in the project. The next promotion path option is 40 Production Development. This option allows you to move the project back into status 40 Production Development and perform development activities against your production path code. This project status does not have any transfer activity rules behind it, since you are just changing the status to get back to the 40 Production Development project status activity rules.

If you look at the work with object management activity rules screen, in the Object Management Configuration application, you will notice that there is a project status of 41 Xfer Production to Prototype under the 41 Xfer to Production to Prototype directory. As we have already discussed in this chapter, when there is a directory with the same project status under it, this tells the software to allow certain development activities. In this case, when your project is in status 41 Xfer Production to Prototype, you can perform gets on your objects.

**Shipped Activity Rules 42 Xfer Prototype to Development**   This set of activity rules is very similar to the 41 Xfer Production to Prototype.

| Project Status | Promotion Path Options |
| --- | --- |
| 42 – Xfer Prototype to Development | 01 – Complete |
| | 40 – Production Development |
| | 41 – Xfer Production to Prototype |
| | 42 – Xfer Prototype to Development |

In this project status, the shipped activity rules allow you to set the project back to status 01 Complete. This will mark the project as completed successfully and release the token. You can also set the project status back to 40 Production Development. This project status has no activity rules behind it, as you are not performing a transfer. It will just move your project back into status 40 Production Development, where there are shipped activity rules set up to allow you to perform development on objects in your production path code.

You can also move your project status from 42 Xfer Prototype to Development to 41 Xfer Production to Prototype. Again, there are no shipped activity rules behind this project status. This just allows you to move your project into another project status where you have different activity rules set up and different promotion options. Think of it as a door into another room. Since we are not transferring any objects when we leave this room to enter another one, we do not need any activity rules on this project status.

When your project is in status 42 Xfer Prototype to Development, you will also be able to perform Gets on your objects. However, all of the Gets will come from the production path code, not the prototype path code.

**Shipped Activity Rules for 45 Pristine Get**   The final set of shipped activity rules are for project status 45 Pristine Get. This project status allows you to perform a Get, using the Get button in the center of the Object Management Workbench window, from the pristine path code. This will allow you to highlight your project status and perform a Get on all of the objects included in the project. However, once you have made a few changes to an object, you may not want to go all the way back to the J.D. Edwards pristine code.

This is why you can grant some of your senior developers the authority to use the Row Exit | Get functionality. This difference with this Get is that it allows the developer to choose what path code he or she wants to get the object from. So, if the developer needs to restore an object, he or she can take it from the PY7333 path code, which will have more recent code. The developer can also perform a Get on an object out of the production path code and review the code to isolate an issue. The developer cannot check into the production path code unless they use project status 40 Production Development. So this is fairly safe and easy-to-use functionality.

| Project Status | Promotion Path Options |
|---|---|
| 45 – Pristine Get | 01 – Complete |
| | 11 – New Project Pending Review |
| | 45 – Pristine Get |

If you choose to move a project from status 45 Pristine Get to 01 Complete, you are marking the project as completed successfully. This project status does not have any activity rules; it just marks the project as completed successfully.

If you choose project status 11 New Project Pending Review, you will just place the project status back into the status that all new projects start in, when you are using an out-of-the-box setup. So, if you restored an object from the pristine path code, you would now be able to work on the project and promote it through the normal promotion path, which we referred to when we discussed the shipped activity rules.

There are activity rules set up so that, when your project is in status 45 Pristine Get, you can perform a Get on the object. This allows you to restore objects from the pristine path code. This also concludes our discussion of the OneWorld shipped activity rules.

# Adding New Activity Rules

Now that we have talked about all of the shipped activity rules that are set up for you out of the box, we can tell you how to add new activity rules. This will allow you to customize the software to meet your company's needs. To start this process, you will need to access the Object Management Configuration application. You will find this application on the Object Management menu (GH9081). Once you are on this menu, double-click the Object Management Configuration application (P98230). This will take you into the Object Management Configuration application. Click the Activity Rules button, which will open the Work With Object Management Activity Rules window, shown in Figure 3-16. Once you see this window, click Find.

Now you can see what activity rules are already defined in the system (for information on the shipped activity rules for OneWorld, see the "Shipped Activity Rules" section of this chapter). You now have to decide what type of activity rules you want to add. We recommend that, before you create a bunch of activity rules, you chart out what you want to do on a piece of paper. You see, the activity rules are the last thing you add in your object management configuration setup. You must first decide whether you are going to add a new user role or not; you then need to add your allowed action setup into the system; and, finally, you can then tell the system where to find information for each action by setting up activity rules.

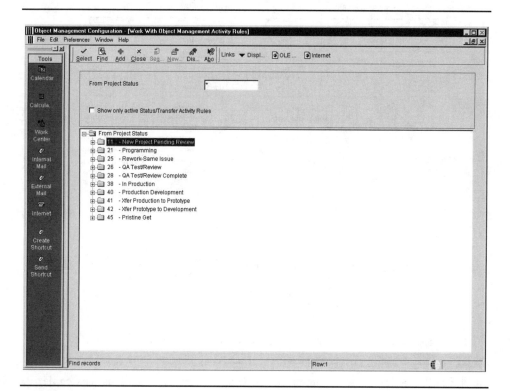

**FIGURE 3-16.**   Working with object management activity rules

We have found that Visio is a great tool to maintain a document showing your object management configuration plan. You simply create a document when you start your object management configuration and then continue to update it as your business's needs change. This will help to ensure you know what OneWorld is set up to do, and that any consultant coming in can quickly get a picture of your configuration. This document can take many different shapes or forms. We have included two example documents in Figures 3-17 and 3-18.

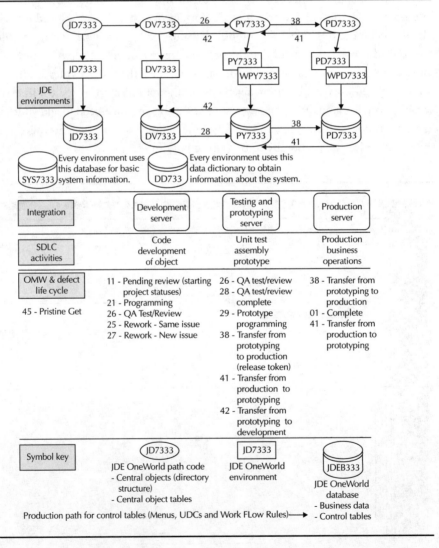

**FIGURE 3-17.**   Software development life cycle and OMW project statuses example diagram using Visio

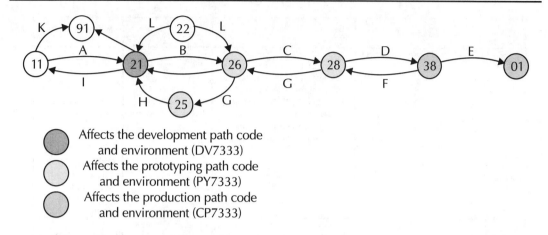

| Transfer Rule | 21<br>DV7333 <=> Local | 22<br>PY7333<=>Local | Activities<br>B<br>DV7333 =><br>PY7333 | D<br>PY7333 =><br>CP7333 | I | L<br>PY7333=><br>DV7333 |
|---|---|---|---|---|---|---|
| APPL | Check In, Check Out, and Delete | | Transfer | Transfer/Release Token | Release Token | |
| APPLVER | Check In, Check Out, and Delete | Check In, Check Out, and Delete | Transfer | Transfer/Release Token | Release Token | Transfer |
| UBE | Check In, Check Out, and Delete | | Transfer | Transfer/Release Token | Release Token | Transfer |
| UBEVER | Check In, Check Out, and Delete | Check In, Check Out, and Delete | Transfer | Transfer/Release Token | Release Token | |
| BSFN | Check In, Check Out, and Delete | | Transfer | Transfer/Release Token | Release Token | |
| TBLE | Check In, Check Out, and Delete | | Transfer | Transfer/Release Token | Release Token | |
| BSVW | Check In, Check Out, and Delete | | Transfer | Transfer/Release Token | Release Token | |
| MENU | Add, Copy, and Delete | Add, Copy, and Delete | Transfer | Transfer | Release Token | Transfer |
| GT | Check In, Check Out, and Delete | | Transfer | Transfer/Release Token | Release Token | |
| WF | Add, Copy, and Delete | Add, Copy, and Delete | Transfer | Transfer | Release Token | Transfer |
| UDC | Add, Copy, and Delete | Add, Copy, and Delete | Transfer | Transfer | Release Token | Transfer |

**FIGURE 3-18.** Software development life cycle and OMW project statuses example diagram using Excel

| User Roles | 11 | 21 | 22 | Allowed Actions 26 |
|---|---|---|---|---|
| Originator | Add and Update a Project | Update Project | | |
| Developer | Delete, Update, and Change Status of Project | Add, Delete, Design, Save, Restore, and Update UBEs and UBE versions; Check In and Out UBEs and UBE Versions; Add, Release Token, and Remove Objects from Projects; Update and Change Status of Project | UBE /Application Versions Add, Copy, Delete, Check In, Check Out, Save, and Restore. | Update Project |
| Quality Assurance | | Get | Get | Design All Objects; Add, Copy, Delete interactive/batch versions, Update and Change Status of Project |
| Manager | Update and Change Status of Project | Add, Delete, Design, Save, Restore, and Update UBEs and UBE versions; Check In and Out UBEs and UBE Versions; Add, Release Token, and Remove Objects from Projects; Update and Change Status of Project | UBE /Application Versions Add, Copy, Delete, Check In, Check Out, Save, and Restore. Get, Update Project, and Change Status. | Update and Change Status of Project |
| PVC Admin | All Actions with All Objects | All Actions with All Objects | All Actions with All Objects | All Actions with All Objects |
| Supervisor | Update and Change Status of Project | Add, Delete, Design, Save, Restore, and Update UBEs and UBE versions; Check In and Out UBEs and UBE Versions; Add, Release Token, and Remove Objects from Projects; Update and Change Status of Project | UBE /Application Versions Add, Copy, Delete, Check In, Check Out, Save, and Restore. Get, Update Project, and Change Status. | Update and Change Status of Project |
| Sr. Financial Systems | Add and Update a Project | Copy, Delete, Save, and Restore interactive/batch versions | | Get and Update a Project |
| Financial Systems | Add and Update a Project | Copy, Delete, Save, and Restore interactive/batch versions | | Get and Update a Project |
| Copr. Report Design | Delete, Update, and Change Status of Project | Add, Delete, Design, Save, Restore, and Update UBEs and UBE versions; Check In and Out UBEs and UBE Versions; Add, Release Token, and Remove Objects from Projects; Update and Change Status of Project | UBE /Application Versions Add, Copy, Delete, Check In, Check Out, Save, and Restore. | Get and Update a Project  Update Project |
| Consultant | Delete, Update, and Change Status of Project | Add, Delete, Design, Save, Restore, and Update UBEs and UBE versions; Check In and Out UBEs and UBE Versions; Add, Release Token, and Remove Objects from Projects; Update and Change Status of Project | UBE /Application Versions Add, Copy, Delete, Check In, Check Out, Save, and Restore. | |

**FIGURE 3-18.**   Software development life cycle and OMW project statuses example diagram using Excel (*continued*)

| 28 | 38 | 25 | 91 | User Roles |
|---|---|---|---|---|
| | | | | Originator |
| | | | Release Token, Update, and Remove Object from Project | Developer |
| Get | | | | Quality Assurance |
| Get, Update, and Change Status of Project | Get, Update, and Change Status of Project | Update and Change Status of Project | Release Token, Update, and Remove Object from Project | Manager |
| All Actions with All Objects | All Actions with All Objects | All Actions with All Objects | All Actions with All Objects | PVC Admin |
| Get, Update, and Change Status of Project | Get, Update, and Change Status of Project | Update and Change Status of Project | Release Token, Update, and Remove Object from Project | Supervisor |
| Update Project | | | | Sr. Financial Systems |
| | | | | Financial Systems |
| | | | Release Token, Update, and Remove Object from Project | Copr. Report Design |
| | | | Release Token, Update, and Remove Object from Project | Consultant |

**FIGURE 3-18.**   Software development life cycle and OMW project statuses example diagram using Excel (*continued*)

## Adding Activity Rules for a New Project Status

You have carefully planned out how you are going to configure your system, and you have found that you want to add a new project status into your configuration. To illustrate this point, we are going to add the project status activity rule of 23 Manager Review. This a shipped project status code, which does not have any activity rules defined for it. If you like, you can also add your own project code, since this is just a user-defined code.

*T I P*

*If you add a custom project status code, you will be adding a new user-defined code value. Since this is the case, you will need to migrate this new user-defined code value to all of your different environments, as different environments can use different user-defined codes. If you do not, anyone accessing OMW functionality may receive a user-defined code error, since your new project status user-defined code would not exist in that environment.*

To add this custom project status activity rule into the system, you will need to do so in such a way that it can be seen as a folder in the Work With Object Management Activity Rules window. To do this, enter the Object Management Configuration application and click Activity Rules. Then click Add in this window. This will open the Project Status Activity Rules window, shown in Figure 3-19. This window is what allows you to add project status activity rules into your system. The fields for this window are discussed in Table 3-6.

In our example, we are adding a project status of 23 Manager Review. To do this, enter project status **23** in the From Status field. You will then enter a **1** in the Active field, **\*PUBLIC** in the User field, and **23** in the To Project Status field. (Creating the status activity rule for 23 to 23 is needed only if you intend to perform actions at this status that will use check in, check out/get, or delete transfer activity rules; otherwise, you can create rules for the statuses that you intend to advance the project to, as we will in this example.) The Description field will default in when you tab out of the To Project Status field. You do not need to enter any values in the From SAR status field or the To SAR Status field. This is because the software action request (SAR) system is for J.D. Edwards internal use only. Once you have filled in these values, click OK. The screen will then be cleared out, so that you can add another project status activity rule.

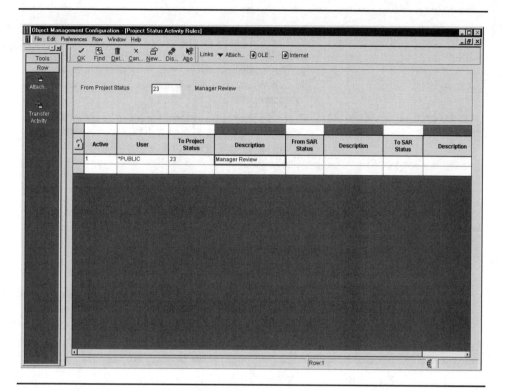

**FIGURE 3-19.** Adding project status activity rules

| Field | Description |
|---|---|
| From Project Status | This field will contain the project status you are adding activity rules for. This field tells the software what project status you are setting up transfer activity rules from and to. This field can also be used to add a new project status into your activity rules. |
| Active | This field will contain a value of 0 or 1. A value of 1 indicates that the activity rule is active. A 0 is a disabled activity rule. OneWorld will ignore all activity rules with a value of 0 in this field. |

**TABLE 3-6.** Project Status Activity Rules Parameters

| Field | Description |
|-------|-------------|
| User | This is the user or group that you are setting up your activity rules for. We recommend you use *PUBLIC for all of your activity rules to cut down on confusion until you have a better comfort level with activity rules. |
| To Project Status | This is the project status that you are setting up project status activity rules to move the project to. If this status matches the From project status, you are then setting up a new directory in the Object Management Activity Rules window. |
| Description | You will see a description of the To Project Status field. |
| From SAR Status | When the project is at the From status and is moved to the To status, the corresponding SAR will be moved to this status. The SAR system is for J.D. Edwards internal use only, so leave this field blank. |
| Description | Here you will see a description of the From SAR status. |
| To SAR Status | When the project is at the From status and is moved to the To status, the corresponding SAR will be moved to this status. The SAR system is for J.D. Edwards internal use only, so leave this field blank. |
| Description | The description is of the To SAR status. |

**TABLE 3-6.**    Project Status Activity Rules Parameters (*continued*)

Once you have finished adding your project status activity rules, click Cancel and you will be taken back to the Work With Object Management Activity Rules window. When you click Find in this window, you will see a new directory for project status 23 Manager Review. This is shown in Figure 3-20.

### N O T E

*It is important to understand that project status activity rules are cumulative. This means that, if you have three rules—one set up for a specific user ID, one for the group that you belong to, and one for *PUBLIC—you will be allowed to advance the project to any of the three statuses. This is different from object transfer activity rules.*

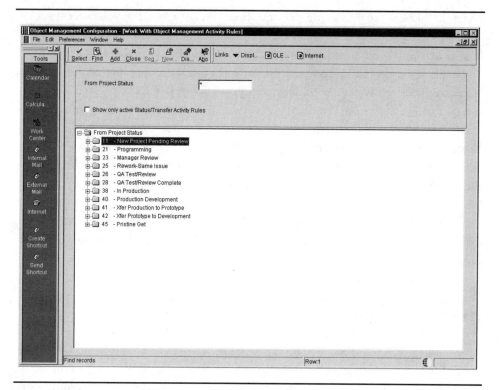

**FIGURE 3-20.** Project status activity rules

## Adding Object Transfer Activity Rules

If you attempt to expand the directory for project status 23 Manager Review, you will notice that there are no project statuses defined below it other than 23 Manager Review, and there are no activity rules behind it. You also may notice that this project status is not listed under any of the other directories in this window. In this book, we have mentioned that you should think of these directories as rooms, and a different project status under the directory as a door to another room. Well, right now you have an isolated room that you can neither enter nor leave.

To hook the project into your promotion status, you will need to highlight the directory that you want to be able to promote your project status from to the new status of 23 Manager Review. In our example, we are going to place this project status under the 11 New Project Pending Review directory. Depending on your needs, you might want to place this project status somewhere else and adjust your project status flow so that your projects must flow through this status before proceeding onward.

To place this project status under the 11 New Project Pending Review directory, highlight the directory node with the plus sign (+) beside it and click Select. This will take you back into the Project Status Activity Rules window. In the grid in this window, you will see the current project status or doors that are listed under the 11 New Project Pending Review directory. To add our new project status, all we have to do is enter 1 in the Active field to tell the system that this rule is active, *PUBLIC in the User field so that this rule applies for everyone, and 23 in the To Project Status field. Once you have entered these values, click OK. You will now be taken back to the Work With Object Management Activity Rules window. Click Find in this window and expand the 11 New Project Pending Review project status. You will now see your new project status 23 under this directory.

This means that when you promote a project out of status 11 New Project Pending Review, you will now see the project status of 23 Manager Review as an option to promote your project to.

To complete the hook into the system, you need to add some activity rules to allow a project to be promoted out of status 23 Manager Review. To do this, highlight project status 23 Manager Review and click Select. This will take you back into the Project Status Activity Rules window. To add a link to another project status, you simply enter 1 in the Active field to tell the system that this rule is active, *PUBLIC in the User field, and the project status that you want to enable your projects to move out of a project status 23 Manager Review. In our example (see Figure 3-21), we are going to place project status 21 Programming. This will allow the promotion of a project from status 23 Manager Review to 21 Programming.

If you now expand the 23 Manager Review directory in the Work With Object Management Activity Rules window, you will see project status 21 under the 23 Manager Review directory, as shown in Figure 3-21.

## Setting Up Activity Rules for Specific Actions for a Project Status

Now that we have our project status 23 Manager Review in the project status promotion flow, we want to give our managers the ability to perform certain actions

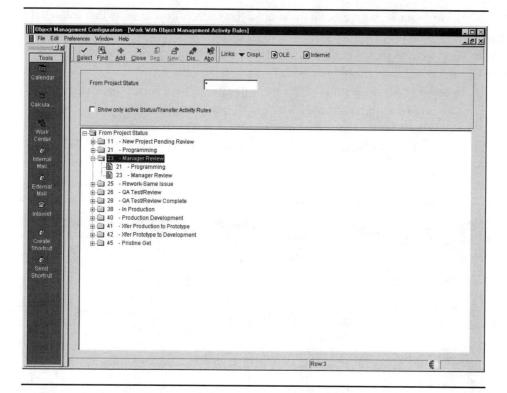

**FIGURE 3-21.**   Project status activity rules for manager review status

while their projects are in this project status. To do this, expand project status 23
Manager Review, highlight project status 23 Manager Review under this directory, and
click Select. This will take you into the Object Transfer Activity Rules window. This
window will allow you to add activity rules for your project status.

*N O T E*

*You must also configure user roles and allowed actions for any new project
status. Please refer to these sections of this chapter for more information.*

In our example, we are going to set up object transfer activity rules that will tell the software to find the information necessary to perform Gets, Check Outs, and Check Ins on objects, as shown in Figure 3-22. However, first let's quickly review the fields on this screen, as described in Table 3-7.

In our example, we want to set up the activity rules for Check Outs, Gets, and Check Ins for project status 23 Manager Review. To do this, we need to enter 1 in the Active field to show the activity rule is active. We then need to enter **\*PUBLIC** in the User field, so that the rule applies to all of the users.

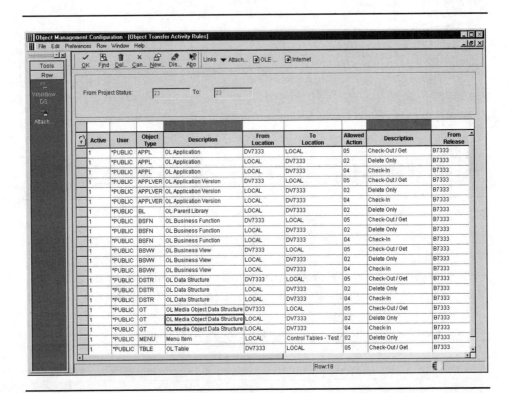

**FIGURE 3-22.** Transfer activity rules

| Field | Description |
|---|---|
| Active | This field will contain a value of either 1 or 0. 1 is to show that the rule is active. 0 tells the system that the rule is inactive, and thus will be ignored. |
| User | This is the user or group that the activity rule is set up for. We recommend using *PUBLIC and then controlling the access to the activity through allowed actions until you feel comfortable with the activity rules. |
| Object Type | This is the object type that the activity rule applies to. |
| Description | This field contains a description of the object type. |
| From Location | This is the location from which the system will read information for the specified allowed action. This can be a path code, a data source, or a special value of LOCAL, depending on the activity rule you are setting up. The LOCAL setting is a special value that tells OneWorld to read from or write to the client workstation's specification files. |
| To Location | This is the location to which the system will write information for the specified allowed action. This can be a path code, a data source, or a special value of LOCAL, depending on the activity rule you are setting up. The LOCAL setting is a special value that tells OneWorld to read from or write to the client workstation's specification files. |
| From Release | This field needs to contain the OneWorld release that you are developing in—B7333, for example. |
| Description | This field contains a description of From Release. |
| To Release | This field needs to contain the release of OneWorld that you are developing in—for example, B7333. |
| Description | This field contains a description of To Release. |
| Allowed Action | This field will contain the action that you are setting up activity rules for. The values that can be used in this field are<br>01 – Transfer Only<br>02 – Delete Only<br>03 – Transfer or Delete<br>04 – Check-In<br>05 – Check-Out/Get |
| Description | This field will contain the description for your allowed actions. |

**TABLE 3-7.**  Object Transfer Activity Rules Parameters

The next step is to choose the object type that we want the activity rule to apply to. There are a multitude of different object types, shown in the table that follows.

| Object Type | Description |
|---|---|
| ACT_DOC (Future Functionality) | ActivEra Documentation |
| ACT_REL (Future Functionality) | ActivEra Task Relationship |
| ACT_RULE (Future Functionality) | ActivEra Qualifier Rule |
| ACT_TASK (Future Functionality) | ActivEra Task |
| ACT_VAR (Future Functionality) | ActivEra Variant |
| APPL | OL Application |
| APPLVER | OL Application Version |
| BL | OL Parent Library |
| BSFN | OL Business Function |
| BSVW | OL Business View |
| DD | Data Dictionary Item |
| DSTR | OL Data Structure |
| GT | OL Media Object Data Structure |
| MENU | Menu Item |
| PRJ | OMW Project |
| TBLE | OL Table |
| UBE | OL Batch Application |
| UBEVER | OL Batch Version |
| UDC | User Defined Code Type |
| UO | User Override |
| WF | Workflow Process |

As you can see, you have a lot of flexibility when you are setting up your activity rules. You can choose exactly what rules you need to set up depending on your business's needs. In our example, we are adding activity rules for applications, application versions, business functions, business views, data structures, generic text, tables, UBEs, and UBE versions. As you can see from Figure 3-23, we have set up these activity rules to have a From location of DV7333 and a To location of LOCAL for the Check-Out/Get allowed actions. This means that when someone performs a Check Out or a Get in this project status, the software will read the DV7333 central object tables and write the information to the workstation's specification files. We have also set up the reverse for the Check In allowed action. This will take information from the client workstation and write it to the DV7333 central objects.

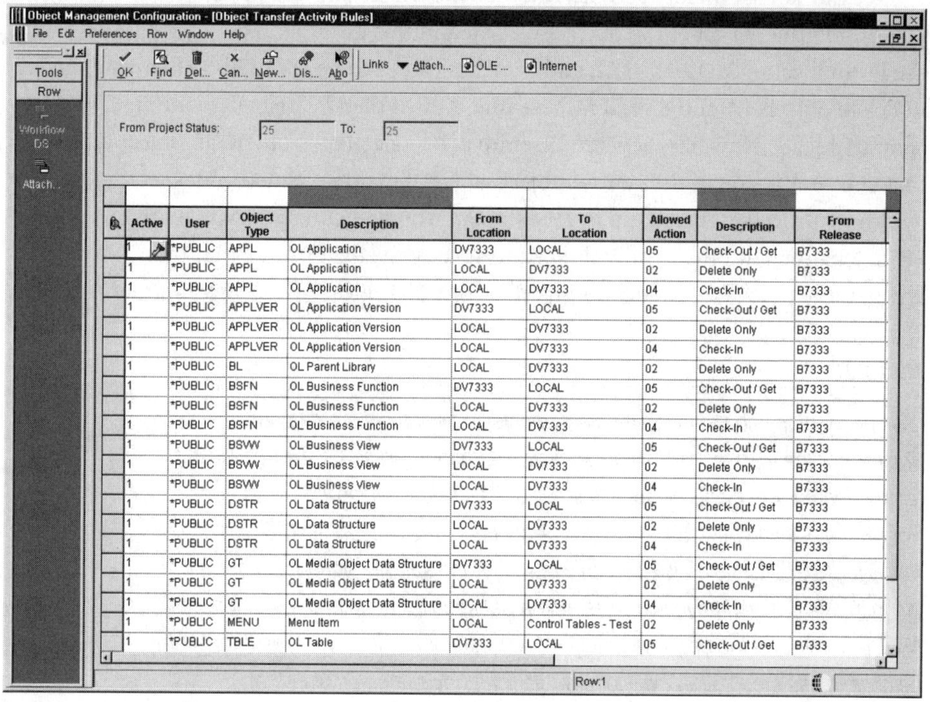


| Active | User | Object Type | Description | From Location | To Location | Allowed Action | Description | From Release |
|---|---|---|---|---|---|---|---|---|
| 1 | *PUBLIC | APPL | OL Application | DV7333 | LOCAL | 05 | Check-Out / Get | B7333 |
| 1 | *PUBLIC | APPL | OL Application | LOCAL | DV7333 | 02 | Delete Only | B7333 |
| 1 | *PUBLIC | APPL | OL Application | LOCAL | DV7333 | 04 | Check-In | B7333 |
| 1 | *PUBLIC | APPLVER | OL Application Version | DV7333 | LOCAL | 05 | Check-Out / Get | B7333 |
| 1 | *PUBLIC | APPLVER | OL Application Version | LOCAL | DV7333 | 02 | Delete Only | B7333 |
| 1 | *PUBLIC | APPLVER | OL Application Version | LOCAL | DV7333 | 04 | Check-In | B7333 |
| 1 | *PUBLIC | BL | OL Parent Library | LOCAL | DV7333 | 02 | Delete Only | B7333 |
| 1 | *PUBLIC | BSFN | OL Business Function | DV7333 | LOCAL | 05 | Check-Out / Get | B7333 |
| 1 | *PUBLIC | BSFN | OL Business Function | LOCAL | DV7333 | 02 | Delete Only | B7333 |
| 1 | *PUBLIC | BSFN | OL Business Function | LOCAL | DV7333 | 04 | Check-In | B7333 |
| 1 | *PUBLIC | BSVW | OL Business View | DV7333 | LOCAL | 05 | Check-Out / Get | B7333 |
| 1 | *PUBLIC | BSVW | OL Business View | LOCAL | DV7333 | 02 | Delete Only | B7333 |
| 1 | *PUBLIC | BSVW | OL Business View | LOCAL | DV7333 | 04 | Check-In | B7333 |
| 1 | *PUBLIC | DSTR | OL Data Structure | DV7333 | LOCAL | 05 | Check-Out / Get | B7333 |
| 1 | *PUBLIC | DSTR | OL Data Structure | LOCAL | DV7333 | 02 | Delete Only | B7333 |
| 1 | *PUBLIC | DSTR | OL Data Structure | LOCAL | DV7333 | 04 | Check-In | B7333 |
| 1 | *PUBLIC | GT | OL Media Object Data Structure | DV7333 | LOCAL | 05 | Check-Out / Get | B7333 |
| 1 | *PUBLIC | GT | OL Media Object Data Structure | LOCAL | DV7333 | 02 | Delete Only | B7333 |
| 1 | *PUBLIC | GT | OL Media Object Data Structure | LOCAL | DV7333 | 04 | Check-In | B7333 |
| 1 | *PUBLIC | MENU | Menu Item | LOCAL | Control Tables - Test | 02 | Delete Only | B7333 |
| 1 | *PUBLIC | TBLE | OL Table | DV7333 | LOCAL | 05 | Check-Out / Get | B7333 |

**FIGURE 3-23.** Activity rules for custom project status 25 Rework-Same Issue

Check in of Batch Versions behaves a little differently than for the other Object Librarian objects. When a batch version is checked out, OMW will use the Check-Out/Get object transfer activity rules defined for the project's current status (or if the user is in the Batch Versions application, the user's default project status). When the batch version is checked in, OMW will use the check-in object transfer activity rule, but it will also check the version into the current sign-on path code in order to make it available to other users. If you would only like the version to be checked into the sign-on path code, you can enter **LOCAL** for both the source and target values. This may be done for the delete rules also so that the new version will be deleted from the sign-on path code; however, keep in mind that this could be dangerous, as you may not want users deleting some versions out of production when they are logged into a production environment. Batch versions are the only object type where LOCAL may be entered for both the source and target locations.

We did not set up any activity rules for the Delete allowed action. If you want to, you can do this for all of the objects we listed in this example. You would just set up the From location to be LOCAL and the To location to be DV7333. When you choose to delete objects from the server, these objects will then be deleted from the DV7333 central objects. Now, if you want to set up a delete activity rule on an object type that does not reside in the central object tables, like user-defined codes, menus, or workflow processes, the setup is very similar. You will still specify LOCAL for the From location, and then you will need to specify the data source that these object types reside in for the To location field—Control Tables – Test, for example.

### N O T E

*It is important to understand that object transfer activity rules are overrides. They follow the hierarchy of 1-Sign on user, 2-Group, 3-\*PUBLIC, if a rule exists for the sign-on user that is higher in the hierarchy, the lower rules will be ignored. For example, if you have two rules, rule A set up for the sign-on user ID and rule B for \*PUBLIC, OMW will use only rule A for the specific signed-on user, ignoring rule B. If you have two rules, rule A set up for a group and rule B for \*PUBLIC, rule A is the only rule that OMW will use for any signed-on user that belongs to this group; OMW will ignore rule B for any signed-on user that belongs to this group. OMW will function the same with a rule for a user ID and a rule for \*PUBLIC. Keep in mind if you create an override rule for a rule that is higher in the hierarchy (such as rule A in the preceding example) and you still want the rule performed that is lower in the hierarchy (such as rule B in the preceding example), you will have to duplicate that rule for the higher hierarchy level (rule A in the preceding example). This is different from project status activity rules. The overrides are recognized for each object type and action. Therefore, you can have an override for one object type and not for the other types, and the rules for the other types will still be recognized.*

**Requirements for Object Transfer Activity Rules on a Status Change**     As mentioned earlier in the chapter, when transferring an application, OMW will attempt to transfer all \*PUBLIC user override records that exist for the application. Therefore, a user override transfer activity rule is required whenever an APPL transfer activity rule is created; otherwise, the application transfer will fail. The configuration application will provide a warning when a transfer activity rule is created for an APPL object, indicating that a user override transfer activity rule needs to be created. If you have already created this rule, you can ignore this warning.

*T I P*

*In the GA release of OneWorld Xe, the object transfer activity rule for user overrides was shipped incorrectly. It was shipped pointing to the Control Tables data source. This will need to be changed to the appropriate central objects data source. There is a breaking news document on the J.D. Edwards Knowledge Garden describing how to do this.*

When you are creating transfer activity rules for Workflow objects, after the grid row has been exited, the Configuration application will display a form requesting you to enter the From and To data sources for the F98811 table. This table contains a BLOB field and is required to be in a "do not translate" data source when located on an AS400. When transferring Workflow objects, you must indicate where these tables are located. If you are not using an AS400, you will need to enter the same From and To data sources that were provided in the Project Status Activity Rules window in the preceding section.

## Copying Activity Rules

Perhaps you do not enjoy typing the same thing over and over again—we are going to cover how to copy activity rules. This is actually a relatively simple process. You first need to determine what type of activity rules you want to copy.

In our example, we are going to copy all of the activity Rules that are set up in project status 21 Programming to project status 25 Rework-Same Issue. This, assuming we set up the allowed actions for this project status, will allow our users to perform the same development activities that they use in project status 21 Programming in project status 25 Rework-Same Issue. For more information on setting up allowed actions, refer to the section "Adding an Allowed Action," earlier in this chapter.

To start this process, go to the Object Management menu (GH9081) and double-click the Object Management Configuration application (P98230). In this application, select the Activity Rules button. This will take you to the Work With Object Management Activity Rules screen. On this screen, click Find to show the directories for the different project statuses and expand the 21 Programming directory. Under this directory, you will see an entry 21 Programming. Select this entry and you will be taken into the Object Transfer Activity Rules window.

You may notice that there is no Copy button in this application. A software action request (SAR) has been entered on this issue requesting that a Copy button be placed into the application. Until that time, we are going to have to do this the old-fashioned way. Simply highlight all of the grid lines that you want to copy, and then press CTRL-C or go to Edit | Copy. This will place the data into your computer's memory. Now close the Object Transfer Activity Rules application by clicking Cancel.

You will now be back in the Work With Object Management Activity Rules window. In this window, expand the 21 Rework-Same Issue directory and select the 25 Rework-Same Issue item. This will take you into the activity rules set up for this project status. Out of the box, this project status is blank. However, we can now just paste our desired activity rules into this project status.

### TIP

*When you click OK to save your work, you may be prompted to enter From and To location values for the F98811 workflow table, even though you have defined From and To locations in your activity rules. This screen prompts you for any Workflow delete transfer activity rules that you may have deleted. Enter the From data source and To data source where your F98811 table resides (on an AS400, this will be a separate data source marked "do not translate").*

### NOTE

*If you are copying object transfer activity rules, you will need to change the From and To location fields to represent the data sources or path codes that you want to transfer objects into.*

## Deleting Activity Rules

We have covered how to add and even copy activity rules, but we still have to talk about how to delete activity rules. In the preceding section, "Copying Activity Rules," we copied a set of activity rules from the 21 Programming project status to the 25 Rework-Same Issue project status. Now let's say, for example, that we no longer need these activity rules. You may either delete the activity rules or disable them if you expect that you may want them sometime in the future and do not want to have to reenter them later. What you would do is click Find in the Work With Object Management Activity Rules window. You would then need to expand the directory for the 25 Rework-Same Issue project status. Once you have expanded this directory, highlight and select the 25 Rework-Same Issue item to bring up the Object Transfer Activity Rules window.

Highlight all of the records that you want to delete and click Delete on the toolbar. You will be asked if you are sure you want to delete these records. Click OK in this dialog box. Now your records are deleted, right? Well, not quite. You see, if you now cancel out of this window, the delete will not be committed to the database. So you need to click OK in the Object Transfer Activity Rules window or you will lose your work.

If you want to completely get rid of a project status directory, in the Work With Object Management Activity Rules window, you need to do a little more work. What you must do is highlight the directory you want to delete and click Select. This will take you to the Project Status Activity Rules window, shown in Figure 3-24. In this window, highlight all of the entries. This will include all of the "doors to other rooms" or entries with other project statuses in the To project field and the entry in the To Project Status field that matches the project status you are attempting to delete. Click Delete.

Again, you will be prompted with a dialog box asking whether you are sure you want to delete these records. Answer OK in this dialog box, and it will appear that your records are deleted. However, you must click OK once again to commit the deletion of your data. If you click Cancel to close the Project Status Activity Rules window, your records will not be deleted.

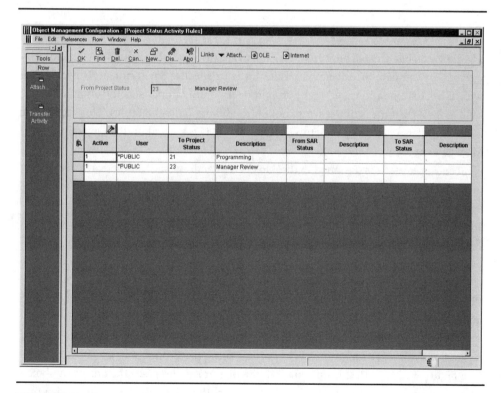

**FIGURE 3-24.** Deleting project status activity rules

*CAUTION*

*If you intend to delete a project status completely, as in the preceding example, be sure to delete the transfer activity rules before deleting the status activity rules, or you will leave orphan records. This will be changed in later releases of OneWorld to delete transfer activity rules when a status activity rule is deleted in order to prevent orphan records.*

You will now be back in the Work With Object Management Activity Rules window. You will notice that you will still see the directory of activity rules that you were attempting to delete. Don't panic—you need to refresh this window by clicking the Find button. You will now see that your directory has, in fact, been deleted.

*CAUTION*

*Be sure to highlight only the records that you really want to delete, since you can delete multiple records at the same time.*

# Activity Rules Director

J.D. Edwards has created an initial, yet somewhat primordial, version of a director or wizard that can help modify activity rules for your specific environment. However, this wizard has its limitations and really should be used only under specific circumstances, such as for a customer's initial setup, not for modifying individual rules. This application is the Transfer Activity Rules Setup Director (P98231), located on the Object Management menu (GH9081).

This application is designed to disable current activity rules and create new rules for a specific object management configuration. The application will work only with three or fewer path codes, and it will not create activity rules for any other project statuses than the conventional 11, 21, 25, 26, 28, and 38. Because of this limitation, the activity rule director is designed to work best when you need to alter your object transfer activity rules to work with fewer than the four out-of-the-box path codes, or if your path codes are named differently than the standard DV7333, PY7333, and PD7333 names. The out-of-the-box path codes are Development, Prototype, Production, and Pristine.

While creating new rules in the activity rule director, you will be asked to fill in a path code reference for your Development, Prototype, Production, and Pristine codes (see Figure 3-25). With this information, the director will replace the out-of-the-box activity rules that are delivered for each of these path codes. Whatever path code you put in development will replace your object transfer activity rules for project status 21.

Whatever you put in your prototype will replace your object transfer activity rules for project statuses 25, 26, and 28; and whatever you put in for your production path code will replace the object transfer activity rules for status 38.

You may be questioning the use of something like this. Well, if you have only two path codes, Development and Production, for example, your shipped activity rules in OMW will fail when you try to advance a project from status 21 to status 26. This is because the object transfer activity rules tell OneWorld to move objects from the DV7333 path code to the PY7333 path code. Well, you don't have a PY7333 path code! You can either go into the object transfer activity rules and change these manually, or you can use the director to change these. If you use the director, you could specify the Development path code to be DV7333 and Prototype path code to be DV7333, while keeping the Production path code at PD7333. This would change the activity rules for movement from 21 to 26 to 28, so that objects would remain in DV7333 until the project is moved from 28 to 38 In Production.

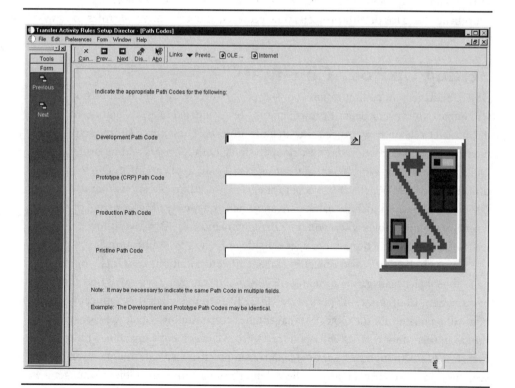

**FIGURE 3-25.**   Transfer Activity Rules Setup Director Path Codes window

This comes in useful for clients with fewer than the four path codes OneWorld is delivered with, or for clients who have custom names for their path codes. The Transfer Activity Rules Director will also make adjustments for OMW objects that use data sources, workflow setup, and the save location.

# Constants

The next topic that we will cover is the OneWorld object management configuration constants. These settings are settings that show through or are constant through the Object Management Workbench. This is why it is so important that you plan these constants out.

## Definition

The constants for OneWorld can be defined as a set of base-level settings that show through or are consistent through the Object Management Workbench software. These settings can be considered the rules for your base setup that the Object Management Workbench uses for default projects, new projects, and assigning user roles to new projects.

## Setting Up Your Constants

Object management configuration "constants" are three very important settings that will impact your users' default project status, newly created projects' status, and the default user role on new projects and default projects. These three simple settings will have a profound impact on day-to-day operations, both for users adding projects in Object Management Workbench and for users in other applications in OneWorld that utilize a user's OMW default projects in the background. Applications that use a user's OMW default project include batch versions when you are creating, copying, or deleting a version; control tables when you are changing menus or UDCs; workflows; user overrides; and data dictionary changes outside of the OMW application.

To set up the OneWorld object management configuration constants, you need to go to the Object Management menu (GH9081). On this menu, you will find the Object Management Configuration application (P98230). Double-click this application and you will be taken into the Object Management Setup window. Click the Constants button in this window. This will open the Object Management Constants window (see Figure 3-26). Although this window is fairly simple, it is also extremely powerful. You see, this window controls many of the default settings within the Object Management Workbench applications, as shown in Table 3-8.

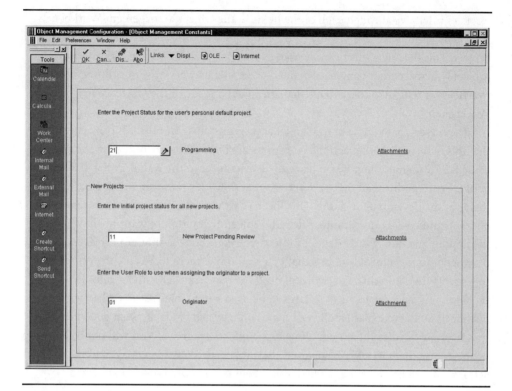

**FIGURE 3-26.**   Object Management Constants window

| Field | Description |
|---|---|
| Project status for user's personal default project | This setting is what controls the project status that a OneWorld OMW user's default project is in. The different project statuses mean different allowed actions and activity rules. Also remember, the default projects cannot be promoted or advanced. The shipped value is 21. |
| Initial project status for all new projects | This setting determines what project status any new projects that are added through the Object Management Workbench will be created at. The shipped value is 11. |
| The user role to use when assigning the originator to a project | This setting controls what user role the persons adding a new project will be set to on that project. The shipped value for this setting is 01 for originator. |

**TABLE 3-8.**   OMW Constants Window Values

Let's briefly go through each of the fields in the Object Management Workbench Constants window. The first value is the project status for the user's personal default project. This default project can be used as a testing area for coding. This default project will also contain any user-defined code, menus, versions, workflows, user overrides, or data dictionary items that are added outside of the Object Management Workbench.

The reason that you want to plan what project status your default project is in is that this will control what actions your users are allowed to perform. The shipped value is 21 Programming. If you leave the constant set to this value, you will allow your users to perform all the same actions that they may perform on a regular project that is at the development status. This means that you will be allowing your users to check in and check out from their default project. If you do not want to allow users to check in and out of their default project, you can create a different project status together with the allowed actions that you would like them to be able to perform at this status. If you do this, you will still need to create transfer activity rules for check in, check out, and delete for this status to be used when objects are worked with outside of OMW (such as batch versions). You may ask yourself, what good are the transfer activity rules if I am not allowing people to use them? You will not be allowing people to use them in OMW; however, they are needed outside OMW, and the allowed actions will not be validated when development outside of OMW is performed.

We just mentioned that, once you set up your object management configuration rules, you can then add a version through the Interactive or Batch Versions application. However, this brings up an interesting problem. You see, throughout this book we have been telling you how the software will assign a token to objects, so that only one user can work on a given object at a time.

You might say, that's great, but that really applies only to developers, right? Well, not exactly. You see, when a business end user adds, copies, or checks out a new version in batch version (P98305), located on the System Administration menu (GH9011), it is placed in that user's default project and a token is assigned to it. The tricky part is that, in the GA release of OneWorld, the only way to release the token in batch versions was to check the object out again and then erase your check out. JDE recognized this limitation, and an ESU is available that will release the token for a version when it is checked in using batch versions.

Until you can obtain this ESU, the system administrators will have to make a decision. The Object Management Workbench is an extremely powerful development tool, set up for true development with the out-of-the-box configuration. It does have an easy-to-use graphical interface; but if your users have already been using OneWorld, they are going to be used to using the Batch Versions application. If you are going to let them into the Object Management Workbench, you will need to ensure you have given them proper training, have project status set up for them to use with the correct allowed actions, and have trained them in the use of this new tool. We mentioned what it would take to set up this type of project status a little earlier in this chapter.

The next field in the Constants window allows you to specify the initial project status for all newly added projects. This is important, as this determines where a new project will enter your project promotion path in the Object Management Workbench. This also will determine, just like the value for the user's personal default project, what actions your users are able to perform, and where the Object Management Workbench will read and write its data from and to. This project status should be the start of your company's software development life cycle. The shipped value is 11. This will allow your organization to create projects and have them at a review status for someone to then move to a development status once they have been approved. If you do not need your newly created projects to be reviewed before moving them to development, you can configure OMW to create projects at a 21 status so that they are immediately ready for development.

The final field in this window allows you to enter the default user role that will be assigned to any newly added Object Management Workbench projects. The out-of-the-box value for this field is 01 Originator. Unless you have modified your allowed actions and activity rules, you will not be able to do much when you are assigned as an originator of a project. This is why you must decide whether this is the role that you want users to assume when they add a project. If it is not and you want the default role to be 02 Developer, you can change it here. However, think carefully about how you want to set this up, as this role will apply to all new projects, including any default projects that are automatically created for new user profiles.

# Tables That the Object Management Workbench (OMW) Uses

We have now talked about how the Object Management Workbench functions; given you the key terms and their definitions; and explained how to set up user roles, allowed actions, and activity rules. Now we are going to dig a little deeper and talk about the relational database tables that the software uses to function. The following table lists all of the tables that the Object Management Workbench uses to store its information on projects and logging. We will go through each of these tables and give you a brief description of each of them. This knowledge will assist you when you run into troubleshooting issues. It is nice to know how the application functions, but it is even better to know what it does under the covers.

| Table | Description |
|---|---|
| F98210 – Logging Header | Contains header information, including the project, object type, object name, time stamps, path codes, data sources, locations, and action type. |
| F98211 – Logging Detail | Contains detailed information on the errors and error codes for the projects and objects included in the F98210. |
| F98220 – Project Master | Contains detailed information on all newly created projects and all default projects. |
| F98221 – Project Users | Includes information on all the Users in OneWorld, the projects they are added to, and the role numbers they are assigned with. |
| F98222 – Project Objects | This log details all OneWorld objects that are added to OMW projects. It includes the object name and type, the path code, object status, token information, and project name. |
| F98223 – Allowed Actions | All the allowed actions assigned to user roles in the object management configuration are detailed in this table. |
| F98224 – Status Activity Rules | Details all project status activity rules. |
| F98225 – Transfer Activity Rules | Details all the object transfer activity rules. |
| F98230 – System Settings | Contains all OMC information other than activity rules and notification subscriptions. |
| F9829 – Notification Subscriptions | All added notification subscriptions are detailed here. |

# Creating a Save Location

We have referred to a save location throughout this chapter. Now let's talk about what a save location really is and why it is important to your company. A save location is new functionality, built into the Object Management Workbench, that can save your company literally tens of thousands of dollars. You see, any time you customize a software package with the scope and functionality of OneWorld, you are investing additional money, time, and effort into this customization. Development by its very nature can cause instability; so those of us who have worked with the software for a while probably have run into the situation where OneWorld developers have corrupted their workstations due to a power spike, bad code, or the fairly common mistake of accepting a OneWorld package without checking in their modifications.

When a full package is deployed, it will replace all of the OneWorld specifications for the affected path code on that workstation. Thus, if a developer forgot to check something in, that developer gets the character-building experience of re-creating that modification.

As valuable as it may be to build the character of your developers, you probably do not want to pay for the same work to be re-created multiple times. This is especially true if you are using an expensive consultant to perform your modifications. However, you also may not want incomplete code checked into the system, as this can cause package build issues. This is why J.D. Edwards development created the concept of a save location.

## Defining a Save Location

A *save location* can be defined as an empty path code that has the sole purpose of holding or saving OneWorld modifications. This path code is not designed for any environment to use; it is designed solely as a holding area for incomplete object modifications. You will not want to ever build a package over this save location path code. This concept allows your developers to save their work nightly to a server; and thus if they lose their machine, they do not lose their OneWorld modifications.

## Creating a Save Location Path Code

We will now walk you through the steps necessary to add a save location into your OneWorld system. A save location path code is not shipped with the software out of the box, as not every company will require a save location. To start this process, you will first want to define a new path code, which you are going to use for your save location.

*T I P*

Although you can create your save location path code to be populated with out-of-the-box J.D. Edwards central object data, you may not want to do this, as this takes up a considerable amount of disk space. We have had great success in creating these tables blank, which cuts down on the disk space requirement, as they really need to contain your company's custom modifications only while these are under development.

The first step in the process of creating your save location path code is, from a client workstation, to go to the System Administration Tools menu (GH9011) and double-click the Database Data Sources application (P986115). You will then be prompted to select a data source in the Machine Search And Select window. Choose your system data source. This will take you into the Work With Data Sources window shown in Figure 3-27. Before you can add your new path code, you must first define a central objects data source that tells OneWorld where this path code's relational database tables will be stored.

In the Work With Data Sources window, click Add. You will now be in the Data Source Revisions window. Here, you need to tell OneWorld where your central object tables will reside. Table 3-9 explains the values in this window.

*TIP*

*You will need to create an owner in your SQL or Oracle database prior to creating the OneWorld data source. If you are on an AS400, you will need to create the library in advance.*

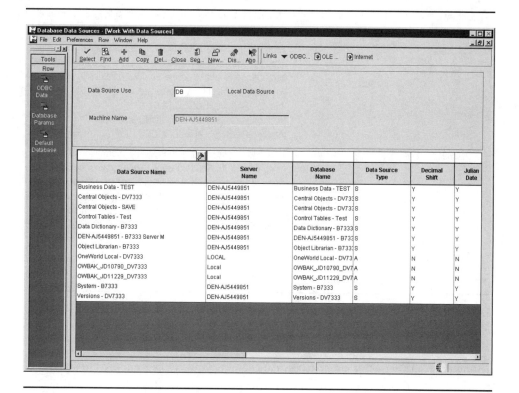

**FIGURE 3-27.**    Work With Data Sources window

| Field | Description/Value |
|-------|-------------------|
| Data Source Use | This field tells OneWorld whether this is a database data source or a logical data source. Enter **DB** in this field for a database data source. |
| Data Source Name | This is the name of your new central objects data source. You can name this data source anything that you desire, but we recommend you use a name that reflects its user; for example, Central Objects – SAVE. |
| Data Source Type | Enter **S** for SQL server, **O** for Oracle, an **I** for client access. This tells OneWorld what type of database your central objects will be stored in. |
| Object Owner ID | If you are using SQL Server or Oracle, enter the name of the database user who will own your central object tables. |
| Library Name | The Library Name field is used for data source tables on the AS/400 only. This field tells OneWorld exactly which library contains the tables defined by the database data source. If you are not using an AS400 to hold your central objects, leave this field blank. |
| Library List Name | This field is generally the server name of the AS400 itself and is used only on AS400 data sources. |
| DLL Name | This field holds the JDEBase DLL, SL, or program name used by OneWorld to create the proper SQL statements and manage the database connection. Valid values to set up your central object data source are<br>Intel to AS400=JDBODBC.DLL<br>Intel to Oracle (Version 8.0)=JDBOCI80.DLL<br>Intel to SQL Server NT=JDBODBC.DLL |
| Database Name | This field is for database connectivity information. If you are using Oracle, this field will need to contain your connect string. If you are using client access or SQL Server, this field will contain the name of your ODBC Data Source, which will be created automatically for you when you finish adding your OneWorld data source. This field matches your data source name when you are using SQL Server or Client Access. |
| Server Name | This is the name of the machine that holds the database containing your central object tables. |

**TABLE 3-9.**   Data Source Revisions Window Values

Once you have finished placing the values into the fields, click OK. If you are setting up a SQL Server or client access data source, you will be prompted to set up your Microsoft ODBC data source. Follow the prompts to set this ODBC up and the

| Field | Description/Value |
|-------|-------------------|
| Platform | This field tells the system what platform you are using to hold your central object tables. The valid values are<br>AS400—IBM AS400<br>HP 9000—Hewlett-Packard 9000<br>LOCAL—Local Client<br>NTSVR—NT Server<br>RS6000—IBM RS6000<br>SUN—Sun Microsystems |
| Use Table Owner | This field needs to checked if you are using Oracle or SQL Server and unchecked if you are using client access to connect to an AS400. |
| Use Julian Dates | This field needs to be checked. |
| Use Decimal Shift | This field needs to be checked. |
| Support for Updates | This field needs to be checked. |
| OCM Data Source | This field should not be checked. |
| AS/400 Blob Data Source | This field needs to be checked if you are going to place your central object tables on an AS400. |

**TABLE 3-9.**    Data Source Revisions Window Values (*continued*)

Data Source Revisions window will be blanked out, allowing you to enter another data source if you like.

*N O T E*

*You will receive a warning that the no tables exist for this data source. Click OK to continue past this warning. You will set up the table in a later step.*

Now that you have added your central objects data source, you can move on to the next step. Close the Database Data Sources application. Now go to the Environments menu (GH9053) and double-click the Path Code Master application (P980042). This will take you into the Work With Path Codes window, shown in Figure 3-28. In this window, click Add, which will take you into the Path Code Revisions window. This is where you tell the system about the new path code you are adding. Table 3-10 shows the values you should enter into the fields in this window.

Once you click OK, you will have told the system about your new path code. However, you are not quite finished setting up this new path code. You still need to create a directory structure on the deployment server for this new path code. To do

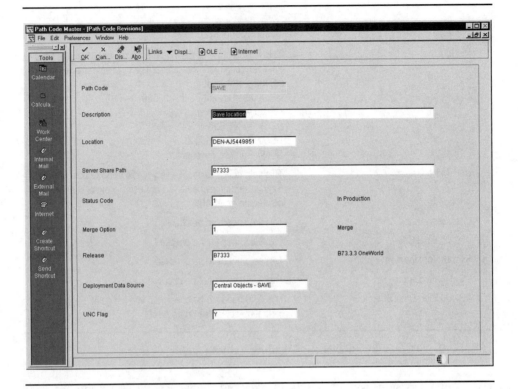

**FIGURE 3-28.** Path Code Revisions window

this, create the directory structure, listed next, on your deployment server under JDEdwardsOneWorld\B7333, where B7333 is the release of OneWorld you are running. This directory will be created during the initial installation of OneWorld:

```
Save (Where Save is the name of your path code)
Bin32
Include
Lib32
Make
Obj
Res
Source
Spec
Work
```

| Field | Description/Value |
|---|---|
| Path Code | Enter the name of your save location path code. We recommend using SAVE as this value. This clearly identifies this path code as a special path code. |
| Description | Enter a description for your path code. |
| Location | Enter the name of your deployment server. |
| Server Share Path | Enter the name of the directory you shared on the deployment server during your OneWorld installation. An example would be B7333. |
| Status Code | Enter **1** in this field. |
| Merge Option | Enter **1** in this field. |
| Release | Enter the release of OneWorld that you are using. |
| Deployment Data Source | Enter the central objects data source you defined in the preceding step. |
| UNC Flag | Enter **Y** in this field. |

**TABLE 3-10.**  Path Code Revisions Window Values

These directories can be blank and will be populated as your OneWorld developers save objects. Although not all of these directories are necessary for defining the save location path code, we recommend you define them all to keep with the standards of adding a new path code. If you want more information on defining data sources and path codes, refer to *J.D. Edwards OneWorld: The Complete Reference.*

You now have to perform a final step in defining your save location path code. This is to actually generate the central object tables in the data source you defined in an earlier step. To do this, you have a couple of options. You can use the generate table functionality built into the Object Management Workbench to generate all 18 of the central object tables by hand, or you can use the R98403 UBE to generate these tables for you. We prefer using the R98403, so we will cover this in our example.

To access the R98403 UBE, go to the Batch Versions application on the System Administration Tools menu (GH9011). Once you are there, double-click the Batch Versions application (P98305). This will take you into the Work With Batch Versions – Available Versions window. Enter **R98403** in the Batch Application field and click Find. This will bring up a list of versions for you to select from.

*In order to copy the F983051 or Versions table for AS400 installations that do not have the central object tables on the AS400, you will need to copy the F983051 by itself. You can use the R98403 report and place the versions data source in the appropriate processing options fields, or you can use the Object Management Workbench to copy the table.*

Highlight the XJDE0019 version and click Select. You will now be in the Version Prompting window. Click Form | Advanced and select override location. Click OK to return to the Version Prompting window and then click Submit to run the UBE. You will now be prompted with a JDE Data Sources window. Select the LOCAL data source to run this job on your workstation. You will then be prompted with the processing options; fill in the values listed next. To function correctly, this report must run locally on your workstation.

1. Leave the first field blank.

2. In the second processing option field, enter the central objects data source that you defined for your save location. This field is what tells OneWorld where to create the tables.

3. In the third processing option field, enter 1. This will ensure that the tables are copied over blank.

4. In the fourth processing option field, enter the name of a central objects data source for one of your existing path codes. We recommend using the pristine path code's data source if you have it loaded.

5. In the sixth processing option field, on the Update tab, enter 1. This will run the UBE in update mode.

6. Leave the seventh field blank.

7. Enter 1 in the eighth field to copy only the tables that exist in your source data source, which you defined in the fifth processing option field.

8. Leave the ninth field blank.

9. Leave the remaining processing option fields blank.

The report will now generate all of your central object tables blank, except for the F983051 and the F98306. Have your database administrator clear these tables for you. You have now set up a new path code to act as your save location.

*CAUTION*

*If you are storing the Versions table (F983051) or any other central object tables on an AS400 you will need to use, do not translate ODBCs. For additional information on these data sources, please refer to the J.D. Edwards Installation Guide.*

# Creating a Save Location Environment

You now have a save location path code, but you still need to create a save location environment. You may be asking yourself, "Why do I need an environment for my save location—won't the path code I just set up give the system the information it needs?" Great question. You need an environment for your save location so that you can save your interactive application or UBE versions. You see, you need an object configuration manager mapping to tell the system where to find the versions table; and to have a mapping, you must first have an environment.

To create an environment, from a client workstation, go to the Environment menu (GH9053) and double-click the Environment Master application (P0094). This will open the Work With Environments window. In this window, click Find, highlight one of your existing environments, and click the Row | Copy Environment button. This will bring up the Copy Environment window. Enter the name of your new environment in the New Environment field. We recommend that this name match the name of your save location path code. Also ensure that the Copy *PUBLIC Records Only check box is selected. This will copy only the *PUBLIC object configuration manager mappings.

Once you click OK, you will have defined a new environment to the system. However, you now must associate that environment with the correct path code. To do this, from the Work With Environments window, highlight and select your new environment. You will now be in the Environment Revisions window. In this window, change the path code to your new save location path code; in our example, this would be SAVE. When you click OK, you will then save your change and be taken back into the Work With Environments window. You can now close the Environment Master application.

Now that you have defined your save location environment and associated it with your save location path code, you must correct the Object Configuration Manager mappings to point to your new path code's central objects data source. To do this, from a workstation, go to the System Administration menu (GH9011) and double-click the Object Configuration Manager application (P986110). You will then be prompted to select a data source; select your system data source.

You will now be in the Work With Object Mappings window. In the query by example (QBE) line, place the name of your new environment in the Environment field and the name of the environment you copied into the central objects data source. Thus, if you copied the development environment, this would be Central Objects – DV7333. The query by example line is the yellow line above the grid in Applications. It can be used to perform searches for data meeting specific criteria. This line is case sensitive and will accept the * as a wildcard.

Your search should return ten records, in OneWorld Xe. Use the SHIFT key and highlight all of these records. Then click the Copy button on the toolbar. This will take you into the Object Mapping Revisions window for each of these records. Change the primary data source to the central objects data source that you defined, for example, Central Objects – SAVE. When you click OK, you will automatically be taken to the next record. Repeat this process for all ten records and you will be taken back to the Work With Object Mapping window.

Now highlight all of the records in the grid again and click the Row | Change Status button. This will deactivate all of these object configuration mappings. Once you have done this, change the primary data source, in the query by example line, to be the central objects data source you added for your save location path code. Click Find, and you should see ten inactive Object Configuration Manager mappings. Highlight these mappings and click the Row | Change Status button to activate these mappings. Now you can now go back and delete the old deactivated mappings, or you can leave them. We recommend you clean these mappings up so that one does not accidentally get activated.

You have one more mapping to correct before you are done setting up your environment for your save location. Blank out the value you have in the Primary Data Source field in the query by example line, and enter **F983051** in the Object Name field of the query by example line. This table holds all of OneWorld's versions. Click Find, and you will be presented with a single record. Highlight this record and click the Copy button. Enter the central objects data source for your save location, which you defined earlier, in the Primary Data Source field. Click OK and you will be taken back to the Work With Object Mapping window. Once you are back in this window, click Find, highlight your new mapping, and click the Row | Change Status button. This will activate your new mapping. You may now delete the old mapping. The process of defining your save location environment is now complete. You can now close the Environment Master application.

# Defining Your Save Location to OMW

We have now covered how to set up a save location path code and environment. However, you still need to tell the Object Management Workbench that this save location exists. To do this, go to the Object Management menu (GH9081) and double-click the Object Management Configuration application (P98230). This will take you into the Object Management Setup window. In this window, click the Save Locations button; the button will look like a large floppy disk.

Once you click this button, you will be taken to the Object Save Locations window. This window is shown in Figure 3-29. This is the window in which you tell the system what path code to use as your save location. In the Location field, enter your development path code—for example, **DV7333**. In the Save Location field, enter

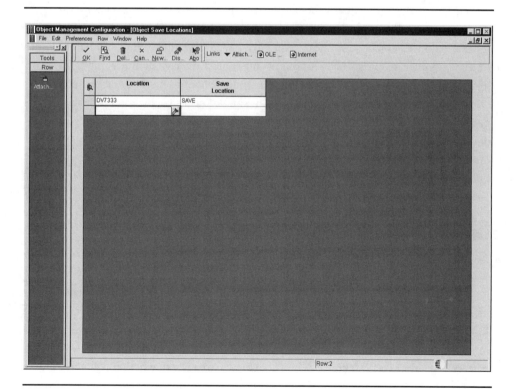

**FIGURE 3-29.** Object Save location

the save location path code that you have defined; in our example, this would be **SAVE**. Click OK, and you will save this definition. When assigning the save location in the Object Management Configuration application, you are associating the sign-on path code with a save path code.

What you have just done is tell the Object Management Workbench software that, for the development path code of DV7333, the save location is the SAVE path code. So any time your developers click Save in the Object Management Workbench application, while working on a project in the 21 Programming status, their object will be saved in the SAVE path code.

You may be wondering what is stopping two different developers from saving the same object, since you do not have to hold the token to save an object? The answer is nothing. The second developer to save the same object will receive a dialog box informing him or her that another user, which it will list, has already saved this object. This dialog box will ask the developer if he or she wishes to overwrite the object or cancel. If the developer chooses to proceed, the object will overwrite the other developer's object. Just in case you have a wild developer who has a habit of overlaying other people's work without asking, object management logging built into the software will tell the system administrator which user saved the object last.

You may also be wondering whether you can define a save location for each path code. The answer is that you could, but why would you want to? All of your development should be taking place in your lowest environment and path code, or the modification will be overwritten when that object is promoted out of your lowest path code.

# OMW Logging Capabilities

Another piece of new functionality that comes with the Object Management Workbench is additional logging. In the prior releases of OneWorld, the only real logging that you had, as a system administrator for development, was the check in–check out log. To say that this logging has been vastly improved is an understatement. In the past, all you could hope for was a record that showed when an object was checked out or in. Now you can see a great deal of information about every action that is performed within OMW, such as when check outs are erased, whether a check in was successful, and how many records were written to the central objects. You can also see the date/time stamps, the OneWorld user ID, and the machine responsible for any logged action.

# Setting Up OMW Logging

To set up your Object Management Workbench logging, go to the Object Management menu (GH9081) and double-click the Object Management Configuration application (P98230). This will open the Object Management Setup window. In this window, click the Logging System button. This will take you to the Object Management Logging System, shown in Figure 3-30.

Out of the box, all of this logging is turned on. As you can see in Figure 3-30, you have two different directories, Log Actions and Log Details. Under these directories are the different types of logging that you can choose from. We will briefly go through these in a moment.

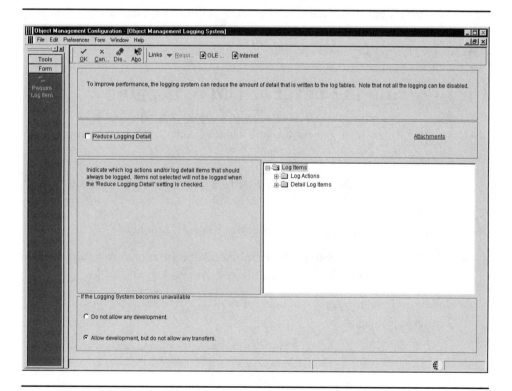

**FIGURE 3-30.**   Object Management Logging window

First, let's cover the check box and radio button in this window. The check box, Reduce Logging Detail, will reduce the logging detail for all of your users throughout the enterprise. This will eliminate most of the detailed logging but still keep a log of the major events, such as object transfers and check ins. This tick box is shipped unchecked, and we recommend that you leave it unchecked until you have had a chance to analyze how much logging detail you require.

The two radio buttons at the bottom of the window control whether your development end users can continue developing if the logging system becomes available. The two choices here are Do Not Allow Any Development when the logging system is unavailable or Allow Development, But Do Not Allow Any Object Transfers when the logging system is unavailable.

When the Do Not Allow Development radio button is checked, no development activity—such as Check Ins, Check Outs, and Gets—can be performed. When you allow development but do not allow any transfers, your development users will be able to perform development activity. However, you will not be able to perform object transfers until the logging system becomes available again.

## Customizing the Level of OMW Logging

Let's return to how to customize or control your logging. Log Actions, the first directory in the Object Management Logging window, contains the major actions that will be logged. These include the following:

- **Transfer**   This is the process of transferring objects from one path code to another.

- **Check In**   This is the process of checking in modifications.

- **Check Out**   A check out is when the object's specifications are copied down from a set of central objects to a client workstation's local TAM files.

- **Delete**   This is the process of deleting an object from the TAM files or the central object tables.

- **Add**   This is the process of adding a new object to the OneWorld system.

- **Copy**   This is the process of copying an existing OneWorld object.

- **Install**   This action is not available in OneWorld Xe.

- **Save**   This is the process of saving modifications to your save location.

- **Restore**   This is the process of restoring an object from the save location to your local TAM specification files on your workstation.

- **Design**   This is the process of going into the design tool for different types of objects.

- **Get**   A Get copies the object specifications from the central objects to the client workstation without a check out having to be performed.

- **Remove Object from Project**   This when a developer drops an object out of a project.

- **Update a Project**   This is when a note is added to a project or the date of completion on a project is updated.

- **Add Object to Project**   This is when a developer adds an object to a project.

- **Switch Token**   This is the action of changing a token from one user and project to another.

- **Release from Token Queue**   This action is when a developer drops his or her place in line for the token on an object.

- **Erases Check Out**   This is when a developer erases a check-out record.

- **Status Change**   This is when a project changes status. When this occurs, an object transfer may or may not take place.

The next directory on this window is the Detail Log Items. Under this directory, you will find all of the detailed logging error codes. These are the logging actions that will give you more detail when an action is performed. These logging actions are listed in Table 3-11.

Now that you know about all of the different types of actions that will be logged, let's talk about how to turn this logging on and off. In the Object Management Logging System window, expand either the Log Action directory or the Detailed Log item. You will now see a list of the different things that will be logged. Remember, all of the logging is turned on out of the box when you install OneWorld. To turn something off, highlight the item and go to Form | Require Log Item. This will change the green check mark to a red X, indicating that the logging for this event is no longer active. You can also double-click the item to turn the logging off. This allows you to easily customize your logging solution to meet your business's needs.

| | |
|---|---|
| Success | Dead Lock |
| Error | Object Is Checked Out |
| Not Supported | Object Already Transferred |
| SAR Integration Disabled | Locked by Vocabulary Overrides |
| Object Already in Project | Not Authorized to Install |
| Object Not in Project | TSE Not Authorized |
| User Already in Project | Transfer Not Compatible |
| User Not in Project | Column Prefix Invalid |
| Adding Invalid Object to Project | Copy Errors |
| Unauthorized Action | Invalid Action for Project Type |
| Status Activity Rule Inactive | Project at Invalid Status |
| Transfer Activity Rule Inactive | Invalid Object ID – Duplicate |
| Project Name Is User ID | Invalid Object ID – Too Long |
| Project Already Exists | Invalid Object ID – Invalid Characters |
| Bad Handle | Errors Cleaning Up Specs |
| Could Not Initialize HUSER | Object Does Not Exist |
| Memory Errors | Unable to Determine OL or Version DS |
| Object Creation Errors | Could Not Initialize PO Data |
| Invalid SAR Number | User Security Not Authorized |
| Can't Create Default Project | Notification System Disabled |
| User Canceled | SAR Creation Error |
| Project Nonexistent | Save Location Not Found |
| Can't Rename Project | No Object to Restore From |
| Invalid Status Change | Other Object in Save Location |
| Invalid String | BSFN Library in Use |
| Invalid Type | Project Already Exists for SAR Number |
| Required Field Is Blank | Role Already Assigned |
| Invalid User ID | Can't Remove User from SAR |
| TAM Errors | Token Is Inherited |
| RDB Errors | Linked Project at Wrong Status |

**TABLE 3-11.**   A List of Detailed Logging Actions

| | |
|---|---|
| OMW RDB Errors | Object Exists in Open Project |
| Parameter Does Not Exist | Object Not Checked Out |
| Token Available | SAR Status Change Error |
| Token Not Available | Inheritance Status Change Error |
| Transaction Rolled Back Per Previous Call | No Transfer Action Requests Exist for Object |
| Transaction Failed to Commit Rollback | Log Failure |
| Transaction Success Ref Decremented | Objects Are Checked Out |
| Transaction Success Commit Rollback | Object Not Checked Out to This Machine |
| JITI Failed | Objects in Token Queue |
| Start Form Dynamic Failed | Source File Does Not Exist |
| Entry Point Not Found | Bad Transfer Action Request |

**TABLE 3-11.** A List of Detailed Logging Actions (*continued*)

*T I P*

*We recommend that you run with all of the logging turned on for a few weeks in order to determine the level of logging that your business requires. After a few weeks, it may make sense to limit your Object Management Workbench logging to reduce the number of records in your logging table.*

# Viewing OMW Logging Information

To view your Object Management Workbench log, go to the Object Management menu (GH9081) and double-click the Object Management Logging application (P98210). This will take you into the Work With Object Management Log window, shown in Figure 3-31. The values for this window are explained in Table 3-12. This window will allow you to access the major logging information on the actions that you set up to trigger an event being logged, in the Object Management Configuration application. Logs can also be viewed from within the main OMW application by selecting the project or object within a project that you would like to view the logs for and clicking the Row | Logging button.

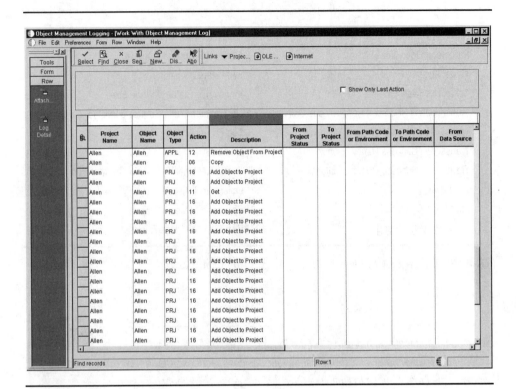

**FIGURE 3-31.** Work With Object Management Log window

| Field | Description |
|---|---|
| Project Name | This column will allow you to see logging for events on specific projects. |
| Object Name | This column allows you to search for and see logging for specific objects. |
| Object Type | This column allows you to see logging events for certain object types. |
| Action | This column allows you to sort on a specific event occurring. |

**TABLE 3-12.** Fields for the Work With Object Management Log Window

| Field | Description |
|---|---|
| Description | This Description field shows you the description of the OMW action. |
| From Project Status | This field will show you the project status that the project and object started in. |
| To Project Status | This field will show you the project status that the project was promoted to, if the project status changed. If the project status did not change, the value in this field will match the value in the To Project Status field. |
| From Path Code or Environment | This field will show the path code that an object is transferred from or the user's path code when a check in is performed, since in the latter case we know that the source was your local specifications. If an Object Librarian object is added, this will show the path code where it was added. If the object added is not an Object Librarian object, this field will be blank. |
| To Path Code or Environment | This field will show the path code that an object is checked into. On a Check Out or a Get, we know that the target was your local specifications, so OMW provides the user's sign-on path code in this field. If a non–Object Librarian object is added, this field will be blank. |
| From Data Source | This field will show the data source that an object is being transferred or checked in from. So, if you are performing promotion of a user-defined code from one environment to another, this field will show the From Control Tables data source. |
| To Data Source | This will show the data source that an object is being moved to for object transfers. |
| Program ID | This will be the name of the interactive or batch application. |
| Machine Key | This indicates the name of the machine on the network that performed the action. |
| User ID | This is the OneWorld user ID that performed the action. |
| Date Updated | This is the date that the action was performed. |
| Time Update | This is the time that the action was performed. |
| Show Only Last Action | This check box tells OneWorld to show only the last logged action on the object or project. |

**TABLE 3-12.** Fields for the Work With Object Management Log Window *(continued)*

You can also change the graphical user interface to assist you in your search. To do this, click the Form | Project Logs button. This will take you into the Work With Project Logs window. This window gives you the same information but has an extra field to allow you to search for your logging events by project name. If you want a little different interface, you can click the Form | Object Logs button. This will open the Work With Object Logs window. This window again gives you the same information, but just in a little different format. This window gives you two fields, the Object Name and Project Name fields, to assist in your search.

Now if you want to see a little more detail on an event that has been logged, from the Work With Object Management Log window highlight the logged event and either click Select or click Row | Log Detail. This will take you into more detail on the logging action.

There are two levels of logging within OMW, project-level logs and object-level logs. Project-level logs are for actions performed on the project and actions for objects that should be reported at the project level, such as adding an object to a project, removing an object from a project, and moving objects between projects. Adding and removing users is also reported in project-level logs. Object-level logs will report events that occurred to the object. Using the project-level logs and object-level logs together can be very helpful. For example, when examining what may have gone wrong with a project status change that involved a transfer, you should look at the project-level logs to see the return value from the status change and, if an object failed to transfer, determine which object incurred the failure. Once you have found the failed object, view the object-level logs for that object in the project to determine what the error was.

# Object Action Notification

You have the ability to set up e-mail notification that will alert users when an action is applied to an object. The user's e-mail address must be defined in the Address Book Who's Who information, and only external e-mails will be sent—OMW does not use the work center. So, if a manager wants to know every time a certain action is performed on an object or a project is promoted, he or she can do so by setting up object notification in the Object Management Configuration application. To set this functionality up, go to the Object Management menu (GH9081) and double-click the Object Management Configuration application. Once you are in this application, click the Object Action Notification button. This will take you to the Object Action

Notification window. Here, there is just a check box labeled Activate Object
Notification to turn this functionality on or off. Select this check box and click OK.
OMW automatically sends e-mail notifications to users when they are added to projects,
are removed from projects, and have been assigned the token after waiting in the token
queue. These messages are sent regardless of whether the notification system has been
turned off.

You will now be back at the Object Management Configuration window. In this
window, click the Notification Setup button. Once notification has been activated,
users may double-click the Object Management Notification application on menu
GH902. This will take you into the Notification Subscriptions screen, shown in
Figure 3-32. This window allows you to set up your object management notification.
To set up notification, simply fill in the fields in the grid line to be notified of what
you desire, and click OK. These fields are described in Table 3-13.

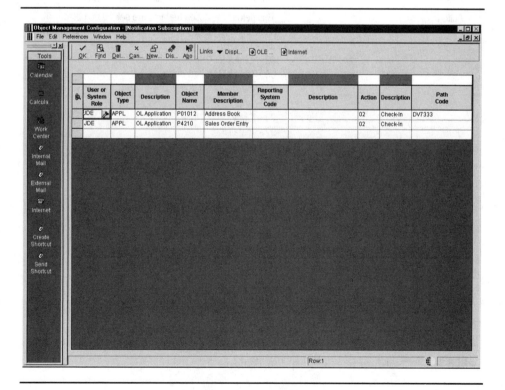

**FIGURE 3-32.**   Object Notification Subscriptions window

| Field | Description |
| --- | --- |
| User or System Role | This is the user or system role that you are setting up object notification for. |
| Object Type | This is the object type that you are setting up object notification for. |
| Description | This is the description of the object type. |
| Object Name | This is the name of the object that you are setting up notification on. |
| Member Description | This is the description of the OneWorld object that you are setting up notification for. |
| Reporting System Code | You can also set up object notification on a system code level. This means that if an action is performed on any object in that system code, the user or group you set up will be notified. |
| Description | This is a description of the reporting system code. |
| Action | This field is the action that you are setting up object notification to occur for. The valid values for this field are<br>01 – Transfer<br>02 – Check In<br>03 – Check Out<br>04 – Delete<br>05 – Add<br>06 – Copy<br>07 – Install<br>08 – Save<br>09 – Restore<br>10 – Design<br>11 – Get<br>12 – Remove Object from Project<br>13 – Update a Project<br>16 – Add Object to Project<br>21 – Switch Token<br>23 – Release from Token Queue<br>30 – Erase Check Out<br>38 – Status Change |
| Description | This is the description field of the action. |
| Path code | You can also limit your notification to specific path codes. |

**TABLE 3-13.**   Notifications Subscription Window

# OMW Reporting Capabilities

This chapter would not be complete if we did not discuss some of the reporting capabilities that are built into the Object Management Workbench functionality. With all of the additional logging functionality built into the software, you also get some additional reporting features. This reporting functionality allows you to monitor your OneWorld modifications, see what users are assigned to projects, monitor your object management logging, and check your object management configuration. These reports can be a very powerful tool for keeping your system running smoothly.

To access these reports, go to the Object Management menu (GH9081). On this menu, you will see a list of OneWorld reports. These reports include the following:

- Project Management Report

- Project Users Report

- Project Objects Report

- Object Management Log Report

- Object Management Log Purge Report

- User Allowed Actions Report

- Consolidated Project/Transfer Active Report

- Transfer Activity Rules Report

- Project Status Activity Rules

- OMW Configuration Report

## Project Management Report

This report is a good report to run to get an overview of all of your OneWorld projects. This report gives you a list of all of your OMW projects and some key information about each. The following table lists the key values that you will get information back on when you run this report.

| Report Column | Description |
|---|---|
| OMW Project Name | This column will show you the name of your Object Management Workbench project. |
| Description | This is the description of the object management project. |

| Report Column | Description |
| --- | --- |
| Project Status | This is the project's status. |
| Project Type | This column will tell you what type of project this is:<br>Bug<br>Enhancement<br>Default<br>Tracking/Parent Bug<br>Tracking Parent Enhancement |
| Project Severity | This is column shows the severity level of your projects:<br>Critical/No Workaround<br>Critical/Workaround<br>Not Critical/No Workaround<br>Not Critical/Workaround<br>Critical Enhancement<br>Enhancement<br>Low-Priority Enhancement |
| System Code | This is the product code of the project. |
| Date Entered | This is the date that the project was entered into the system. |
| Planned Completion Date | This is the planned completion date for the project. |
| Completion Date | This is the actual date that the project was completed. |
| SAR Number | This field will be blank, as the SAR system in OMW is currently reserved for internal use only. |

# Project Users Report

The Project Users report gives you information on your OneWorld users. It tells you what projects they are working on and the estimated number of hours before these projects are completed. The columns for this report are listed here:

| Report Column | Description |
| --- | --- |
| User ID | This column will show the OneWorld user ID. |
| Alpha Name | This will show the alpha name associated with the OneWorld user ID. |
| OMW Project Name | This is the name of the project that the user is listed as an owner of. |
| Description | This is the description of the OMW project. |
| User Role | This is the role that the OneWorld user is assigned on the project. |
| Project Lead | This field is for future functionality. |
| Date Assigned | This is the date that the user was assigned to the project. |

| Report Column | Description |
|---|---|
| Time Assigned | This is the time that the user was assigned to the project. |
| Estimated Hours | This is the estimated time the project will take the user to complete. |

# Project Objects Report

This report gives you a list of the objects that are included in the Object Management Workbench projects. This is a good report for the system administrator to use to track the objects that are being modified in the system.

## R98222B – Purge OMW Project

This report will remove all objects from a project. This can be very helpful if you have a project with a large number of objects that you would like to clear of all objects, but this project will work for default projects also. The sign-on user will need to make sure that he or she plays a role in the project before running this report. When running this report, you will enter the processing option value indicating the project that you would like to remove the objects from. The report that is generated will display each object in the project and the result status of whether it was successfully removed.

# Object Management Log Report

Surprise! This report shows you your Object Management Workbench log errors. The processing options in this report allow you to report on all of the actions on each object or report only on the last action performed on each object. There is also a processing option that will allow you to show only the header information or the header and detail information, shown here:

| Report Column | Description |
|---|---|
| OMW Project Name | This is the name of the object management project. |
| Object Name | This is the name of the object. |
| Object Type | This is the type of object. |
| OMW Action Description | This is the description of the action taken. |
| User ID | This is the OneWorld user ID. |
| Date Updated | This is the date that the object was updated. |
| Time Updated | This is the time the project was updated. |

| Report Column | Description |
|---|---|
| From Pathcode/Env | This column will show the path code that an object was taken from for a check out, transferred from, added to, or deleted from. |
| To Path Code/Env | This column will show the path code that an object was checked into, added, deleted from, or transferred into. |
| From Date Source | This will show the From data source that an object is moved from. |
| To Data Source | This is the data source that an object is moved to. |
| From Project Status | This is the project status that the project is coming from. |
| To Project Status | This is the project status that the project moved to. |

If you have this report list out the detail, you will also have blocks of data that will show you the detailed logging information. This makes the report a little harder to read, but it gives you a great deal of information about your system.

### NOTE

*You may want to apply data selection to this report, as the logging table will grow to be quite large.*

## Object Management Log Purge Report (R98210A)

This report will purge all of the information from your object management logging tables, the F98210 header record table, and the F98211 detail logging information table. Your company may want to create an archive and purge strategy for this file. This report has some very powerful processing options on it. You can run this report in either final or proof mode, you can purge both the head and detail logging records, or you can just purge the detail records. You can also enter a processing option value to control the days you purge your logs from. Thus, you can go back only a few days, or you can purge all of the records in your logging file.

## User Allowed Action Report (R98223A)

This report will show you the allowed actions that are set up for your different user roles. This report can help your system administrator keep track of your company's object management configuration. The following table shows you the columns that this report will give you.

| Report Column | Description |
|---|---|
| User Role | This column shows you the user role. |
| Description | This is the description of the user role. |
| Object Type | This is the object type that the allowed action is set up for. |
| Description | This is the description of the object type. |
| Project Status | This is the project status that you are setting up your allowed action for. |
| Description | This is the description of the project status. |
| OMW Action | This is the action, e.g., check out, that you are setting up an allowed action record for. |
| Description | This is the description of the OMW action. |

# Consolidated Project/Transfer Activity Rules (R98230B)

This report shows the project and transfer activity rules that have been set up for your object management configuration, as shown next. This is another tool in your system administrator's bag of tricks.

| Report Column | Description |
|---|---|
| Active Flag | This flag shows whether the activity rule is active or not. |
| User ID | This is the user or group that the activity rule is set up for. |
| From Project Status | This column shows the project status that the transfer activity rule is set up to come from. |
| Description | This is a description field for the project status. |
| To Project Status | This is the project status that the activity rule is set up to move to for object transfers. |
| Description | This is the description field for the To project status. |
| From SAR status | This field will be blank, as the SAR system is for JDE internal use only. |
| Description | This is a description of the SAR status. |
| Object Type | This is the object type that the activity rule is set up for. |
| Source Release Number | This column should show the release of OneWorld that you are running on. |
| Source Location | This is the data source that the objects are being read from. |
| Target Location | This is the target data source to which objects are written. |
| OMW Action | This is the action that the activity rule is set up for. |

| Report Column | Description |
|---|---|
| Description | This is the description of the activity rule. |
| Release Token Now | This will tell you whether the token will be released during an object transfer. |

## Transfer Activity Rules Report (R98230C)

This report shows you what transfer activity rules have been set up in your object management configuration. The following table shows the report columns that you will get when you run this report.

| Report Column | Description |
|---|---|
| Active Flag | This will show whether the activity rule is active or not. |
| From Project Status | This shows you the project status that the activity rule is set up to come from. |
| To Project Status | This shows you the To project status for the activity rule. |
| User Id | This is the user ID or group that the project status is set up for. |
| Object Type | This is the object type that the activity rule is set up for. |
| Source Release Number | This is the release of OneWorld that the object was developed in. |
| Source Location | This is the data source where information for the action is read from. |
| Target Location | This is the data source that information is written to. |
| OMW Action | This is the action that the activity rule is set up for. |
| Release Token | This column will tell you whether the token will be released on an object transfer. |

## Project Status Activity Rules Report (R98230D)

This report shows the activity rules that are set up for specific project statuses. An example would be the activity rules set up to allow OneWorld development to take place in project status 21 Development, shown here:

| Report Column | Description |
|---|---|
| Activity Flag | This column will tell you whether the activity rule is active or not. |
| User ID | This column will show the user or group that the activity rule is set up for. |
| From Project Status | This column shows the project status that the activity rule is set up from. |

| Report Column | Description |
|---|---|
| Description | This is the description of the From project status. |
| To Project Status | This is the To project status that the activity rule is set up for. |
| Description | This is the description of the To project status. |
| From SAR Status | This column will be blank, as the SAR system is for JDE internal user only. |
| Description | This is the description of the From SAR Status. |
| To SAR Status | This field will be blank, as the SAR system currently is used for JDE internal use only. |
| Description | This is the description of the To SAR Status. |

# OMW Configuration Report (R98230E)

This is a very powerful report for your system administrator, as it provides a summary of your object management configuration setup. The following table shows some the information that you will get out of this report:

| Report Column | Description |
|---|---|
| Object Management Constants | This area of the report shows you the object management constant settings that you have set up. |
| SAR System Integration | This area shows whether the SAR system is turned on. This value should be 0 for no. |
| Object Action Notification | This area shows whether you have object action notification set up. |
| Notification Subscriptions | This area of the report shows the subscriptions that are set up for object notification. This section will show you the user, object type, the OMW object name, product code reporting, the OMW action, and the path code that is set up for notification. |
| Logging System | This area of the report shows whether you have reduced the logging detail and, if development is disabled, whether the logging system is unavailable or whether logging is allowed but no transfers are allowed. |
| Log Actions | This area shows you what actions will cause an event to be logged and whether the logging is enabled for that event. |
| Log Detail Items | This area shows the detailed logging events and whether logging for them is enabled. |

# Summary

In this chapter, we have covered a lot of ground. We have discussed what the out-of-the-box setup is for the Object Management Workbench and what this means to your company. We have also covered what each different piece of the Object Management Workbench configuration is and how to set it up. This included a discussion of the user roles, allowed actions, and activity rules. We ended this chapter with a discussion on the reporting capabilities of the Object Management Workbench. This chapter should get you started on your object management configuration setup and inform you of the key definitions that you must make as you set your system up.

# CHAPTER 4

# Strategic Change Management

What Is a Software Development Life Cycle?

What Do I Need to Keep Track Of?

Standard OMW Configurations

Advanced Object Management Configurations

U p to this point, we have spent a lot of time discussing the details of the Object Management Workbench and how to configure your OMW change management system. We would now like to take a few moments to step back and discuss the strategy of change management at a higher level. You see, in order to truly take advantage of the Object Management Workbench's change management functionality, you must first have a high-level understanding of change management itself.

To discuss change management at this level, we will cover what a software development life cycle is and why your company should follow one. We will discuss what types of changes you need to keep track of and how this ties into OMW configurations. We will also share some advanced object management configurations with you to give you a flavor of what the software can truly do with the correct level of planning.

# What Is a Software Development Life Cycle?

Let's start by discussing what a software development life cycle (SDLC) is and why your company should care about it. To those companies who do not modify their software packages very much, a software development life cycle concept is strange and new. They often wonder if they can go without implementing any type of software development life cycle. We recommend that, no matter how large or small your company, you institute some kind of SDLC. This will save your company a lot of time and effort when tracking down issues.

## Definition of Software Development Life Cycle

A software development life cycle is an approach to the development, modification, and promotion of objects in a system. Now, this system does not have to be a OneWorld implementation. You can apply the concepts that we will discuss in this chapter to any number of different types of applications. This has become very important with the growth of J.D. Edwards Extended Process Integration (XPI), which allows you to achieve full integration between the OneWorld software and another software package, such as the Extended Business Processor (XBP) between OneWorld and Ariba. If you customize these integrations, you will want to track these changes. The software development life cycle that your company develops can afford you the ability to do this. This is why having some kind of documented SDLC is so important to the success of implementing the OneWorld product and other software packages.

# Why Is the Software Development Life Cycle Important to Your Company?

It just would not be our style to leave you with only a definition of the software development life cycle. Let's talk in real-world terms about why having an SDLC is important to your company. The authors realize that time and effort really equate to dollars when you are talking about implementing a software package. Well, that is what a SDLC does: it saves your company money.

Since this book is about functionality in the OneWorld software package, we will use this as our example. Let's say that your company has implemented OneWorld Xe software, and you have discovered an issue that requires a fix from J.D. Edwards. This fix is in the form of an electronic software update (ESU). You now have someone ready to apply this fix to an environment, but to which environment do you apply the fix? You have a development environment, that your OneWorld developers are using, but they did not find the issue. You also have a prototyping environment, in which your business users test the software's functionality, but they also did not discover the issue here. Finally, you have your live production environment, where the issue was discovered.

Since you run your business in the production environment, you probably do not want to apply the ESU to this environment. So you apply the ESU to the prototyping environment, which your business users use for acceptance testing. They test the fix, and then it is promoted into the production environment. Everything is great, right? Wrong—suddenly everything stops working. The reason for concern is what happens when a project is promoted out of the development environment that includes an object from the ESU. Since this fix was not applied to the development environment, the changes for the fix on this object are lost. Now you have a fix that may include hundreds of objects, only a few of which were overlaid. This is makes the issue extremely difficult to debug and troubleshoot.

Now that you have decided that you need to apply the ESU or change to the development environment, you are ready, right? Well, not quite yet. You see, you need to schedule any ESUs that you apply to the development environment. This is because, when you apply an ESU, the software will perform one of three actions. If the object in the fix is new, it will add the object into the system. If the object is already in the system and you have not marked it as a modified object that you want to keep, the object will be deleted and replaced by the object contained in the ESU. If you marked the object as a modified object that you want to keep your modification on, the object will be merged.

Once you merge an object, you are not out of the woods. You see, any merged object will need to be retrofitted. This can be accomplished using the standard design aid tools and the visual ER compare tool in the Object Management Workbench. If you have changed an object, J.D. Edwards will keep your changes, as long as you follow their object modification rules, which can be found in the J.D. Edwards developers guide and the OneWorld upgrade manuals. If you would like details on what is required to perform a OneWorld upgrade, refer to *J.D. Edwards OneWorld: The Complete Reference* (Osborne-McGraw/Hill, 2000).

You may be thinking that it could take an awful lot of work, time, and money to implement a fix that may or may not resolve the issue your company is having. We agree with you. That is why we recommend that you build an ESU testing path code and environment into your software development life cycle. This way, you can apply an ESU to base J.D. Edwards code and then test to see if the issue is resolved. If it is not, you can pursue the issue with J.D. Edwards customer support. If you have modified the objects that are affected by an ESU and then the ESU does not work, J.D. Edwards customer support will be unable to assist you, as they will not be able to tell if it was your modification or the ESU that is causing the problem. The visual ER compare tool can be helpful in this case. However, you can compare the old code to the new to retrofit the change delivered from J.D. Edwards.

As you can see from this real-world example, if you do not have a well-thought-out and documented software development life cycle, you will be costing your company time and money that it does not have to spend. We have seen projects stagger due to confusion as to how changes are implemented into the system. They have also seen this confusion adversely affect some companies' production environments.

## Recommended Points of Review for Changes

Before we get too deep into the weeds on what you need to track for your change management effort to be effective, let's take a minute to talk about some of the recommended processes and procedures for reviewing your proposed changes. After all, if you are going to place a change into your system, don't you want the input of the people who can tell you the true effect of the change to the system?

We would answer, yes, absolutely, to this question. How do you do this? Well, the easiest way is to design some checkpoints that a change request needs to go through before being applied to your system. These checkpoints will include impact analysis and contingency planning.

There are several ways to perform these tasks, depending on your company's size, its environment setup, and the scope of your OneWorld development effort. In this example, we will start at the beginning of the request for an ESU. The request will be logged with your system administrator in some manner. This request could take the form of an e-mail message or even an entry into some kind of issue tracking system. However your company decides to log these requests, the authors recommend that you track them.

The reason for tracking these requests is simple: this information will provide metrics around your system. These metrics will help to ensure that you have an adequate development and system administration staff to handle the requests. This tracking will also enable you to show the cost of implementing some of these changes and how quickly the changes have been made. We recommend tracking at the very least the time, date, name of the requester, detailed description of the request, contact information, who was assigned to the request, close date, close time, and resolution.

Once a request like this one is received, you will then need to ensure that it is reviewed by the correct people to assess the possible impact on the system. We recommend that you have some kind of review board to discuss and schedule changes to the system. We have seen this review board called many different things: a change management board, a release management board, or even a weekly project meeting. We recommend that this review board meet weekly to discuss any changes to the system.

What you call this meeting is really up to you. However, you will want to ensure that this meeting, or board, addresses certain key concerns. The first is having the correct individuals in the room. You should have your development manager, your system administrator, a representative from your business (that is, the end users), and the project manager. When you have these people available, you can actually get a good feeling for what is happening in your system and the impact a change may have on it.

In our example, the business or end-user group has requested an electronic software update be applied to fix an issue. The system administrator can bring a list of affected objects to the meeting (such a list is available when you download the ESU). The development manager can then tell you if these objects have been modified, the time it will take to retrofit these objects, and the impact to the time line of the development effort.

With this type of information, your team can then determine the best time to apply this change. You can schedule the system administrator's time to apply the ESU, ensure that you have backups available, and see that the appropriate people are dedicated to applying the change. This approach will also assist you in keeping your costs under control. We have seen projects go over budget because little or no planning went into the time it takes to apply patches or changes into a system.

This meeting will also ensure that you have a contingency plan. Let's say that the ESU is applied but does not fix the issue or causes another issue. You will want to ensure that plans and people are in place to roll the ESU off your system. You will also then be able to determine who is responsible for testing and signing off on the electronic software update.

To reiterate, one of the main ingredients to ensure the success of this meeting is the representation of the proper groups. You absolutely must have representation from your system administration, business, and development groups. If you do not, you will not know the possible impact on these groups when applying a patch or change. They might be in the middle of a critical process that could be severly impacted.

Another advantage of having these groups represented is that it allows you to receive and give feedback on your company's entire change management process. Since all of the groups are represented, they can work together to ensure that changes are applied in a timely and effective manner. The authors recommend post mortem reviews of any major changes, such as ESUs, service packs, and other updates to the system.

During these reviews, you can determine what has gone well and which processes and procedures need improvement. This review process does not have to be long or involved; it is just to ensure that there is not a more efficient manner of accomplishing the same goal. An example of this modification approval process is shown in Figure 4-1.

# Applying Emergency Fixes to the System

What about a critical or emergency fix? That is a great question. Unfortunately, this is real life and you cannot forecast or plan for everything. There will be times when an emergency fix needs to be implemented. Now, some people will argue that using the system modification approval process model we just described will take too long and will be inefficient. This is actually not the case. You want to ensure that you use this procedure, especially for any emergency fixes.

We are not telling you to have your end users wait a week so that you can hold your release management meeting. What you need to do is have the ability to put together an emergency meeting if necessary. This means that everyone who sits on your release management board needs to have a backup person who is authorized to make decisions if the original member is unavailable or out of the office.

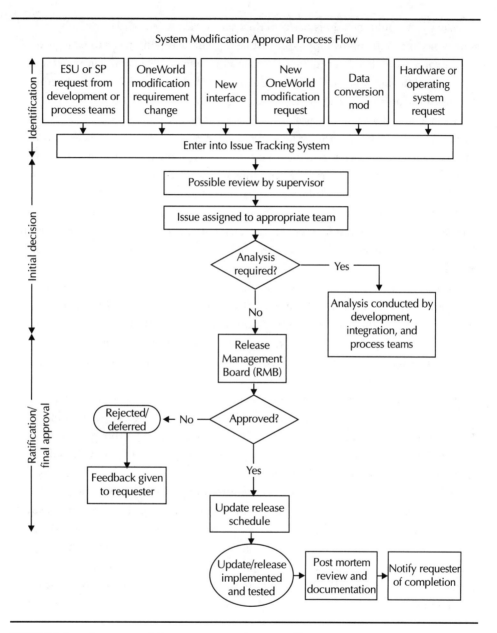

**FIGURE 4-1.** System modification approval process flow

What you would then do is perform the exact same procedure described by the system modification approval process, just faster. The issue still needs to be logged so that you ensure that you can have the correct people involved and you know what has changed in your system. Once the issue is logged, you can hold a quick meeting to determine the possible impact of implementing the fix.

When an emergency fix comes through, a lot of people are tempted to take some shortcuts to get the fix into the system quickly. We cannot stress enough that this is not recommended. One common misconception is that applying the fix directly into the production environment is faster and thus will resolve the issue more quickly.

Let us dissolve this myth right now. That is right, we said "myth." You may get lucky for a little while when placing a fix into your production environment. However, your luck will not hold out forever. This means that one day, when you look down the tunnel and see the light at the end of it, that light will be an express locomotive heading right at you.

Let's cover what will most likely happen if a fix is implemented in the production environment. If this fix is an ESU, and if any of the objects in the ESU have been modified, applying the ESU will not work without a retrofit effort taking place. You see, if the ESU affects a custom modification that your developer has made, you can give the developer access to development tools in the production environment, and that person will be able to retrofit the object.

However, the first time you promote one of the affected objects from a lower environment, you will lose that developer's change. Some people say, "No problem, we will just manually enter the change in all of the path codes." Although this is possible, to do it complicates tracking changes in your system, and you will find yourself asking what code is in what path code.

A final point is that, following this procedure, you are making a programming change in your production system. Those of us who code know that programs always run flawlessly the first time, right? Well, not exactly! Why, then, would you risk your production data, which in essence is your business, to an untested change? What happens if the change causes a data corruption issue? Well, you've just corrupted your production business data. Do not fall into the trap of thinking that you do not have enough time to do it right the first time, but that you have enough time to do it over. This almost always costs your company more time, money, and pain.

Even an emergency fix should be implemented in the development environment and promoted to the prototyping environment, tested, and then promoted into the production environment. After all, if you have a data corruption issue, wouldn't you rather find an issue in your lower environments, where you can easily refresh the data?

If you have worked with OneWorld awhile, you are probably saying, "But I need to build a new package for every path code that I promote the object through!" The answer is yes, you do. Don't fret; we are not telling you to build a full package, which can take from six to twelve hours. You can use update packages for any emergency fix. That way, you can also deploy the fix to a select group of people to quickly test it prior to rolling the fix out to all of your users. The authors have been able to take a fix and promote it through all of the required path codes with package builds in one day. This depends upon the complexity of the fix, but even the largest objects do not take long to transfer through the different path codes. Figure 4-2 shows the modification migration that should occur when you make any modification or fix.

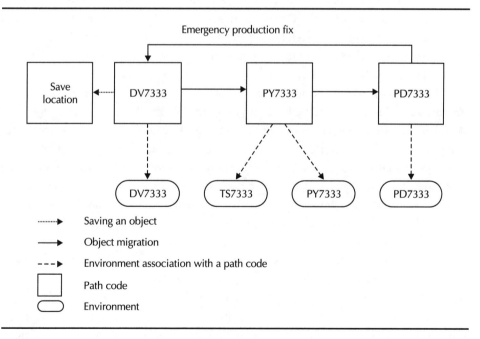

**FIGURE 4-2.** Emergency object promotion

**N O T E**

*If your modification or ESU only affects objects that are run on the client workstations and not an enterprise or application server, then you can perform a get on the project. This will bring all of the changes down to the tester's workstation without having to build a package. However, you will need to compile any business function or named-event rule change. If even one object needs to run on the server, you are better off just building an update package.*

As you can see, the emergency promotion procedure looks very similar to the standard promotion procedure. What is the difference? Well, the difference is that the former happens a lot faster. The modified objects will also be in all of your path codes, so you do not have to guess where the fix is a few weeks later. The fix will also have been tested against data that is not live production.

Let's briefly review the high-level procedure document shown in Figure 4-2 and flush it out a little. A request for an emergency fix comes in and is approved for application by your designated contacts. Once this has taken place, a developer is assigned to the project by the OneWorld development manager or supervisor. If another project holds the token for the affected objects, the manager will switch the token to the emergency fix Object Management Workbench project. This will enable the assigned developer to start working on the emergency fix.

Now the question may occur to you, "What if I have code in those objects that is not ready to be promoted?!" Well, that is part of the beauty of the Object Management Workbench. As a developer, you do not want to check an object in until it is complete; you can simply save the object to the save location every night before you go home. That way, if your workstation crashes, you will not lose your work. This also means that if another developer needs to work on some of your objects, you can simply save your changes to the save location and another developer can check the objects out, which will now have only code that is ready to promote.

This developer adds the objects to a project, which is labeled appropriately, and performs the fix. Once the developer has implemented the fix and has performed unit testing on his or her workstation, it is now ready to be checked into the development path code. At this point, the project has a status of 21 Programming. It is then promoted to a status of 26 QA Test/Review. Promoting the project to this status will transfer the objects from your development path code to your prototyping path code (in the standard OMW configuration).

At this point, you can build an update package including the objects in the emergency fix project, or the tester can select the project and click the Get button.

The transfer activity rules will bring the specifications down to the local machine from the prototype path code. If there were any control table changes, they would have been promoted into the prototype set of control tables. Since most OneWorld configurations are mapped directly to these control tables, the new user-defined codes or menus would be seen immediately. Although this type of test is very quick, you may need to compile some objects in order for the test to work correctly. Before you start using this approach, you should be aware that if there are any objects that need to be installed on the server, such as a table change, a business function, a data structure, a business view, or a report (UBE), you are better off building an update package. This is because you will want to test the modification on your server prior to promoting the change into the production path code. This test will usually be performed in the PY7333 environment, not the TS7333 environment. This is because this is the environment that normally contains the data that is the closest to the production environment. This test will help to ensure that the fix does not have an adverse or unexpected effect on your business data.

Once this test is completed, you then promote the project to a status of 38 In Production. The change to this project status transfers the objects from the prototyping path code to your production path code. Now that you have the fix in you production path code, you need to build one more update package and deploy it out to your production users. You have now transferred the fix all the way to the production environment, and you know which path codes the modified objects are in, so you know that you will not have an object overlaid by another object promotion at a later date.

Although this may look like a lot of different time-consuming steps, it really is not. Normally, an emergency fix will not affect a large number of objects, and those that are affected can be transferred in a matter of minutes. Update packages also do not take long to build. So the real question is this: is saving a few minutes worth risking your business?

# What Do I Need to Keep Track Of?

Although you know that change management is keeping track of changes to the system, you may be asking yourself, "What do I need to keep track of?" Well, the answer is, anything that will affect your system. This includes operating system changes, hardware changes, software patches, ODBC updates, changes to any bolt-on products, and the promotion of any changes from one environment to another.

It will occur to you that this will require a lot of time and effort. We will not argue with you on this point: to truly perform a good level of change management, your company will need to dedicate some time and effort. This means that you will need to have buy-in from your project sponsor and management.

Although this may seem like a difficult argument or sell, really it is not. The question your company's management has to answer is, how much risk are they comfortable with in regard to their production system? The authors have seen a company lose about thirty-five percent of their system's efficiency due to improper change management.

The company placed a database patch, a new disk array, and new memory into their production system, while moving databases to different machines, all at the same time. What happened was that they had to reboot their production server about two to three times a day. This cost them efficiency and money. The problem turned out to be incompatible memory in the server, but since no real change management was applied to implement these changes, it was very hard to find what was really causing the issue. This scenario is a strong argument for change management, as it took this company about four days to finally determine the cause.

## Hardware and Operating System Changes

Changes to the operating system and hardware are fairly commonplace and don't need to be tracked or really scheduled, right? Well, as the preceding real-life example shows, this is not the case. Any changes to your operating system or to the hardware configuration of your production system need to be tracked and scheduled. You do not want to implement these changes when you are in the middle of closing a quarter!

The first step to tracking these types of changes is to gather a baseline to measure from. You can then create an operating system change document and procedure. A good time to gather this baseline information is during the conference room pilot or prototyping effort. This is when your application users are setting up your business models in OneWorld. During this time, you will be running on a smaller set of hardware and installing the hardware that will eventually support your production effort. This means that you will discover if you need any PTFs for your AS400, NT service packs, or Unix patches to be installed.

Once you have this baseline determined, you will need to place this information in a controlled document. (An example of this type of document is shown in Figure 4-3.) What do we mean by a controlled document? We mean that change management will be applied to the changes on this document. This means that the document will not be updated until an operating system fix has been approved and applied. The document will show not only what the fix was and when it was applied, but who applied it. This

| Server Name | Server Type | IP Address | Operating System | OS Patches | MDAC If Applicable | Date Applied | Operator Name |
|---|---|---|---|---|---|---|---|
| Peg | Intel® NT | 10.1.1.1 | NT 4.0 | SP 6a | 2.1 | July 15th | Alex |
| Condor | AS400 | 10.2.2.2 | V4R5 | SF5341 | NA | July 25th | Alex |
| Condor | AS400 | 10.2.2.2 | V4R5 | SF6791 | NA | August 21st | Alex and Frank |

**FIGURE 4-3.** Example of hardware change

tracking mechanism will allow your company to quickly isolate any changes that were made to the system when an issue comes up and determine if the change caused the issue, which helps to reduce your system administration costs and helps to reduce the time between when an issue is reported and when it is resolved.

# Environments and Architecture

Another piece of this puzzle is keeping track of your OneWorld environment setup and system architecture. An example of an environment and system architecture document is shown in Figure 4-4. In this figure, you can see how an architecture diagram is useful to show how your servers are laid out. This is extremely useful in bringing new members of your project team up to speed on the system.

The next section of this document should contain a list of your server names, IP addresses, operating systems, service pack or patch levels, and the purpose of each server, for example, production enterprise server. This purpose statement should also list the environments, path code, and any third-party integrations that the server is used to implement. This document can be and normally is also used as the hardware change control document discussed in the previous section.

You should also have a section in this document that shows your OneWorld environment setup. This will include a list of your environment names, data sources, printers, default UBE servers, path codes, subsystem jobs, package build schedule, package deployment schedule, and scheduled night jobs. This sounds like keeping track of a lot of information, and it is. By performing this task, however, you will have the documentation in place to hand the system off from your technical project team members to production support. All of your procedures will be tested, tried, and best of all neatly documented for someone new to the product to follow. This will save your company vast amounts of time in spinning up your production support personnel.

Architecture diagram

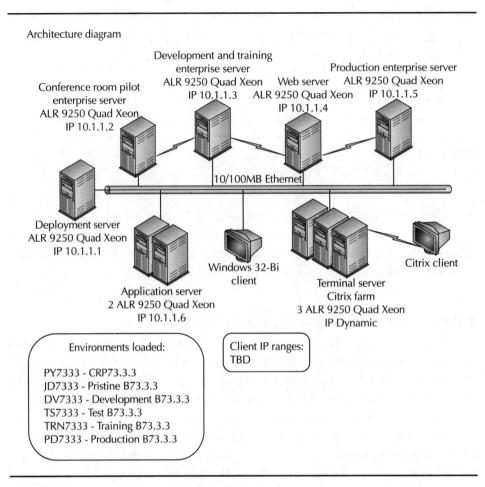

Development and training
enterprise server
ALR 9250 Quad Xeon
IP 10.1.1.3

Web server
ALR 9250 Quad Xeon
IP 10.1.1.4

Production enterprise server
ALR 9250 Quad Xeon
IP 10.1.1.5

Conference room pilot
enterprise server
ALR 9250 Quad Xeon
IP 10.1.1.2

10/100MB Ethernet

Deployment server
ALR 9250 Quad Xeon
IP 10.1.1.1

Windows 32-Bi
client

Citrix client

Application server
2 ALR 9250 Quad Xeon
IP 10.1.1.6

Terminal server
Citrix farm
3 ALR 9250 Quad Xeon
IP Dynamic

Environments loaded:

PY7333 - CRP73.3.3
JD7333 - Pristine B73.3.3
DV7333 - Development B73.3.3
TS7333 - Test B73.3.3
TRN7333 - Training B73.3.3
PD7333 - Production B73.3.3

Client IP ranges:
TBD

**FIGURE 4-4.**   Example architecture diagram

# OneWorld Objects

Now we need to discuss the different OneWorld objects that you need to track. If you have been working with the product for a while, you might say that you already know what these objects are. However, we are going to catch you here, since the definition of what an object is in OneWorld has changed with the addition of the Object Management Workbench to the software.

In the past, OneWorld objects were defined as applications, business functions, business views, UBEs, data structures, tables, and media objects. These were the types of objects that you could create, copy, delete, or modify using the object librarian. By replacing the object librarian with the OMW, J.D. Edwards has expanded the definition of a OneWorld object. This was done to assist you in understanding what should be tracked through the system and why.

The new OneWorld objects are data dictionary items, user-defined codes, workflow items, menus, user overrides, and versions. These objects are tracked through the OMW, just like the traditional object librarian objects. When a project is promoted to a status code that transfers objects to another path code, these objects will be promoted to the next environment as well. The reason that these are now defined as objects is that these objects have an effect on how the system behaves.

An example would be a custom menu and a version. Let's say that you've added a custom menu and you want to promote this menu into your production environment. Once you have moved the menu, everything is great, right? Well, not quite—you see, that custom menu probably calls some custom interactive or batch versions. If these versions have not been promoted with the menu, your end user will receive an error when attempting to execute the application or report. You could also see an issue arising if a processing option was changed and the version was not promoted; in that case, the application or report would not function as the user expected. This is why all of these objects need to be tracked using the OMW application. This will ensure that you have the correct objects in the correct places to ensure that the system performs in the manner that you need it to.

# XPI or Third-Party Integration

Although OneWorld is a fairly robust product, your company may have some very specialized needs. To meet these needs, you might use J.D. Edwards' new XPI (Extended Process Integration) product. Another option would be a bolt-on product or a third-party integration using a point-to-point method.

**N O T E**

*Extended Process Integration, or XPI, is powerful message broker software that enables J.D. Edwards to write adapters to integrate with other software packages. This message broker technology means that you have only one integration point instead of many. It also means that you can use this broker to integrate several different pieces of software into your system for full end-to-end integration. If you want, you can also write your own adapters to access other software packages.*

When you add these products into your OneWorld system, you are making changes to the system that you will need to track if you are to have change management controls on your system. When you apply an update, an upgrade, a service pack, or even an operating system change, you will want to ensure that you are not negatively affecting these integrations.

This is a little easier when dealing with XPI, as the XPI functionality calls J.D. Edwards' business functions, so you can look to see if the business functions or data structures that your adapter is using have changed when you think about applying an update or upgrade. When you have a third-party or bolt-on integration, you will need to analyze your integration points and determine which changes are more likely to impact these integrations.

## Documentation

We have discussed the need to track several different types of objects and how certain documents will assist you in keeping your system under control. However, we have not really talked about the documentation itself. When you are using this type of documentation to make key strategic business decisions, you need to ensure that the documentation is accurate and up to date.

You can do this by using change management controls on your documentation as well. Now, this does not mean that once you have the documentation in place, it can never change or that you need to add a lot of bureaucracy to accomplish this. All this really means is that you need to have a master set of documents that everyone refers to. That way, you know that everyone is playing from the same sheet of music.

We have seen some clients use third-party tracking systems, such as PVCS, to achieve these controls. However, most clients will simply use a network share drive and password-protect the master document. That way, only authorized individuals, such as your document owners, can update the documents. You can also link a Web page, which your end users and management can refer to, to this directory structure. This ensures that the documents' integrity is protected.

## Standard OMW Configurations

Okay, now that we have talked about what you need to keep track of in your environment, let's take a step back and talk about how all of this information plays into a standard OMW configuration. After all, most clients using J.D. Edwards OneWorld will have only four path codes and four environments. With this in mind, let's cover what this means for your strategic approach to change management and the configuration of the OMW.

The shipped environment and path code names are as follows:

- Standard Environment Names

  - JD7333   Pristine Environment

  - DV7333   Development Environment

  - PY7333   Prototyping Environment

  - PD7333   Production Environment

- Shipped Path Codes

  - JD7333   Pristine Path Code

  - DV7333   Development Path Code

  - PY7333   Prototyping Path Code

  - JD7333   Production Path Code

Now, with this in mind, you need to discern how to apply good change management practices to these environments and path codes as they apply to your organization. We have touched on some of these points in the course of this chapter, but now we are going to pull all of them together. We will address how development activities, electronic software updates, and service packs fall into this configuration.

# Standard Project Configuration

In Figure 4-5, you can see the path codes and the migration flow that are commonly used for the standard project configuration. You will also see the major out-of-the-box object management project statuses listed in this figure. It shows what path codes are affected during each project status. We will go over exactly how these path codes are affected in the following sections.

## New OMW Projects

With an out-of-the-box standard configuration, all development work is set up to be done in the DV7333 environment and path code at a project status of 21 Programming. However, when an OMW project is added, with the shipped configuration, your project status will be 11 New Project Pending Review, and the person who added the project into the system will default to a user role of 01 Originator.

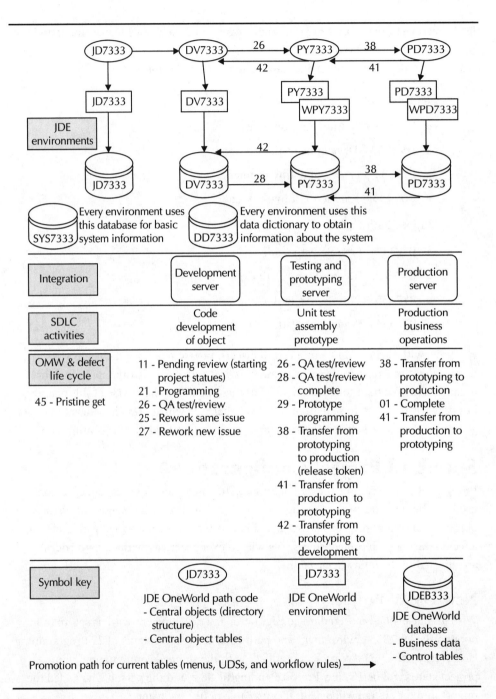

**FIGURE 4-5.**    OMW migration and major project statuses document

At this project status (11), all you can do is update the project. What this means is that all that person can do is add notes to the project, add category codes to the project, change the project description or system code, and update the planned start and completion dates of the project. This project status was developed by J.D. Edwards to give you the ability to add change requests directly into the OneWorld system. These requests can then be reviewed by a developmental manager and approved or rejected.

The downside to this is that any time you add a new project, the project will be set to a status of 11 Pending Review, and your role on the project will be set to 01 Originator. In order to perform any development work, including adding the desired objects into the project, you will need to change your role from 01 Originator to 02 Developer or add yourself to the project in the developer role. You will then have to promote this project to a status of 21 Programming in order to perform any development.

Another thing to consider with the out-of-the-box configuration is that all of your end users' default projects will default into a status code of 21 Programming. However, they will be assigned a user role of 01 Originator. This means that your users will not be able to check any objects in or out in OMW. This is because no allowed actions are set up for the user role of 01 originator for a project status of 21. The only allowed action that is shipped out of the box is to allow users to update a project. If users want to add objects to their default projects and use the design tools, they will need to add themselves to the project as an 02 Developer or change their user role to 02 Developer.

Before we move on to discuss the project status of 21 Programming, let's briefly discuss some of the options that a user will see when that user advances a project out of a status of 11 Pending Review. With the out-of-the-box Object Management Workbench configuration, anyone who has access to the OMW application will be able to change their user role to whatever they desire. This is because you need to set up row security in order to limit what user roles and thus privileges your users are allowed to assign themselves.

When users assign themselves a user role of 02 Developer, 03 Manager, 06 PVC Administrator, or 09 Supervisor, they will have the rights to advance a project out of the project status of 11 Pending Review. When this action is performed, they will be able to advance the project to more than just a project status of 21 Programming.

They will be able to advance the project status to 40 Production Development, 45 Pristine Get, or 91 Entered in Error. The project statuses of Pristine Get and 91

Entered in Error are not much of a concern. A project status of 45 Pristine Get allows the user to perform only gets from the pristine path code. The project status of 91 Entered in Error shows that the project has been cancelled. The status of 40 Production Development is a different story. This project status gives your user the ability to perform development work in the production path code. You should change the 11 to 40 transfer activity rule from *PUBLIC to a specific administrator's ID or an administrative group. This will help to ensure that only authorized users are allowed to use this project status.

## Project Status of 21 Programming

This project status is what tells the Object Management Workbench what tables to write to when a check in, check out, delete, save, restore, or addition of an object is performed. Here is the way this is determined: the software looks at the user role assigned to the project, it then looks at the allowed actions for that user role, and finally the system looks to see what the activity rules are for the project status. The activity rules are what tell the system where to copy data from and write it to during a check in, check out, get, save, restore, or other development activity.

All of your OneWorld developers should have access to the OMW and be allowed access to a user role that has the appropriate privileges in a project status of 21 Programming. With an out-of-the-box configuration, this will be a user role of 02 Developer.

## Project Status of 26 QA Test/Review

With the shipped allowed actions, only the 02 Developer, 03 Manager, and 09 Supervisor roles are allowed to advance a project out of the status of 21 Programming. They will be able to move the project back to a status of 11 Pending Review, move it forward to a status of 26 QA Test/Review, or cancel the project by setting the status to 91 Entered in Error. The thing to keep in mind strategically is that changing a project from a status of 21 programming to 26 QA Test/Review will transfer the objects from the DV7333 path code to that of PY7333. This means that when this takes place, you should not be performing any package builds, and the testing team needs to be aware of any objects coming forward that may affect their testing.

The OneWorld system administrator should also be aware of projects being advanced into this status so that packages can be built, over the PY7333 path code, for the testing team to use. One of the most successful approaches to this is to have a package build schedule that is agreed upon by the development, testing, and business leads. This schedule then ensures that everyone knows when a new package will be available with any new changes.

The testing team can then schedule their activities with a greater degree of confidence. Using a package build strategy also saves on a lot of disk space on your deployment and enterprise/application servers. This is because if you stick to a package build schedule, you will know when you can delete an old package, and thus you will avoid unnecessarily using up a lot of disk space on your deployment server. You always want to have what you know is a good package to roll back to. This is why you should use the A and B approach when building full packages.

### T I P

*If your modification consists only of objects that are used solely on the client workstations and does not require your enterprise/application server to be updated, then you can avoid building a package. This can be done by assigning your testers to the OMW project, which will be in a status of 26 QA Test/Review, and having them perform a get on the project. This will bring all of the specifications down to those testers' workstations, where they can compile those specifications and perform their tests.*

If you have an emergency fix, you can then build an update package. Once you have tested your next full package build, you can delete the update package. The changes that you built the update package to capture now exist in the next full package. This will conserve disk space and spare you confusion over what package has what objects in it and why it was built. The authors highly recommend that a package build schedule be used in your implementation.

Many people have faced the issue of promoting a modification all the way through their software development life cycle, with thorough testing, only to discover an issue in the production path code. Now they have to scramble to get a new fix all the way through the software development life cycle to fix the new issue. To avoid this, you can create a backup path code. This path code will be integrated into your promotion path so that you can roll modifications out of the production environment, if they cause issues.

The 26–28 status change can be very helpful for implementing this type of backup for a company's production objects. Before objects are transferred from the PY7333 path code to PD7333 path code at the 28–38 project status change, you could transfer the same objects from PD7333 to a backup path code. For this example, let's call it BU7333; it can be an empty path code created in exactly the same manner as a save location.

When the tester signs off on the project and advances the status from 26 to 28, objects will be transferred from PD7333 to BU7333. BU7333 will now contain the objects in their state previous to the new fix or enhancement. Then when the manager advances the project from 28 to 38, PD7333 will be updated with the objects from the new fix or enhancement out of the PY7333 path code. You can then set up a custom project status to restore these objects from the BU7333 path code into the PD7333 path code. A backup of the affected objects prior to a fix being rolled into your production path code can assist in restoring the production environment to smooth operation in a timely manner.

## Project Status 28 QA Test/Review Complete

Once your testing is complete, you can reflect this change by moving the project to a project status of 28 QA Test/Review complete. This tells you that the testing is complete and has been signed off on. Although this project status does not perform any real actions, such as an object transfer, it is a very important project status.

The reason this status is so important is that it represents the testing team's sign-off on a modification. This also means that you can run shipped OneWorld reports to show you all of the projects that have been signed off on by your testing team and moved into this project status. You can find these reports on the Object Management menu (GH9081).

With the shipped object management configuration, only the 03 Manager, 04 Quality Assurance, and 09 Supervisor roles can advance a project out of a status of 26 QA Test/Review. This means that once a project gets into a status of 26, the developer role no longer has any allowed actions set up and thus does not have the rights to perform actions on a project at this status. This is important in a strategic sense, since this is the point where the developer is placed into the background on the project.

It is also important to note that, while in a project status of 26 QA Test/Review, these user roles cannot check any objects out or in. Although gets can be performed and some user roles will have the ability to go into the design aid to review code, no code can be checked in by these user roles at this project status. This is important because it ensures that changes are not introduced into a higher environment and your software development life cycle is not broken.

### NOTE

*The user role of 06 PVC Administrator can perform any action at any project status. This is why this user role should be used only by your OneWorld system administrator, and security should be implemented to ensure that other users do not use this role.*

Let's say that the testing team finds an issue with the project. The roles just listed can also set the project status to 25 Rework Needed. This lets the developer know that the project has been rejected by testing and that he or she needs to perform additional work. The developer, manager, and supervisor role can then advance the project from a status of 25 Rework Needed issue to a status of 21 Programming, where a fix can be performed, and the project can then again be advanced to a project status of 26 QA Test/Review.

## Project Status 38 In Production

The next project status is the most important. When a project status is changed from 28 QA Test/Review complete to 38 In Production, the objects contained in that project are moved into your production environment and path code. With the shipped allowed actions, only the 03 Manager and 09 Supervisor user roles are able to move this project to the 38 In Production status. When you move objects into the projects and thus into the production environment, you will need to schedule a package build and deployment to see some of these changes. This is another reason why you should maintain a package build and deployment schedule. You should also attempt to schedule your project's moving into production in such a way to ensure that you do not accidentally interfere with a production activity, such as a quarterly close.

### CAUTION

When a batch or interactive version is moved into the production environment, any processing option changes that were made take effect immediately for the versions contained in the project.

J.D. Edwards has provided you with the ability to move a project backward as well. If you have a project in a status of 28 QA Test/Review Complete, you are not restricted to only moving the project to a status of 38 In Production. You may also move the project back to a status of 26 QA Test/Review. This capability allows you to move your projects backward and forward as necessary.

The reason that you can do this and not break your software development life cycle is that the token on an object will not be released until a project is moved into a status of 38 In Production, set to a status of 91 Entered in Error, or the token is manually released. This means that this object can be checked out from this project only during that time. This feature ensures that no new changes are introduced by another project containing the same object. If developers working on another project attempt to check the object out, they will be prompted to queue up for the token. This means that they cannot check the object out and back in until the token is released.

## Project Status 01 Complete

Once a project is in a status of 38 In Production, it is in the production environment. However, you may change the project status from 38 In Production to 01 Complete or back to 28 QA Test/Review Complete. The project status of 01 Complete is a reporting status that shows that the project has been in production for a period of time and no issues have been reported. Again, you can run reports of this project status to show how many projects have been completed in your OneWorld implementation.

It is important to note that the status of 01 Complete has an important meaning in OMW: it is the only status that OMW will recognize as being "closed." The Object Management Workbench does not allow a status to be moved out of 01 Complete. The reason that a project being "closed" is important is that when an object is marked to be deleted completely, OMW will check to see if the object exists in any open projects to prevent the object from being deleted while someone is working on it. OMW will look for the object in any project that is not at 01 Complete status.

The other project status under discussion, 38 In Production, has some strategic risks associated with it. At this point, you have released the tokens for all of the objects in this project; if you move this project back to a status of 28 QA Test/Review Complete, the objects in the PY7333 or DV7333 path code might not be the same. This is why the authors recommend instead moving a project that has reached a status code of 38 In Production to a status of 28 QA Test/Review Complete; you should add a new project to fix the issue with the original project. This makes it easier to track the objects in your system.

## When the Token Is Released

In the standard configuration, the token is released at a status 38 In Production and then an object is transferred into the production path code. When you release the token, you are indicating to other developers that they are free to make additional changes to the object and that the project, having released the token, has been completed. This ensures that an object's integrity is protected, because no one but the developer who holds the token for the project can change this object. This action ensures that you do not allow one developer to step on another developer's code and thus cause problems on that object.

The only other project status in an out-of-the-box OneWorld configuration that will release the token is the project status of 91 Entered in Error. This project status indicates that the project or modification has been canceled and that objects are available for another project to modify. Thus this project status helps to ensure that an object does not remain forgotten and stagnant while holding the token.

## Deleting Objects

With the old Object Librarian (OL), when you attempted to delete an object, you were prompted with a screen asking for a password. If you did not have this password, you could not delete an object. This password was written into the OneWorld code so that it could not be changed or set by the system administrator. This solution did help to discourage people from deleting objects out of the object librarian. However, once this password was compromised, which it was from the start because you could get it from J.D. Edwards customer support, anyone could delete any object out of the system, unless OneWorld action security was put into place.

This security problem is why this feature has been changed with the OMW. You will no longer be prompted to enter a password when you click the Delete button. J.D. Edwards is now assuming that you will set up the appropriate allowed actions within the OMW configuration application, with the appropriate combination of application security to restrict the delete functionality to only those people who really need it. If you do not take the time to set this up, there is nothing to stop users from deleting any object, including a J.D. Edwards object. If you find that a J.D. Edwards object has been deleted, you will need to restore the object from another path code or restore your central object tables from a tape backup. You need to be aware that the out-of-the-box configuration is to have no security set up on this button.

# Advanced Object Management Configurations

Now that we have discussed the out-of-the-box standard Object Management Workbench configuration, let's move on to discuss some of the more advanced configurations that the authors realize J. D. Edwards cannot possibly preconfigure in the OMW. That is why they made the OMW extremely configurable.

## Custom Environments and Path Codes

Several customers using OneWorld Xe have nonstandard environments and path codes. If you fall into this category, do not worry. You can still use the OMW; you just need to understand that there will be additional system setup tasks. This may include defining custom user roles, allowed actions, project statuses, or activity rules.

### Custom User Roles

You will need to add custom user roles if the shipped user roles do not meet the needs of your company. Say, for example, that you have business analysts that you want to enable to access the OMW to check versions in and out but no other objects. One option to resolve this is to add a new user role. In this example, you could add a user role of 10 Business Analysts.

## Custom Allowed Actions

If you set up a new user role, it will be fairly useless unless you grant this user role the ability to perform certain allowed actions. When thinking about custom allowed actions, you will need to keep in mind what project status you will want to set the allowed actions up for and exactly what you want to allow each user role to do at the different project statuses. An example of this might be allowing the user role of 01 originator the ability to check versions in and out of a project status of 11 New Project Pending Review.

## Custom Project Statuses and Activity Rules

If you want to add a custom project status, you will need to do this before you are allowed to set up any allowed actions on this project. As you consider adding a new project status, draw out your environments, path codes, and project status on a sheet of paper. Then ask yourself how this new project status fits into your software development life cycle. This exercise will assist you in determining whether you really need to add the project status code.

If you do require this project status, this exercise will show where the project status should be placed into the software development life cycle. It will also help you to determine what user roles should be able to perform actions in this project status or promote projects into or out of this project status. Finally, you will be creating the documentation for the new configuration.

# Sandbox Environment and Path Codes

Some clients are large enough to feel that they need an area in which they can test different things without fear of impacting the entire system or critical work. This has often been referred to as a *sandbox* environment and path code. We have seen this approach implemented from time to time.

Normally, what will occur is that the client will go live with one module first, such as financials. They will still have modifications and testing activities going on, which they do not want to interfere with. However, they would like to start to set up some other module to see if they want to implement it in the future, say, for example, manufacturing. In order to do this, some clients set up a sandbox environment and path code. This allows them to test new business processes freely by changing key processing options and thus control data freely.

If you are thinking about attempting this, however, you need to first ask, "Can I afford to take on the system maintenance involved with an additional environment and path code?" This maintenance includes package builds, printer definition, environment setup, and all of the other normal maintenance associated with a OneWorld environment and path code. You will also need to determine whether you are going to save any data setup, versions, menus, user-defined codes, or modifications from this sandbox. If you are, you need to come up with a plan for moving these changes into your standard development life cycle when you are finished with the sandbox.

## Training Environment and Path Code

A *training environment* is a common requirement for clients using the OneWorld software. Some clients simply associate the training environment with their prototyping path code (PY7333). Although the authors agree that a training environment is a good idea, associating it with your PY7333 path code might not be the best idea. This is because if you change any processing options during your training class, you have not only affected the manner that the software behaves in your testing environment, but you have also affected your prototyping environment, since they also share the PY7333 path code. Also, if you add versions during your training or change an application during a development training session, you can impact your testing and prototyping efforts.

The authors recommend that instead of associating a custom training environment with an existing path code, you create a custom path code. This recommendation assumes that you have the hardware and administration resources to maintain this environment and path code. The reasons for using a custom path code as well as a custom environment are simple. You now have the ability to totally refresh this environment and this path code at will. Also, any changes that are made to this environment and this path code will not affect the other environments in the system.

Not only does this approach give you the ability to teach your end users how changing processing options can assist them in responding to changes in the business, but you can also train new developers on how to perform modifications in OneWorld. What enables this training is that you will have a tape backup of this environment and path code that you can simply refresh after each training session. This ensures that you can teach consistent and predictable classes using the system without interfering with the operation of the business or the testing of new modifications.

# Handling Control Data

Another area that is often changed depending on the clients' needs is how control data is handled. When we use the term *control data,* we are referring to user-defined codes, menus, workflow rules, and versions. Many business users will argue that these are data and not objects, and the items from J.D. Edwards could be truly defined as data.

Not all businesses will be able to add all of their menus, user-defined codes, workflow rules, or versions in the development environment and promote them through to the production environment. Some clients have business processes that require them to have the ability to enter user-defined codes daily. This provides a bit of a challenge for the change management team; they know that these items or objects need to be tracked and exist in all of the environments or issues. However, they also realize that if the business cannot use the system, then no revenue will be generated.

Most often a compromise will be made. The authors have seen several different approaches used. One of them was where all versions would be entered and tested in the PY7333 environment before being moved into production. These versions would also be transferred back to the development environment once they had been tested. Another site had only a handful of power users who could add menus, workflow rules, or user-defined codes. Every month or so when a subset of the production data was copied into the PY7333 and DV7333 environments, to ensure realistic data was being used for testing, the user-defined code, menus, and workflow files would also be copied back. Prior to this happening, any user-defined codes or menus entered by the development staff would be entered into the production environment if they were ready to be used or documented and manually reentered into the DV7333 environment.

These custom setups do require that you have all of your change management procedures nailed down, tested, and documented. Although these custom configurations give the business users the freedom to accomplish their jobs and although they may be required, it is easy to introduce issues into the system by missing a user-defined code, menu, version, or workflow rule.

When deciding what is best for your company, you should think of change management as a spectrum. At one end, you have absolute change management, which means that there are a lot of tracking mechanisms in place and thus changes may move more slowly through the system. This is a very stable configuration, but it may not be appropriate due to the time it takes to implement a change. At the other end, you have no change management. In this configuration, changes can happen immediately, but you also have a highly unstable system. What you need to determine is what level of risk your company is willing to accept, and then you will be able to find where your company lands in this spectrum. Most companies land about three-quarters of the way up the spectrum. They have enough change management in place to ensure stability, but not so much as to interfere with truly critical business activities.

# Summary

In this chapter, we have discussed some of the strategic issues that you will face as you determine what your Object Management configuration needs are for your company. These strategic decisions are the foundation that you will build your system upon.

This is why we discussed the importance of understanding the software development life cycle and the impact it can have on your company. This is also why we talked about the types of changes to the system that you should keep track of, including hardware and software changes. We also discussed the importance of managing your system documentation. Finally, we discussed the standard object management configurations and some of the more advanced configurations. During this discussion, we discussed some of the questions that you will need to ask and have answered in order to have a successful change management effort.

# CHAPTER 5

# Object Management Workbench Case Study

Case Study of a Small OneWorld
  Development Effort

Company Overview

Case Study of a Large OneWorld
  Development Effort

In the preceding chapters, we have discussed how to determine what the software development life cycle (SDLC) is and how to configure the Object Management Workbench (OMW) to meet this life cycle. Now that you are comfortable with the OMW and how to configure it to meet your development and business needs, we can talk about what we have observed and configured at various companies to meet their development needs using the OMW. This chapter is dedicated to discussing what two different companies did to meet their software development requirements.

The first company in this case study is a smaller firm that did not require heavy modifications to the delivered OneWorld software system. This company's main modifications were custom OneWorld reports. They have very few OneWorld developers and no custom environments or path codes. The second company is a large company that has a large team of OneWorld developers who are currently making and will continue to make additional modifications to the software. This company is concerned with the matter of incorporating several custom environments and path codes into their OMW configuration.

# Case Study of a Small OneWorld Development Effort

During your J.D. Edwards OneWorld implementation, you will likely come across changes that you'd like to make to the vanilla system. These changes are quite often due to current business processes not matching up to delivered functionality. Depending upon the staff you have on hand, as well as other factors, you will want to put some careful thought into whether you want to modify the system, or change your process to meet the delivered functionality by way of workarounds. At the very least, most likely, you will have additional reporting writing needs, and thus you will want to implement change management procedures. In the following example, we are assuming that your development efforts are small and you will be using the standard configuration for Object Management Workbench, as well as the standard environments available for user sign-on.

Alongside any development effort, there are a multitude of risks, or issues and concerns. You can nearly eliminate quite a few of those risks by following the change management processes already configured for you. OMW eliminates risks such as check-in location errors, improper object changes, overwriting priority changes, and incorrect object transfers. There are, of course, certain manual processes that must still occur, but we'll make this as painless as possible. Other development project risks include proper user training, go-live schedules, access to confidential data, and inaccurate development time estimates, to name a few.

# Company Overview

The company we will be using in our small development effort example, Company A, employs around 1,000 persons and does one billion dollars worth of business per year. They are using the Financials Suite to track all accounting data, as well as the Distribution Suite for tracking inventory and sales. In the future, they would like to implement the Manufacturing Suite to include quality and shop floor management. There are no plans to implement Human Resources or Payroll. These processes are done by a third party and will be integrated at a later date using Extended Process Integration (XPIe). Company A farms and produces sugar beets for specially granulated sugar distributed throughout the United States. All processing and packaging is done at their farm. Although there are around 1,000 employees, those that need to access the OneWorld system will be up to 75 consecutive users. Of those users, five are developers, and two are system administrators. There will be a need to implement HTML clients prior to go-live, allowing for easier and quicker access into the system specifically for entering orders and doing inventory availability look-ups.

The development effort at Company A is limited in scope due to other tasks required of their developers. There is, however, a definite need for additional financial reports to be created so that the company can report according to industry-specific requirements. Company A has no plans to hire additional developers but is venturing on bringing in Firm Z for assistance. Because you have a development effort, you will need someone to head this up. That person needs to be able to track all custom objects in a structured manner and manage items such as deadlines, transfer procedures, and package build schedules. Doing custom development is not an easy task, and it can sometimes become tiresome to keep track of objects and development efforts in an effective manner. By using, at the very least, the standard OMW configuration, you can more easily track your changes, know when to build packages, and make sure that erroneous data isn't transferred into production.

## Standard Configuration

The standard configuration used at Company A is described in the paragraphs that follow. A developer will create a project in OMW. That project will be entered at status 11 New Project Pending Review. At this status, the developer will assign owners to the project. Also note that you will want to come up with a naming convention for your projects so that they can be tracked more easily. Possibly implement dates into the Project ID field, or follow some suggestions that were made in Chapter 2, under "Working with Projects." Owners that should be included in the project at this time include, at the very least, developer and manager. At status 11 New Project Pending Review, further analysis is done and functional and technical design specifications are written. These specifications include information such as the purpose of the new object, meaning what function will the new object or objects perform; the risks and limitations of the object(s); a business process flow; and any issues and assumptions; as well as the new applications, forms, event rules, affected tables, and conversion information. Company A has developed standard documents that are in use for gathering this information; you may want to consider a similar approach.

**N O T E**

*With the standard configuration, if you enter a project at status 11 New Project Pending Review, and that project is no longer needed, it can be deleted only while at status 11 New Project Pending Review. Projects may also be moved to status 91, meaning they were canceled or entered in error. In both cases if your project contains an object, the token is automatically released.*

If you set up object notification, the manager will be notified if the project status changes. At Company A, the e-mail system is not integrated with OneWorld, and thus management control is contained within OMW setup and configuration, as well as with manual processes. Manual processes include, but are not limited to, informing management of a project status change and updating management about objects affected by the development effort. Managers should also be monitoring the system to see what projects are new and the status of existing projects. This can be done simply by searching on the Manager (02) or Supervisor (09) user ID and role, by typing the user ID in the user field, and 02 or 09 in the role field on the OMW form.

From status 11 New Project Pending Review, the project is then advanced to status 21 In Programming, where development is done. In the standard setup, only those users assigned as Developers will have access to check out, check in, mark objects for deletion, copy and add objects, or advance projects. Tokens may also be released and switched at this stage; however, those actions are limited to only those owners who play a Manager or Supervisor role. You will want to implement security so that those users who are not developers are not permitted into the OMW system.

Company A has set up user groups to implement this type of security. For more
information about security setup, please refer to *J.D. Edwards OneWorld: The Complete
Reference*, by Joseph Miller, Allen Jacot, and John Stern (Osborne/McGraw-Hill, 2000).

**N O T E**

*Non–Object Librarian object changes are automatically added to the default
project. These objects must be moved to the actual project if the change is
required for the custom object process. For example, Company A has made a
change to their sales order entry process. They have added new values to sales
category codes and perform edit checks on these values. In order to properly
transfer the new category code values, this information must be moved from the
default project it was added to upon an Add or Change operation, to the actual
OMW project.*

When a developer at Company A has completed development of an object, as well
as unit testing (which is a test of the object's functionality within the product suite in
which it is intended to be used), the project it is contained within can be advanced to
status 26 Testing. For example, a developer at Company A has created a new variance
report on financial data (R5511121). That report is based on information contained
within the Account Balances table (F0902), as well as the Account Ledger (F0911).
A unit test is performed using General Accounting data. Since developers have access
to transfer their own projects to testing, this is done by clicking the Advance Project
button in the center column of action buttons. This action kicks off a transfer from the
development environment (DV7333) into test or PY7333, in the case of Company A.
One important note to make is that if the user wishes to save their work without
checking the object in, thus not affecting the current development environment, the
save and restore locations have also been configured. At Company A, the save location
is SV7333. SV7333 is not an environment that you can sign into; rather, it is used only
for saving, restoring, and backing up object data. The system administrator, seeing the
status change, will check to see that the object was transferred successfully and will
then build a package.

At status 26 Testing, a package build is done and system testing is performed
on the custom object. A system test is, using the preceding variance report example,
similar to a unit test, except that a greater number of accounts are used in testing.
A system test for a change to the accounts payable (AP) voucher process, for example,
would include a unit test, testing AP functionality within that system only (product

code 04), and a system test, which includes testing all other end processes, such as procurement (product code 43) processes and data that may be affected by the change. Company A also creates and checks in additional interactive and batch versions at status 26 Testing. If this is done, the system administrator is informed via a manual process so that those objects are built on the server.

In order to request a package build, developers must send information such as project ID, object type, object name, and requested by for an Object Librarian object and information such as project ID, object type, object action (add, change, delete, copy), and requested by for non–Object Librarian objects. A standard form has been created that is required for all requests. If you decide to use a manual process, you may want to create a standard procedure for package builds. Using OMW object notification and having a build schedule, however, would greatly improve this process.

After testing is complete, either by the developer or by a quality assurance team (a separate user role [Owner]), the project is advanced either to status 28 QA Test Review Complete or to status 25 Rework-same issue. If rework is needed, the project is demoted from status 25 back to 21 In Programming, and the software development life cycle begins again.

### TIP

*It is not uncommon to have the quality assurance analyst (tester) perform a Get or an Advanced Get on the object prior to transfer, such that additional tests can be performed and you are assured the users are getting what was asked for in the functional design specifications.*

Because Company A does not have object notification enabled, there is not an automated process for informing the manager, or even the system administrator, that an object was transferred and tested. Company A uses manual forms to request a package build and to inform management and quality assurance analysts, or even end-user testers, of the availability of a custom object. All object transfers and builds are tracked in an Excel spreadsheet along with issues that arose and were resolved during the software development life cycle. The build request was discussed previously.

In standard setup and configuration, if testing is successful, the object is then advanced by the manager or supervisor from status 28 QA Test/Review Complete to status 38 In Production. The object transfer process is kicked off again, and the object is promoted from test (PY7333) into the production environment (PD7333). An update package is built and deployed to all clients needing the custom object.

The full parent package is also recompressed so that the next full installation will include the modification.

From status 38 In Production, a manual sign-off of the custom object(s) occurs, and the project is advanced to an 01 Complete status. At this time, the functional and technical design specifications are also signed off on. The technical design is such that if the object were to be deleted, another developer could use the design to re-create the object.

### *N O T E*

*It is recommended that all design specifications be completed and signed off on prior to beginning development, and that minor modifications be made as you advance through the software development life cycle; however, please note that this, quite often, is not the case. To encourage you and to stress the high importance of these documents, we urge that they be completed, even if only at the end of the life cycle.*

Once a project at Company A reaches status 01 Complete, the software development life cycle is considered complete. If any problems are found in the newly created object(s), a new project is created, and the software development life cycle, or project life cycle, begins again.

### *T I P*

*You will want to use an issue-tracking spreadsheet or database to track all issues that arise, including requests for additional modifications. By tracking your issues, you will begin to build a listing of common issues at your company, and prior resolutions to those issues.*

# Case Study of a Large OneWorld Development Effort

In the previous chapters, we have discussed how to determine what the software development life cycle is, what user roles should be employed, allowed actions, and activity rules. We have shown you examples of how to work with the object management software. Now we can really look closely at how a large company took this information and used it to meet their specific needs.

# Company Overview

This company is a large manufacturing organization that manufactures and sells products around the world. This means that the company deals with a user community that is scattered across the globe. The company was setting up financials, distribution/logistics, and manufacturing. They were also attempting to integrate several legacy systems into their OneWorld system. This was being set up as a back office integration.

Since this company supports a large number of developers, quality assurance testers, and business analysts, they had a requirement for many custom environments and path codes. This means there is additional setup for the OMW configuration.

To determine how to handle change management at this company, with their OneWorld implementation, a series of meetings were held to communicate the business development needs. In these meetings, the company's software development life cycle was created. From this software development life cycle, we were able to determine necessary environments, path codes, Object Management Workbench project statuses, user roles, and other necessary components of the Object Management Workbench configuration.

# Environments

During the course of several meetings with the various development, testing, and user groups, the required environments were determined. Since the development effort was considered large, the number of required environments was also comparatively large. The following environments and path codes were determined to be necessary:

| Environment Name | Path Code |
| --- | --- |
| JD7333 – Pristine Environment | JD7333 |
| PRO7333 – Prototyping Environment (Sandbox Environment) | PRO7333 |
| WIP7333 – Work in Progress Environment | WP7333 |
| DV7333 – Development Environment | DV7333 |
| INT7333 – Interface Environment | INV7333 |
| TS7333 – Testing Environment | PY7333 |
| TRN7333 – Training Environment | TRN7333 |
| CNVAU733 – Conversion Environment | WIP7333 |
| CNVSIG733 – Conversion Environment | WIP7333 |
| CNVMA733 – Conversion Environment | WIP7333 |
| PD7333 – Production Environment | PD7333 |
| PY7333 – Prototyping Environment | PY7333 |

As you can see from this list, there are a great number of environments and path codes to deal with here. Let's briefly go through each of these to give you an idea why the company felt they needed these to meet their business needs.

- The Pristine Environment and path code are required to give the company a set of pristine J.D. Edwards objects and business data. Their definition of pristine also included Electronic Software Updates (ESUs), which are applied to the pristine environment and path code first, to ensure that an issue was resolved by an ESU and that the ESU did not introduce undesired results in another mission-critical process.

- It was determined that a sandbox, or playground, environment and path code should be set up to allow the company's business process team to test new business models. This was also a configuration for an application suite that will go live later without impacting the true business model that is set up in the PY7333 environment and path code. This environment and path code was PRO7333, which was not inside the software development life cycle, and thus very little was saved from this environment.

- The Work in Progress (WIP7333) environment and path code is this company's development environment. This is where developers perform all of their OneWorld development and unit testing. The new objects are tested by the developer and not tested in a package including other modifications in progress.

- The Development Environment and path code (DV7333) are used for testing the developers' modifications along with other projects that are ready to be promoted. The developers test their modification, after receiving a package, on the server and on the workstation. This helps to ensure that if one modification made by a developer had a problem with another modification made by another developer, it would show up quickly and early in the testing process.

- The Interface Environment and path code (INT7333) were set up to accommodate testing of the multiple interfaces between legacy systems and the OneWorld system. Although the interface team uses only certain business functions, they do not want to share the development environment for fear that they might have a business function changed on them and waste time trying to track the error down.

- The Testing Environment (TS7333) was created so that the testing team had an area where they could run through their test scripts and affect only their own set of business data. This company uses the J.D. Edwards Automated Testing Tool, or Autopilot, to assist in their testing process.

- The Training Environment and path code (TRN7333) was created to train the client's end users on the use of the new OneWorld system. This environment is isolated outside of the software development life cycle, and a refresh strategy was created to refresh this environment with a subset of production data and production object specifications. This ensures that the training is realistic for the end users. The fact that the environment has its own path code allows the training department to create exercises that change processing options, add versions, and even modify objects using the development tool set.

- The three Conversion Environments (CNVAU7333, CNVSIG733, and CNVMA733) were set up to convert data from a legacy AS400 system into the correct format for OneWorld Xe to read the data. This path code shares the WIP7333 path code, as the conversions required that custom table conversions be written.

- The Production Environment and path code (PD7333) are being used as the company's production environment for their end users.

This is a lot of information to absorb, so we have included a picture of how these environments tie together. Figure 5-1 shows how the environments relate to each other and gives you a rough idea of how things are designed to move through the system.

# Object Management Workbench Configuration

Due to the fact that this company has a lot of custom environments and path codes, they needed to set the OMW up to know about these environments and path codes. To do this, they first needed to determine where each of these environments and path codes fell into the software development life cycle. They then needed to assign project statuses so that the Object Management Workbench could recognize the different environment and path codes.

## Major OMW Project Statuses

To illustrate how this was accomplished , we are going to go through the different project statuses and explain how they related to the environments and path codes described previously. With this client, the initial status of a new project is 21, or

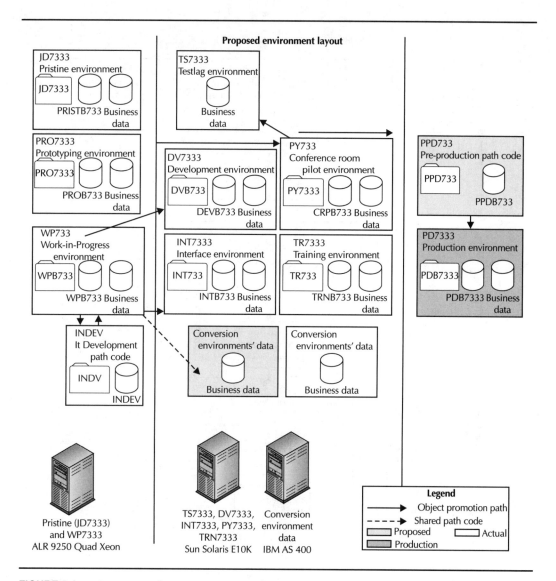

**FIGURE 5-1.** Overview of company's environments

In Programming. When a modification is proposed, the modification approval process shown in Figure 5-2 is followed. Once a modification is approved, and a requirements document submitted, then and only then is a project entered into the OneWorld system.

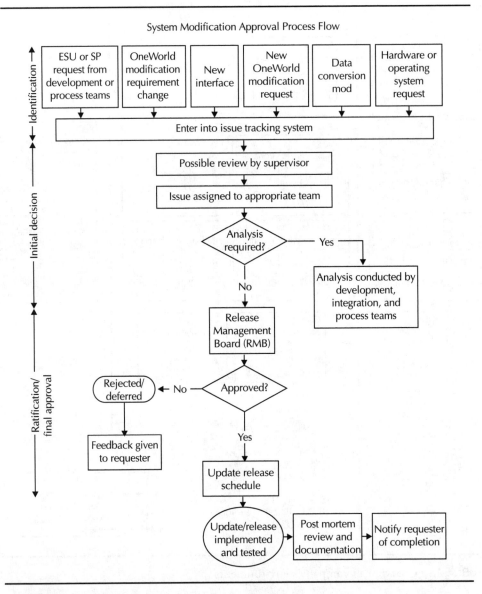

System Modification Approval Process Flow

**FIGURE 5-2.** Modification approval process

Now that you have an idea of how the modifications are approved and implemented, we will go through all of the different project statuses that the company uses. The diagram shown in Figure 5-3 illustrates all of these different project statuses, the types of activities that are performed in each of these project statuses, the affected environments, and path codes.

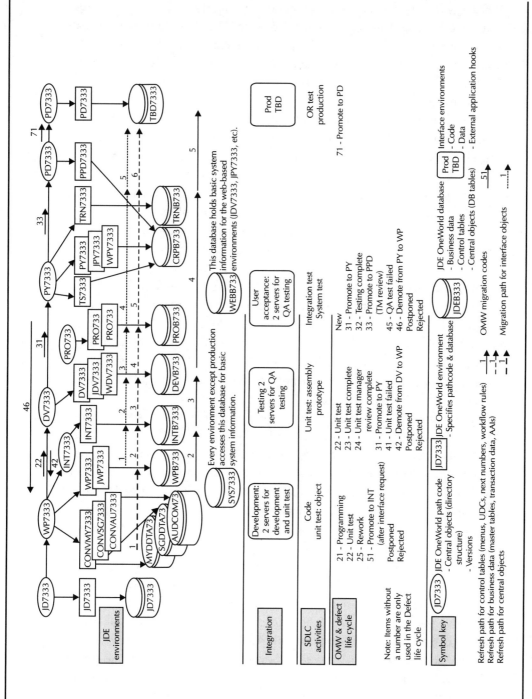

**FIGURE 5-3.** Project statuses for a company with a large development effort

When a developer adds a new project into the system, the project is set to status 21, or In Programming. This project status affects the WP7333 environment and path code. The project allows the developers to perform modifications, check out, check in, perform a project status update, and conduct other development activities.

The next project status, 22, or Unit Test, is used to transfer objects into the DV7333 environment and path code. After this transfer takes place, a full package is built, on a weekly basis, and deployed to the developer's workstations. This allows the developers to perform a functional test on their modifications on both the server and their client workstation. In this project status, the developers cannot check objects out or in; however, they can perform Gets against an object as well as use the design tools to review the behind-the-scenes processing (the object's code). A developer performs unit tests and advances the project status to 23 Unit Test Complete.

At a project status of 23 Unit Test Complete, this indicates that the developer has completed the unit test. At this point, a tester from the test team performs a functional test of the modification on a test workstation. Once this test is complete, the project is moved into a project status of 24, or Unit Manager Review.

At status 24 Unit Manager Review, the testing team manager decides when the modification can move into the PY7333 path code for additional testing. When the testing team is ready to accept the modification, they then inform the manager and move the project status to a status code of 31 Promote to PY. This project status transfers the objects contained within the project from the DV7333 path code and environment to the PY7333 path code.

A full client and server package is built when the project is at status 31 Promote to PY; it is then deployed to all necessary locations. Again, the package builds take place only on a weekly basis. If an emergency fix is requested, an update package is built and deployed. This project status also transfers the menus and user-defined codes into the TS7333 environment. This gives the testing team the correct user-defined codes and menus to test with, which allows the testing team to execute their testing scripts. This company uses the J.D. Edwards Automated Testing Tool, or Autopilot, to assist in their testing procedures. Autopilot helps to reduce the costs of testing modifications made to the software. Once all testing is complete, a package is deployed and tested by the end users. This would not be the first time a user has seen the modification. While the modification was being developed, in a project status of 21 In Programming, the developers send the user screen shots and even have the users take control of their workstations to perform limited testing.

Once user acceptance testing is passed and signed off on by the appropriate business representatives, then and only then is the project moved on to the next project status. This project status is 33 Promote to PPD. The project can be promoted into this project status by only a few select individuals. When a project is promoted into this status, the objects are transferred from the PY7333 path code and environment into the PPD7333 path code and environment.

The PPD7333 path code and environment was created solely to act as a holding location for modifications. This allows other projects to be promoted into the PY7333 path code for testing without forcing a transfer into the production environment and path code. This also allows modifications to be queued up and rolled slowly into the production environment and path code when the company is ready to accept the modification. Since this company is a manufacturing company, they routinely freeze all modifications into their production environment, usually during the fourth quarter.

Once the decision is made to move the modification into the production environment, the project status is changed to status 71 Promote to PD. To transfer a project into this status code, the approval of the company's information systems department management is required. Once this approval is received, the project status is changed to 71 Promote to PD. This transfers the objects from the PPD7333 path code and environment into the production (PD7333) path code and environment.

When this project status is reached, a full package build and deployment is scheduled. This scheduling and coordination helps to prevent issues with the deployment of changes to the production workstations and servers. Once the project has been in production for a while, and the staff is comfortable that the modification was successful, the project status is set to 01, or Completed.

## Demotion Project Statuses

Although it is rare, sometimes an object may need to be demoted from the production environment and path code down the software development life cycle. Great care needs to be taken when performing this demotion. This is because when a project is promoted into the production environment, the token is released. This object can then be part of another modification that is coming up through the different path codes. When you demote a project, you could possibly overlay a single object of another project. This could cause undesired results; so, for these reasons, extreme caution needs to be taken when demoting objects through the path codes.

The large company example set up the following project statuses to handle demoting of objects from the production path code to the lower environments and path codes. They have created the project status of 46 Demote from PY to WP. This will take an object from the PY path code and move it down to the WP7333 path code. This allows the users/developers to avoid accidentally overlaying part of another modification. Another project status that the company has set up is 42 Demote from DV to WP. At the time of this case study, this company did not have a project status code to demote objects out of the production path code or environment. If an issue was found with a modification once it was in the production path code, the company would enter a brand new OMW project to address the issue and move it through the software development life cycle.

## Project Statuses for Test Failure

The last set of project statuses that we will discuss are the project statuses that are used to handle a modification failing a test, prior to being promoted into the production environment and path code. When a project is promoted into the project status of 22 Unit Test, if the quality assurance or tester discovers an issue, they then set the project status from 22, or Unit Test, to 41, or Unit Test Failed. The developer then reviews the issue; and if they agree that there is a problem with the modification, the project status is set to 25 Rework-Same Issue. The developer then addresses the issue that the tester has found and promotes the project back to status 22 Unit Test. If the developer did not agree that there was an issue, the project is set back to status 22 Unit Test, from the previously assigned status 41, or Unit Test Failed.

When the project is promoted into status 31 Promote to PY, the project's objects exist in the prototyping environment and path code (PY7333). If the testing scripts failed or the user acceptance test fail the project status is set to 45 QA Test Failed. If the developer agrees that there is an issue, the project status is set to 25 Rework-Same Issue, then to be promoted back through the software development life cycle.

### N O T E

When a project is set to status 25 Rework-Same Issue, the objects are not promoted to a lower environment or path code. This is because the token has yet to be released, so no other project is allowed to modify the objects.

# Summary

In this chapter, we have shown you how two different companies created and configured the Object Management Workbench to meet their software development life cycle. We have discussed how a smaller company, without much of a development effort, uses the Object Management Workbench to meet their needs, and how they use the different project statuses. This type of setup and configuration allowed the company to instantly know the statuses of all of their modifications in their system.

We also discussed a company with a larger development effort. This company works in multiple custom environment and path code settings. This means that they needed to carefully plan custom project statuses to deal with the modifications in their system. This planning and setup allowed them to easily track the modifications to their system.

# Index

*References to figures and illustrations are in italics.*

## INTERNATIONAL CONTACT INFORMATION

**AUSTRALIA**
McGraw-Hill Book Company Australia Pty. Ltd.
TEL +61-2-9417-9899
FAX +61-2-9417-5687
http://www.mcgraw-hill.com.au
books-it_sydney@mcgraw-hill.com

**CANADA**
McGraw-Hill Ryerson Ltd.
TEL +905-430-5000
FAX +905-430-5020
http://www.mcgrawhill.ca

**GREECE, MIDDLE EAST,
NORTHERN AFRICA**
McGraw-Hill Hellas
TEL +30-1-656-0990-3-4
FAX +30-1-654-5525

**MEXICO (Also serving Latin America)**
McGraw-Hill Interamericana Editores S.A. de C.V.
TEL +525-117-1583
FAX +525-117-1589
http://www.mcgraw-hill.com.mx
fernando_castellanos@mcgraw-hill.com

**SINGAPORE (Serving Asia)**
McGraw-Hill Book Company
TEL +65-863-1580
FAX +65-862-3354
http://www.mcgraw-hill.com.sg
mghasia@mcgraw-hill.com

**SOUTH AFRICA**
McGraw-Hill South Africa
TEL +27-11-622-7512
FAX +27-11-622-9045
robyn_swanepoel@mcgraw-hill.com

**UNITED KINGDOM & EUROPE
(Excluding Southern Europe)**
McGraw-Hill Education Europe
TEL +44-1-628-502500
FAX +44-1-628-770224
http://www.mcgraw-hill.co.uk
computing_neurope@mcgraw-hill.com

**ALL OTHER INQUIRIES Contact:**
Osborne/McGraw-Hill
TEL +1-510-549-6600
FAX +1-510-883-7600
http://www.osborne.com
omg_international@mcgraw-hill.com